# Windows® 7 Plain & Simple

*Jerry Joyce*
*Marianne Moon*

PUBLISHED BY

Microsoft Press
A Division of Microsoft Corporation
One Microsoft Way
Redmond, Washington 98052-6399

Library of Congress Control Number: 2009932320

ISBN: 978-0-7356-2666-9

Printed and bound in the United States of America.

11 12 13 14 15 16 17 18 19 QGT 7 6 5 4 3 2

Distributed in Canada by H.B. Fenn and Company Ltd.

A CIP catalogue record for this book is available from the British Library.

Microsoft Press books are available through booksellers and distributors worldwide. For further information about international editions, contact your local Microsoft office or contact Microsoft Press International directly at fax (425) 936-7329. Visit our Web site at www.microsoft.com/mspress. Send comments to mspinput@microsoft.com.

**Acquisitions Editor:** Juliana Aldous Atkinson
**Developmental Editor:** Sandra Haynes
**Project Editor:** Valerie Woolley
**Typographer:** Kari Fera
**Proofreader/Copy Editor:** Alice Copp Smith
**Manuscript Editor:** Marianne Moon
**Technical Editor:** Jerry Joyce
**Indexer:** Wright Information Indexing Services

Body Part No. X15-74124

[2012-06-08]

# Contents

**3** **Accessing and Organizing**      **27**

**4** **Running Programs and Gadgets**      **53**

## Personalizing

**83**

## 6 Exploring the Internet

**115**

## Working with Multimedia 175

## Using Voice and Sounds 199

## 14 Setting Up 271

# Acknowledgments

This book is the result of the combined efforts of a team of skilled professionals whose work we trust and admire and whose friendship we value highly.

Kari Fera, our talented typographer, did the work of two people and did it graciously, as always. Kari, who has worked on our books for many years, not only refined and produced the graphics but also laid out the complex design, wrestling with problems ranging from limited space to logical arrangement of numbered steps. We deeply appreciate her excellent work.

Our dear friend Alice Copp Smith has helped us improve every one of the 16 books we've written. Alice does so much more than proofread and copyedit: Her gentle and witty chiding on countless yellow sticky notes makes us groan (and laugh) but teaches us to write better and, always, to get rid of those danglers!

For many years we have been fortunate indeed to have worked with indexer *par excellence* Jan Wright, whose indexes reveal in microcosm the soul of each book. We've always called Jan the Queen of Indexing, and she richly deserves this exalted title as the recipient of the American Society for Indexing's H. W. Wilson Award for Excellence in Indexing, an annual award given for the best index submitted in 2009. Congratulations, Jan!

We thank this dedicated and hardworking trio for their exceptional work and their unwavering good humor in the face of grueling deadlines.

At Microsoft Press we thank Juliana Aldous Atkinson for asking us to write this book, and we also thank Valerie Woolley and Sandra Haynes for their valuable insight and helpful suggestions.

Thanks to David Villarina at NextWindow for his help with the multi-touch driver so that we could fully appreciate the multi-touch features of Windows. Thanks also to the Microsoft Windows team for letting us play with the fun and interesting games, the screen saver, and the programs in the Microsoft Touch Pack, and for letting us use the graphics of the games.

Thanks also to the Seattle Audubon Society for allowing us to use images from their beautifully designed Northwest Shade Coffee Campaign Web site.

On the home front, we thank our brainy, beautiful grandchild Zuzu for love, laughter, and many hours of Monopoly, Birdopoly, and Dogopoly, at which she routinely beats both of us and winds up with more money than the bank. We thank her too for allowing us to use her lovely owl drawing in section 11 of this book. We also thank puppies Baiser and Pierre for graciously allowing us to publish their private playlist.

Last but not least, we thank each other—for everything.

# 1

# About This Book

If you want to get the most from your computer and your software with the least amount of time and effort—and who doesn't?—this book is for you. You'll find *Windows 7 Plain & Simple* to be a straightforward, easy-to-read reference tool. With the premise that your computer should work for you, not you for it, this book's purpose is to help you get your work done quickly and efficiently so that you can get away from the computer and live your life. Our book is based on the Windows 7 Home Premium edition running on a desktop, notebook, pen-based, or multi-touch-based computer that is, or can be, connected to the Internet. If you're running another edition of Windows 7, you can still use all or most of the information you'll find here. However, we do talk about some features that aren't included in either the Starter or the Home Basic edition, and we don't deal with some additional features that you'll find in Windows 7 Professional, Enterprise, and Ultimate editions.

## No Computerspeak!

Let's face it—when there's a task you don't know how to do but you need to get it done in a hurry, or when you're stuck in the middle of a task and can't figure out what to do next, there's nothing more frustrating than having to read page after page of technical background material. You want the information you need—nothing more, nothing less—and you want it now! *And* it should be easy to find and understand.

That's what this book is all about. It's written in plain English—no technical jargon and no computerspeak. No single task in the book takes more than two pages. Just look up the task in the index or the table of contents, turn to the page, and there's the information you need, laid out in an illustrated step-by-step format. You don't get bogged down by the whys and wherefores: Just follow the steps and get your work done with a minimum of hassle. Occasionally you might have to turn to another page if the procedure you're working on is accompanied by a *See Also*. That's because there's a lot of overlap among tasks, and we didn't want to keep repeating ourselves. We've scattered some useful *Tips* here and there, pointed out some features that are new in Windows 7, and thrown in a *Try This* or a *Caution* once in a while. By and large, however, we've tried to remain true to the heart and soul of the book, which is that the information you need should not only be available to you at a glance—it should also be *plain and simple!* So, whether you use Windows 7 on one home computer, on several computers that are part of a home network or a homegroup, or in a home office, we've tried to pack this book with procedures for everything we could think of that you might want to do, from the simplest tasks to some of the more esoteric ones. We've also tried to find and document the easiest way to accomplish these tasks. Windows 7 often provides a multitude of methods to achieve a single end result—which can be daunting or delightful, depending on the way you like to work. If you tend to stick with one favorite and familiar approach, we think the methods described in this book are the way to go. If you like trying out alternative techniques, go ahead! The intuitiveness of Windows 7 invites exploration, and you're likely to discover ways of doing things that you think are easier or that you like better than ours. If you do, that's great! It's exactly what the developers of Windows 7 had in mind when they provided so many alternatives.

## A Quick Overview

Your computer probably came with Windows 7 preinstalled, but if you do have to install it yourself, the Setup wizard makes installation so simple that you won't need our help anyway. Next, you don't have to read this book in any particular order. It's designed so that you can jump in, get the information you need, and then close the book (but keep it near your computer!). However, that doesn't mean we scattered the information about with wild abandon. The tasks you want to accomplish are arranged in two levels. The overall type of task you're looking for is under a main heading such as "Finding a Web Page," "Creating Quick Access to a File or Folder," and so on. Then, in each of those sections, the smaller tasks within the main task are arranged in a loose progression from the simplest to the more complex. OK, so what's where in this book?

Section 2 covers the basics: starting Windows 7 and shutting it down; starting programs and working with program windows; using shortcut menus; working with files, folders, and libraries; and getting help if you need it.

Section 3 focuses on accessing and organizing your files and folders: moving, copying, deleting, compressing, classifying, sharing, and archiving them; copying files to CDs or DVDs; recovering deleted items; creating new libraries; and using removable memory devices. We also provide illustrations of the many window view settings for Windows 7, with explanations about when and why you'd choose one view over another, and then how to go about changing the view to suit your particular needs.

Section 4 is all about running programs. We take a look the Ribbon, whose tabs put at your fingertips everything you need to compose professional-looking documents, and we introduce you to Calculator. We also look at some of the other programs that come with Windows 7: the On-Screen Keyboard, the Sticky Notes program, the Windows Journal, the Snipping Tool for capturing screen images, and a bunch of useful little gadgets you can keep on your Desktop. There's a short section here for MS-DOS fans, and another about running older programs.

Section 5 is where you'll go to make your computer truly yours. You can customize just about everything in Windows 7, including your Desktop background, screen saver, folders, Desktop icons, account picture, taskbar, and Start menu. You can check out some alternative ways of working, and, if you sometimes work in another part of the world or use another language, you can customize your keyboard to that area and language.

Section 6 helps you explore the Internet with Internet Explorer. Here's where we talk about finding a specific Web page or returning to a favorite site, finding all sorts of information on the Web, saving a Web page or copying information from it, and setting your own home page or pages. We also discuss controlling those annoying pop-up windows, and deleting your browsing history to keep your Web surfing private.

Section 7 is devoted to playing games, including Chess Titans, Mahjong Titans, and six other familiar games to keep you challenged and entertained, as well as three games—Comfy Cakes, Purble Shop, and Purble Pairs—that will delight the youngest members of the family. If you want to venture out into cyberspace, you can do friendly battle with an opponent over the Internet.

Section 8 explores the many options Windows 7 gives you for viewing and working with your photographs and other pictures. You'll find detailed explanations here that will help you choose which of the many photographic tools is exactly right for what you want to do. We show you how to use an add-on program's editing tools to crop your pictures, change

their resolution, remove "red eye," and create impressive panoramic photos. We also talk about using the Paint program to draw your own pictures.

Section 9 deals with multimedia, and we include detailed information about using Windows Media Player and Windows Media Center. You'll learn how to create playlists, copy CD music, synchronize your media with portable devices, share your media libraries, create video DVDs, record live video, download video from your camera, and make a movie.

Section 10 is about sounds—controlling the volume of the sounds your computer makes, creating sound files, designing your own sound themes, associating sounds with events, and so on. However, the majority of this section is devoted to Windows 7's speech-recognition system that makes it possible for you to direct your computer with voice commands. Alternatively, you can have a program called Narrator read aloud the contents of your computer screen—a valuable feature if your eyesight isn't what it once was!

Section 11 answers questions about printing your documents or setting up your printer. Windows 7 makes it a snap to print your photographs, and we also show you how to print readable Web pages. We also talk about creating documents in the XPS format, which makes it possible for your documents to look exactly the same regardless of the computer you use to open or print them. We also discuss scanning and digitizing documents, images, and anything—feathers, flowers—with an interesting texture or pattern.

Section 12 covers the many ways in which you can communicate, including sending and receiving faxes. We discuss e-mail clients, Webmail, and Windows Live Mail so that you're clear about their differences and the ways in which each of them works. It's quick and easy to send photos and documents via e-mail, and you'll learn about connecting with your contacts and creating a contacts group so that you can send the same information to a group of people.

Section 13 is about networking. Here, we talk about the types of networks you might encounter, with special emphasis on the advantages of setting up and using a homegroup. You'll learn how to share files and folders, and how to connect to your network in several different ways, including creating a VPN (Virtual Private Network) connection, connecting over the phone, connecting to public wireless networks, and even connecting to a network without having a network.

Section 14 is about setting up your computer. This is where you'll find information about transferring your files, folders, and settings from one computer to another without losing any information. You'll learn how to turn Windows features on or off and how to set up your homegroup, modem, Windows Live programs and Windows Live Mail, Internet access and connections, Backup program, Fax, local and network printers, and any other hardware.

Section 15 deals with Security, with a capital "S"! Here, we cover all the ways you can protect yourself and your computer. We show you how to set up secure passwords to deny access to your computer when you're not around, restrict user rights, use parental controls to keep children safe, protect yourself from spyware, set up a firewall to prevent intrusions from the Internet, protect your personal information on the Internet, increase your protection against dangerous e-mail viruses, and install critical fixes.

Last but not least, section 16 concentrates on doing some maintenance to tune up Windows once in a while, modifying settings to optimize the way your computer works, and adjusting settings for pen and touch input. And if something does go wrong with your system, we help you diagnose and fix the problem or, if necessary, show you how to get help to get the system running properly again.

## What's New in Windows 7?

What's new for you depends on which operating system you've been using. If you've been using Windows XP or an earlier version of Windows, you'll find many new remarkable and powerful features to enhance your time on the computer. If you've been using Windows Vista, you'll already be familiar with many of the features in Windows 7, but you'll find many of them much friendlier and easier to use.

The first thing you'll notice is that Windows 7 doesn't look like Windows XP. An impressive feature of Windows 7 is its Aero Glass appearance. If your computer's hardware supports this feature, parts of windows and other Windows elements can be transparent, semitransparent, or colored as you want. You can see dazzling 3-D effects when you switch between windows, and everything on your screen looks really clear and sharp. You'll notice improvements in other visual effects, including the increased clarity of pictures and videos, and you'll see some significant differences between the features of Windows 7 and those of Windows XP. For example, the Start menu doesn't have all those cascading submenus to navigate, and the folder windows aren't cluttered up with different toolbars; instead, the toolbar that remains changes its content depending on the types of folders or files contained in the windows. You'll also notice that the menus seem to have disappeared. Fear not! They're still there (just press the Alt key) but are hidden and mostly unnecessary. You'll see that folder windows can have different panes so that you can easily navigate among folders, see detailed information about an item, and even peek at a preview of a file without opening the file. Available previously only in special editions of Windows, the Media Center and Tablet PC tools are now included in Windows 7. With Media Center, you can watch movies and even live TV. You can record shows, play music, and make your computer the center of your entertainment world. The Tablet PC tools are specialized tools that give you the power to do most of your work directly on the screen, especially if you use the Ink feature, which enables you to use your own handwriting in your programs.

Another remarkable feature of Windows 7 is its ability to conduct any type of search from almost anywhere on your computer. If you need to find a document, just search for it from the Start menu or from within any window. If you're saying, "Well, what's so new about *that?*", try this: Press the Windows key, and then type part of the name of any program, folder, or file. The Windows key opens the Start menu, and, as you type, the results of your search appear on the Start menu. Type another letter or two, and the search results get narrowed down.

You'll find other features that make working on your computer easier than ever, including links in each window—some set up by Windows and others you create yourself—that allow you to jump to your favorite locations. There's also the Address bar, which helps you locate all the different places you want to explore. Windows 7 has grouped many of the tools and features you need into task-oriented centers. For example, there's the Mobility Center, which helps you set up your portable computer when you're on the road; the Network And Sharing Center, which helps you configure, control, secure, and navigate your network; the Ease Of Access Center, which helps you modify computer settings to improve your access to the computer; and the Action Center, where you track all your security and maintenance needs and make whatever adjustments are required.

If you've used Windows Vista, you'll find all sorts of additions to make your work easier. The new Jump Lists on the taskbar and Start menu reduce the number of steps it takes to find and open files or execute your most commonly used actions. You'll find the taskbar to be much improved—you can attach your frequently used programs directly to it, so starting a program is just a click away. Finding files is also a lot easier, with files of the same type arranged in common libraries regardless of where they're stored. This means that a Pictures Library will hold all your pictures, whether they're in your My Pictures folder, your Public Pictures folder, or some other folder you've included in that library. Windows creates libraries for your documents, music, pictures, and videos, but you can also create additional libraries. The libraries are also shared with Media Player and Media Center, so all your music, photos, and videos will always be available. You can even share these libraries over your home network with other computers running Windows 7 by creating a *homegroup*. A homegroup is a new networking tool that makes sharing files, printers, and other devices simple and easy. Windows 7 is loaded with new wizards that step you through some of the more complex operations, and new troubleshooters that help you solve problems. A powerful but annoying security feature that was introduced with Vista—the User Account Control (UAC)—has been substantially improved and made a lot less annoying! Designed to prevent either malicious or accidental damage to your system by requiring Administrator approval for many actions, Windows 7's UAC not only greatly reduces the number of times this approval is required but also lets you set the level of protection you want.

Sometimes just a few simple changes make your work on the computer a lot easier. Windows 7 introduces three features that make working with windows much more pleasant: Aero Snap, Aero Shake, and Aero Peek. Aero Snap helps arrange the windows by snapping to certain sizes—taking up the left half of the screen, for example, by dragging the window to the left edge. Aero Shake is one you've got to try: When there are multiple windows open on the Desktop, just use the mouse to grab one by the title bar, shake the window a bit, and all the other windows become minimized. Aero Peek is controlled by a little bar at the end of the taskbar: Point to this bar, and all the windows become transparent so that you can see the Desktop. Click the bar, and all the windows become minimized.

Windows 7 also has some features for specialized equipment. If you have a computer that supports multi-touch input, many Windows features really come alive. And with the Play To feature in Media Player, you can send your multimedia to different devices—another computer, a networked photo frame, or even an Xbox 360 console. You'll also find much more support for and information about those devices that you can attach to your computer.

One of the most notable changes in Windows 7 is what *isn't* included. You might have become used to using Windows Mail, Photo Gallery, MovieMaker, and Messenger. These programs no longer come with Windows, but enhanced versions of them, as well as some additional programs, are available for download as part of the Windows Live Essentials suite. Another missing part for some people is Internet Explorer; in much of Europe, for example, Internet Explorer isn't included in Windows. It's up to the computer manufacturers to decide which browsers are available on new computers. However, you can always download Internet Explorer from Microsoft.

So what's new for *you* in Windows 7? Aside from all the new tools and features we've just described, perhaps what's new in Windows 7 is a feeling of renewed confidence that you can easily and safely do what you want on your computer without worrying that someone or something will cause you all sorts of trouble.

## A Few Assumptions

We had to make a few educated guesses about you, our audience, when we started writing this book. Perhaps your computer is solely for personal use—e-mail, surfing the Internet, playing games, and so on. Perhaps your work allows you to telecommute. Or maybe you run a small home-based business. Taking all these possibilities into account, we assumed either that you'd be using a stand-alone home computer or that you'd have two or more computers connected so that you could share files, a printer, and so on. We also assumed that you have an Internet connection.

Another assumption we made is that—initially, anyway—you'd use Windows 7 just the way it came, and that your computer is capable of using all the features of Windows 7, meaning that your computer supports the Aero Glass transparent appearance. Also, although we assumed that you'd be using your mouse to execute commands and navigate around your computer, we know that many people prefer to accomplish just about every task by using the keyboard only.

If you decide to change the appearance of Windows 7—by reverting to the look of a previous version of Windows, for example—or to hide some screen elements and display others, you can quickly and easily customize almost everything. However, because Windows 7's default setup makes accomplishing your work so easy—and because our philosophy is that work should be as stress-free and pleasant as possible—the default setup is what we've shown in the procedures and graphics throughout this book.

## A Final Word (or Two)

We had three goals in writing this book:

- Whatever you want to do, we want the book to help you get it done.

- We want the book to help you discover how to do things you *didn't* know you wanted to do.

- And, finally, if we've achieved the first two goals, we'll be well on the way to the third, which is for our book to help you *enjoy* using Windows 7. We think that's the best gift we could give you to thank you for buying our book.

We hope you'll have as much fun using *Windows 7 Plain & Simple* as we've had writing it. The best way to learn is by *doing,* and that's how we hope you'll use this book.

# 2 Jump Right In

Windows 7 is designed to work for you, not you for it. You'll find that there are often several ways to accomplish one task. Why? Because people work differently. Because different tasks have different requirements. And because you want to find the way that works best for you, get your work done quickly, and then get away from the computer and live your life!

The procedures described in this book are simple and straightforward, and you can often use automated methods to get the more complex tasks done easily. This section of the book covers the basics: starting Windows 7 and shutting it down, starting programs, switching users without having to shut down all your running programs, accessing your documents, arranging your open windows, using the mouse, getting online help, and so on. There's also a handy visual glossary on the following two pages that will help you become familiar with the various features of the Windows 7 environment.

You'll want to feel comfortable with the basics before you do any customizing, so don't change anything yet. The best way to learn about running programs, managing windows, and getting help if you do get into trouble is to jump right in and try things out.

# What's Where in Windows 7?

Windows 7 is your working headquarters—the operating system that lets you run different programs simultaneously and share information among programs if you need to. Most of the programs you'll be using have common characteristics that were designed to work together in the Windows 7 environment so that once you learn how to do something in one program, you'll know how to do it in other programs.

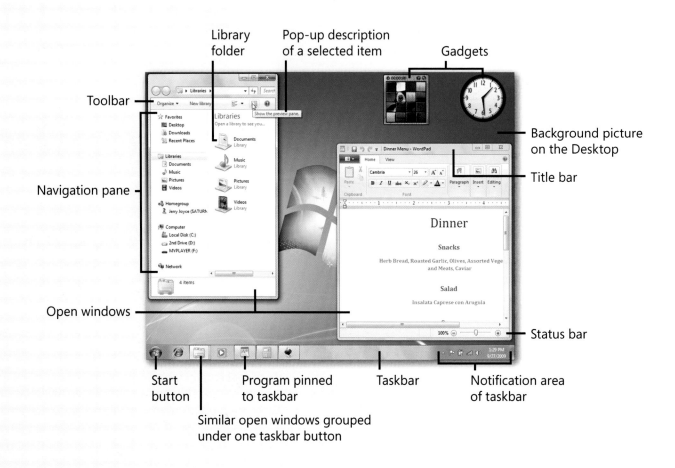

Library folder

Pop-up description of a selected item

Gadgets

Toolbar

Navigation pane

Background picture on the Desktop

Title bar

Open windows

Status bar

Start button

Program pinned to taskbar

Taskbar

Notification area of taskbar

Similar open windows grouped under one taskbar button

Take a look at the different parts of the Windows 7 environment displayed on these two pages—what they do and what they're called—and you'll be on the road to complete mastery. The way Windows 7 was set up on your computer, as well as the many ways in which you can customize

Windows 7, can make drastic changes to the look of your Desktop, but the basic concepts are the same. And, if you need to, you can always come back to this visual glossary for a quick refresher on Windows 7 terminology.

Shortcut menu

Account picture

Aero Glass appearance

Subfolder (folder inside another folder)

Desktop icon

Start menu

Running program

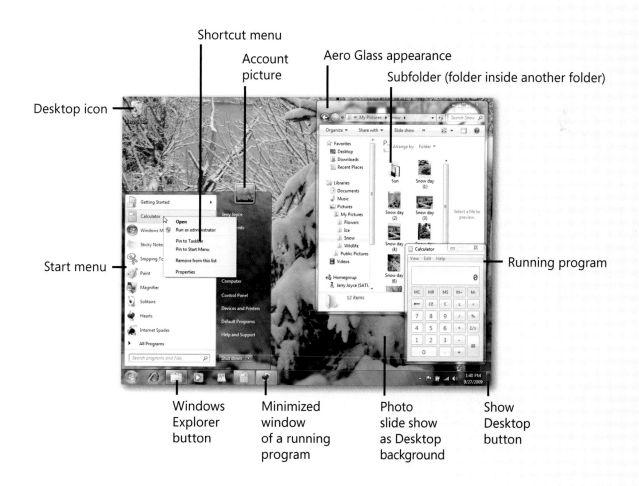

Windows Explorer button

Minimized window of a running program

Photo slide show as Desktop background

Show Desktop button

# Starting Up

Windows 7 and your computer are designed to exist in more states than just being on or off. If you've been gone for a while, if you've unplugged your computer, or if you're using it for the first time, you'll need to bring it to life from its "off" state. Just like humans, Windows 7 and your computer both love to sleep. In the computer world, "sleep" is a state in which the computer stores your information on the hard disk and keeps it in memory, enters a very low-energy state, and then returns to full activity very quickly.

## Start or Wake Up a Computer

1. Move the mouse or press a key on the keyboard to see whether the computer is really off or just sleeping, or if it's simply resting with the screen off.

2. If the power button or power indicator is blinking, press the power button to wake up the computer.

3. If the computer is really turned off, turn on the computer, the monitor, and any peripheral devices—your printer, for example—and wait a moment for Windows to load.

4. Click your user name.

## How to Get Your Computer Going

| Its state | What you can do |
|---|---|
| Off | Press the power button, and log on. |
| Sleep | Press the blinking power button or lift the laptop cover, and log on if required. |
| Hibernate | Press the power button, and log on if required. |
| On, with a blank screen | Move the mouse or press a key. |
| On, with a screen saver | Move the mouse or press a key, and log on if required. |
| On, locked | Enter your password, or click Switch User to log on using a different name. |

---

**Caution**

Personal accounts are very powerful. Each user of the computer has his or her own folders for storing documents, and each user has individual and specific settings. You should never use someone else's account! If you do, everything from files to e-mail messages could be misplaced or lost.

**See Also**

"Leaving Your Computer" on the facing page for information about putting the computer to sleep, turning it off, restarting it, or locking it.

# Leaving Your Computer

If you walk away from your computer for more than a few minutes—or even for a few seconds if your computer is accessible by others—you'll want to either lock the computer or switch it to a low-power state that saves energy. When locked, the computer can still function, but your files, settings, and programs aren't accessible and can't be viewed by others.

If you want to grant access to another user, you can let the other person log on and use his or her own settings. If you need to be away from the computer for extended periods, or you want to add features or move the computer to a new location, just turn it off.

## Leave It

1 Click the Start button.

2 If the action you want is displayed, click the appropriate button.

3 If the action you want isn't displayed, point to the arrow and choose the action you want:

- Switch User to keep your programs running in the background (but inaccessible until you log on again), allowing another user to log on.

- Log Off to close all your programs but leave the computer running so that another user can log on.

- Lock to deny access to anyone except those you've authorized to log on to this computer.

- Restart to shut down the computer and then restart it.

- Sleep, and wait for Windows to save your work and then go to sleep.

- Hibernate, and wait for Windows to save your work session and turn off.

- Shut Down to close all your programs and turn off the computer.

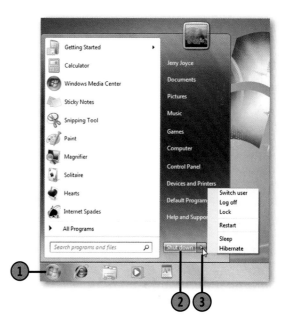

**See Also**

"Customizing the Start Menu" on page 99 for information about customizing which action is the default and is shown on the appropriate button.

# Starting a Program

The real work of an operating system is to run software programs. Windows comes with a wide variety of programs, and you can install additional (and often more powerful) ones. Most programs are listed on the Start menu, but Windows gives you several ways to start your programs so that you can choose the way you like best. The programs listed below are only some of the programs that come with Windows. You'll find descriptions of the others elsewhere in this book.

## Start a Program

**1** Do any of the following:

- Click the Start button or press the Windows key, and choose a program from the Start menu.
- Click the program if it's shown on the taskbar.
- Click the Start button or press the Windows key, type the first few letters of the program you want to run, and, after the search results on the Start menu show the program, press Enter or click the program.
- Click the Start button, point to All Programs, click any relevant folders to display or expand their content, and click the program you want.
- Point to and then double-click the program icon on the Desktop.
- Click Windows Explorer on the taskbar, navigate to the location of the program or file associated with the program, and double-click the program or file.
- Click a library on the Start menu, locate the file that's associated with the program, and double-click the file.
- Insert the disc or removable drive that contains a program designed to run from the disc or drive, and choose to run the program.

**2** Use the program, and close it when you've finished.

## Frequently Used Windows 7 Programs

| Program | Purpose |
| --- | --- |
| Calculator | Does arithmetical, programming, statistical and date calculations as well as conversions. |
| Character Map | Inserts special characters from installed fonts. |
| Internet Explorer | Functions as a Web browser and an HTML document viewer. |
| Magnifier | Magnifies sections of the screen. |
| Notepad | Creates, edits, and displays text documents. |
| Paint | Creates and edits bitmap pictures; imports and edits scanned images and digital pictures. |
| Sound Recorder | Creates digital sound files. |
| Media Center | Plays, records, and organizes multimedia. |
| Media Player | Plays sounds, music, and videos. |
| Math Input Panel | Converts handwritten equations and formulas into type. |
| WordPad | Creates, edits, and displays text, Rich Text Format, and some Word documents. |

# Accessing Your Documents

The Documents Library is an inventory of your documents on the computer. Only documents stored in folders that have been included in the Documents Library are listed.

## Open a Document

**(1)** Click the Start button, and choose Documents from the Start menu to open the Documents Library.

**(2)** Click a file to select it.

**(3)** Review the properties of this file.

**(4)** Click the Show The Preview Pane button to review the contents of this file. Click the button again to close the preview.

**(5)** Double-click the file to open it, or press Enter to open the selected file.

**(6)** Click the Close button when you've finished.

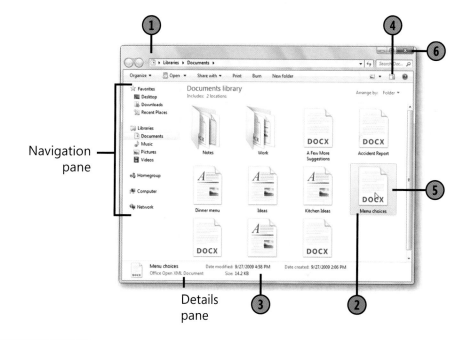

Navigation pane

Details pane

### See Also

"Using Jump Lists for Quick Access" on page 25 for information about using Jump Lists to access files when starting a program.

"Windows Views" on page 28 and "Changing the Window View" on page 30 for information about changing the way files and folders are displayed.

"Add a Folder to a Library" on page 50 for information about adding a folder to an existing library, and "Create a New Library" on page 51 for information about creating new libraries.

### Tip

Each user of the computer (provided he or she has logged on) has a separate Documents folder, as well as other personalized settings. Files in your Documents folder, as well as those in the Public Documents folder, are automatically included in your Documents Library.

# Mouse and Keyboard Maneuvers

Windows lets you work the way you want. You can move around, choose items, and do much of your work using only the mouse, only the keyboard, or a combination of the two. With the mouse, you can jump directly to the point you want, grab and move things, and quickly choose commands. With the keyboard, you can do most things by using keyboard shortcuts or by moving around using the Tab key or the arrow keys. The way you work is up to you, and you might find that a combination of the two methods gets things done quickly, efficiently, and, most important, comfortably for you.

## Mouse Moves

**Point:** Move the mouse until the mouse pointer (either a small arrow-shaped pointer or a tiny hand) is pointing to the item you want.

**Hover:** Point to an item and keep the mouse stationary.

**Click:** Point to the item you want, and then quickly press down and release the left mouse button.

**Double-click:** Point to the item you want, and then quickly press down and release the left mouse button twice, being careful not to move the mouse between clicks.

**Right-click:** Point to the item you want, and then quickly press down and release the right mouse button.

**Select:** Point to an item, and click to select it. To select an icon when the system is set to open an item with a single click, point to the icon but don't click. A selected item usually is a different color from other similar items or is surrounded by a frame.

**Multiple-select:** To select a list of adjacent or sequential items, click the first item, hold down the Shift key, and click the last item. To select or deselect *nonadjacent* items, hold down

the Ctrl key and click each item you want. (Note that not all windows and dialog boxes permit multiple selection.)

**Drag:** Select the item you want. Keeping the mouse pointer on the selected item, hold down the left mouse button and move the mouse until you've "dragged" the item to the desired location; then release the left mouse button.

## Keyboard Moves

**Keyboard shortcuts:** Press two or more keys in combination or consecutively. Keys you press in combination are linked with a plus sign, so Ctrl+C means hold down the Ctrl key and press the C key, and then release both keys. Keys you press consecutively are separated by a comma or commas, so Alt, F, X means press and release the Alt key, press and release the F key, and then press and release the X key.

**Windows key:** A special key that displays the Windows logo. Press it by itself to open the Start menu. Many programs have keyboard shortcuts that use the Windows key.

**Arrow keys:** Four keys, each with an arrow pointing in a different direction. Use them to move the highlight, the insertion point, or the selection in the direction of the arrow.

**Tab key:** This key has various functions. In a document, it inserts a tab character or moves you to the next column; in a window or dialog box, it moves you from section to section. To go in the opposite direction, press Shift+Tab.

## So Many Ways to Do It

To modify the way the mouse works, see "Customizing Your Mouse" on pages 92–93 and "Customizing Your Folders" on pages 100–101. To work without the mouse or keyboard, see "Directing Your Computer with Voice Commands" on pages 206–207, "Dictating Text" on pages 208–209, and "Letting Your Computer Do the Talking" on page 212.

# Files, Folders, and Libraries

Everything you have on your computer is contained in files. These are those strange digital files composed of zeroes and ones that are useless without the right program to translate them. Fortunately, in most cases, if you have a file on your computer, you also have at least one program that can use it. You have operating-system files that make Windows run, application files that run the programs you use, and data files that store the information used by the programs. In most cases, you'll do the majority of your work with data files. For example, if you have a digital picture, it's a specific type of data file that can be used by programs such as Paint or Windows Live Photo Gallery. If you have a Word document file, the data file contains all the words and formatting that you can access by using Microsoft Word.

The way Windows and programs quickly recognize the type of file is by the part of the file's name called the *extension*. This is the last few letters of the name, the part that follows the period. For example, a file called *mystory.txt* is a text file, as indicated by the *.txt* file extension. You might not always see the file extension in Windows Explorer, depending on your settings, but Windows and the programs can always see it and know to open it as a text data file in Notepad, WordPad, or Word.

Folders are ways to organize your files and group them together by type. For example, you might want to keep all your documents, including any Word documents, text files,

PDF files, Excel files, and so on, in your My Documents folder, and all your picture files in your My Pictures folder. You can create additional folders and, for an even greater level of organizing, create folders inside folders, often called subfolders. By creating folders and placing specific types of files in them, you can set up whatever method of organization you want.

One difficulty with creating multiple folders used to be gaining quick access to their content. Not anymore! Let's say you're looking for a Word file, which could be in your My Documents, Public Documents, or your newly created Work Documents folder. Now, with Windows 7, when you go to your Documents Library—provided you've added the Work Documents folder to the Documents Library—you'll see the content of all three of these folders in one place, making it easy to locate the file. The same is true for the other libraries—all your pictures will be shown regardless of their location, and so on. You can also control which folders are included in each library, so if you want to keep certain items out of the library, such as all those confidential memos, you can put them in a folder that hasn't been added to the library.

You can also create your own libraries and designate which folders you want to be included. For example, if you have a big project, you might create one folder for text, another for art, and a third for data. Add each of these to your Project Library, and you'll see all the files in one place.

# Quickly Finding a Program, File, or Folder

You know it's there somewhere, but where? Instead of wasting time digging through all the menus or folders you think might hold that program, file, or folder you need, why not have Windows 7 do the searching for you? With the Search feature, not only can you search for a program, file, or folder name or even part of its name, you can also search for words that are contained in a file.

## Search for the File or Folder

① Click the Start button, and start typing in the Search box the name, or part of the name, of the file or folder you want, or text that you know is contained in the file.

② As you type, you'll see the search results. If there are too many results, type more of the name to narrow the search, or include the file extension if you know it.

③ If you see the file or folder you want, do either of the following:

- Click it if you want to run the default action for that type of file or folder. For a document, this means to open it in its default program; for a program, it means to run the program; for a folder, it means to open the folder.

- Right-click the file, and choose the action you want from the shortcut menu.

④ If you don't see the file or folder, do either of the following:

- Click See More Results to open a window containing all the search results, and then locate your file or folder.

- Click a type of file to open a window with all the results for that type of file, and then find your file or folder.

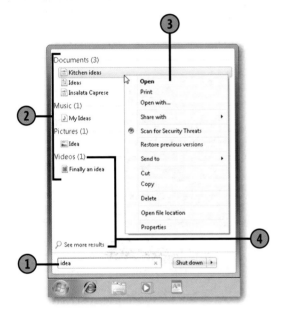

**See Also**

See "Changing Search Options" on page 321 for information about customizing the way Windows searches files and folders.

**Tip**

When you search from the Start menu, Windows searches for files and folders throughout your computer. However, by default, it searches for file content only in locations that are indexed. If you want to search for files by content anywhere on your computer, you can change the way Windows searches and which locations are indexed.

# Searching a Specific Location

A computer can end up containing a lot of files. Instead of scrolling through a long list of files, you can search the library and even add other restrictions to further narrow the search. You can also search locations on your network.

## Refine Your Search

① Click Windows Explorer on the taskbar to open a window if one isn't already open.

② Navigate to the location you want to search.

③ Click in the Search box and type your search text.

④ If you can't easily find the item, click in the Search box again, select a search filter, and enter the information to refine your search. Add any other search filters you want to use, and select or enter the value for the filter.

⑤ Find your file in the window.

**See Also**

"Changing Indexing Options" on page 322 for information about customizing the way Windows indexes files and folders.

**Tip**

To remove a search and restore the full content of the window, click the X at the right of the Search box.

**Try This!**

Create and run a search that you know you'll probably want to redo in the future. Click the Save Search button, and name the search. In the future, click the search in the Favorites section of the Navigation pane of any window. Windows will run the search and will show the updated results.

# Accessing Everything

Windows Explorer is the gateway to your computer's contents. It displays the icons that represent all your local storage areas: removable disk drives, hard disks, CD and DVD drives, and so on, as well as your homegroup and other shared network files. From here you can access your libraries or venture as deep into the folder structure of your computer as you dare.

## Open Any Folder

① Click Windows Explorer on the taskbar to open a window.

② If the location you want to go to is visible, click it.

③ If the location isn't visible, move the mouse over the Navigation pane and click the right-pointing arrows to display the folders or items contained in each item. Continue clicking the arrows until the location you want is displayed.

④ Click the location to display its contents in the window.

⑤ To open a folder or a file in the window, double-click it, or, if the folder or file is already selected, press Enter.

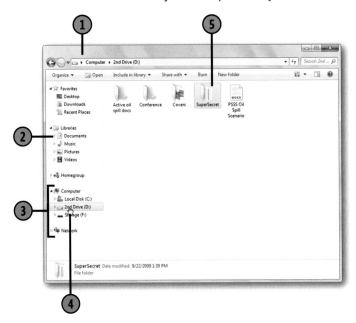

**See Also**

"Accessing Your Homegroup" on page 249 and "Sharing with Your Homegroup" on pages 250–251 for information about accessing files in your homegroup, and "Connecting to a Network Computer" on pages 256–257 for information about accessing files over a network.

**Tip**

To open a file that you used recently, point to the program that you used on the Start menu and choose the file from the list that appears. If the program is on the taskbar, you can also right-click it to see the list of recently used files.

## Explore

**①** Do either of the following:

- Click a location to return to it.

- Click a down arrow to see a list of locations you can go to, and click a location to go to it.

**②** Click the Back button to return to the previous window, or click the Forward button, if available, to move to a folder you visited previously and then left using the Back button.

**③** Click Recent Pages to see a list of windows you visited since opening Windows Explorer.

**④** Click a link in the Favorites section of the Navigation pane to go to that location. Click Recent Places to see a list of locations you've visited recently.

**⑤** To open a folder in a new window, hold down the Ctrl key and double-click the folder.

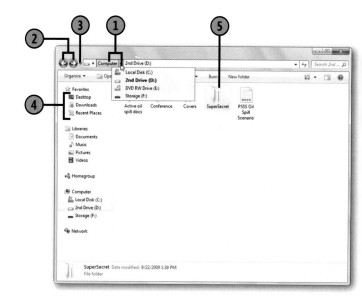

**See Also**

"Add a Link" on page 39 for information about adding your own destinations to the Favorite Links list.

**Tip**

When you use the Address bar to navigate, you're using the traditional "path" structure in which items are organized in a hierarchy—for example, a drive contains certain folders, a folder contains subfolders, those subfolders contain more subfolders, and so on.

# Switching Among Open Windows

Whatever your working style, it's likely that you'll end up with more than one window open on your computer—your Documents Library window and the Network window, perhaps, or a couple of program windows. Instead of closing one window to get to another, you can simply switch windows.

## Select a Window

1. On the taskbar, point to either Windows Explorer to locate a folder or library window, or to a program to locate files that are open in that program.

2. Use the thumbnail image of the window to confirm that it's the one you want. If you can't tell from the thumbnail whether you're looking at the correct item, move the mouse over the thumbnail to see a full-screen preview of the window.

3. Click the thumbnail on the taskbar to switch to that window.

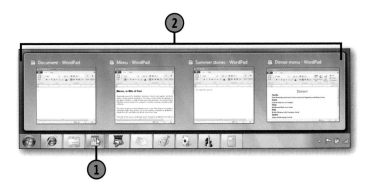

## Switch Windows

1. Hold down the Alt key and press the Tab key to display the open windows. Continue pressing the Tab key while holding down the Alt key to cycle through the open windows.

2. Release the Alt key when the window you want is selected.

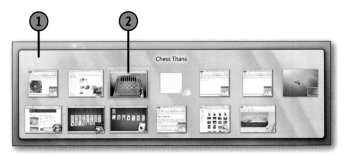

**Tip**

The icon on the taskbar for a program with multiple files open has a stacked appearance instead of the flat appearance of a program pinned to the taskbar with no open files.

**Try This!**

Hold down the Windows key and press the Tab key. Each window will be shown in 3-D. Continue holding down the Windows key and pressing the Tab key until the window you want is on top.

## Hide the Windows

**①** Move the mouse pointer over the Show Desktop button to use the Aero Peek feature and to see the Desktop and the outlines of the open windows.

**②** Move the mouse pointer away from the Show Desktop button to display the windows again.

**③** Click the Show Desktop button to minimize all the open windows.

**Tip**

If you don't see the windows in 3-D when you use the Windows and Tab keys, and don't see the thumbnail and full-screen previews, then either your computer doesn't support the Aero Glass features or these features have been disabled.

**Try This!**

With more than one window visible on the screen, point to the title bar of a window, hold down the left mouse button, and shake the window until all the other windows become minimized. This is the Aero Shake feature that's similar to the Aero Peek feature.

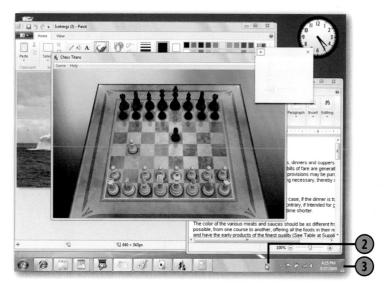

# Managing Windows

"Managing" a window means bossing it around: You can move it, change its size, and open and close it. Most programs are contained in windows. Although these windows might have some different features, most program windows have more similarities than differences.

## Use the Buttons to Switch Between Sizes

① Click the Maximize button, and the window enlarges and fills the screen. (If the window is already maximized, you won't see the Maximize button.)

② Click the Restore Down button, and the window gets smaller. (If the window is already restored, you won't see the Restore Down button.)

③ Click the Minimize button, and the window disappears but you can see its name on a button on the taskbar.

④ Point to the icon for the window, and click the window you want. The window zooms back to the size it was before you minimized it.

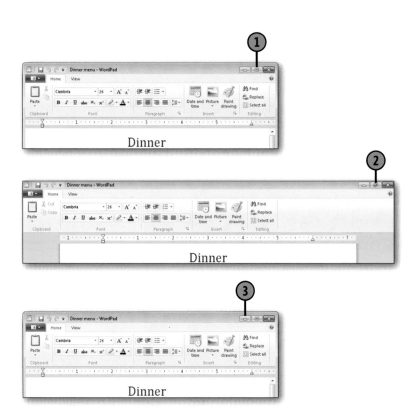

**Tip** ✓

To automatically arrange all the windows on your Desktop, right-click a blank spot on the taskbar, and choose the arrangement you want from the shortcut menu.

# Use the Mouse to Move and Resize a Window

**1** Do any of the following:

- Move a window by pointing to the window's title bar, clicking and holding down the left mouse button, and then dragging the window to a new location.

- Move a window to the left until the mouse pointer touches the edge of the screen, and then release the mouse button to resize the window so that it takes up the left half of the screen.

- Move a window to the right until the mouse pointer touches the right edge of the screen, and then release the mouse button so that the window takes up the right half of the screen.

- Move a window until the mouse pointer touches the top edge of the screen, and then release the mouse button to maximize the window.

- Double-click the title bar to restore a maximized window or a window moved to take up half the screen to its original size. For other windows, double-clicking the title bar will maximize the window.

**2** To resize the window to any size you want, move the mouse over one of the borders of the window until the mouse pointer changes into a two-headed arrow. Drag the window border until the window is the size you want. If the mouse pointer reaches the top of the screen, the bottom of the window will automatically be resized to reach the bottom of the screen.

**See Also**

"Managing Windows Arrangements" on page 320 for information about disabling both the Aero Snap and the Aero Shake features.

**Tip**

The automatic resizing of a window when the mouse pointer reaches the right, the left, or the top of the screen is called Aero Snap. This feature works only if your computer is capable of supporting the Aero Glass features.

# Using Shortcut Menus for Quick Results

Windows 7 and the programs that work with it were designed to be intuitive—that is, they anticipate what you're likely to want to do when you're working on a particular task, and they place the appropriate commands on a shortcut menu that you open by clicking the *right* mouse button. These shortcut menus are *dynamic,* which means they change depending on the task in progress.

## Use a Shortcut Menu Command

**1** Right-click an item.

**2** Choose a command from the shortcut menu to accomplish the task at hand. If the item or action you want isn't listed on the shortcut menu:

- From the shortcut menu, choose an item whose name has an arrow next to it to see whether the item or action you want is on one of the shortcut menu's submenus.

- Check to be sure you right-clicked the proper item.

- Check the program's documentation or Help files to verify that what you want to do can be accomplished using the item you right-clicked.

### Tip

The tasks listed on the toolbar in a library or folder window are also dynamic, depending on the types of files in the library or folder, but they usually provide actions that are less specific than those listed on a shortcut menu.

### Tip

When in doubt, right-click! If you're not sure how to accomplish what you want to do, right-click the item in question, and you'll usually see an appropriate command on the shortcut menu.

### Try This!

Right-click a blank spot on the Desktop, and note the commands on the shortcut menu that appears. Right-click a blank spot on the taskbar. Open the Start menu, and right-click an item. Continue experimenting by right-clicking the Recycle Bin icon and other items on the Desktop, and various files and folders in folder windows. Amazing, isn't it?

# Using Jump Lists for Quick Access

Jump Lists, a new feature in Windows 7, are designed to give you quick access to what you need. The Jump List for Windows Explorer contains locations that you frequently visit. A Jump List for a program such as WordPad or Paint lists your most recently used files. A Jump List for some of the other features—the Getting Started feature, for example—lists common tasks. Jump Lists exist in two places: on the taskbar and on the Start menu.

## Use a Taskbar Jump List

① Right-click the program you want to use to access the item.

② Click the item you want to open.

## Use a Start Menu Jump List

① Open the Start menu and point to the program you want to use to access the item. (Only programs that display right-pointing arrows have Jump Lists.)

② Click the item you want to open.

**See Also**

"Customizing the Start Menu" on page 99 for information about enabling and customizing the Jump Lists.

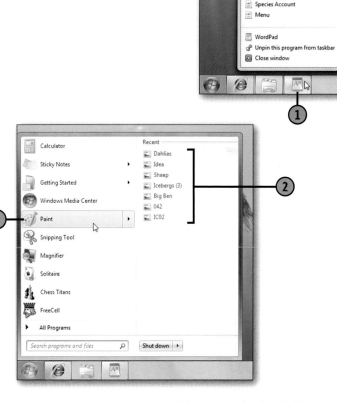

# Getting Help

What are big and colorful; packed with information, procedures, shortcuts, and links to online information; and sadly underutilized? The Help programs! Of course, they couldn't possibly replace this book, but you can use them to find concise step-by-step procedures for diagnosing and overcoming problems, and to explore many aspects of managing Windows. You can access Help from the Start menu or from within a program.

## Find the Information

(1) Click the Start button, and choose Help And Support from the Start menu to open the Windows Help And Support Center.

(2) To search for a specific item, type a keyword, keywords, or a short phrase in the Search box, and press Enter.

(3) Click the link to the most relevant topic. If the item has subtopics, click the subtopic you want.

(4) Review the content of the Help topic.

(5) To check out the information that's available, click the Browse Help button to see all the topics in Help. Click a topic, and browse to display a list of items you can choose to view. Click a link to the main topic of interest. If the item has subtopics, click the subtopic you want.

(6) To find other resources for help, click the More Support Options button.

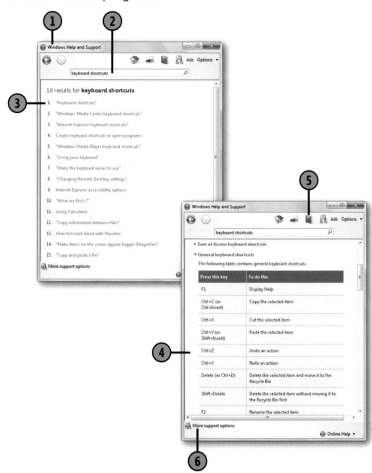

**Tip**

To get help about the window, dialog box, or program you're using, press the F1 key.

# 3

# Accessing and Organizing

We all know that to work productively, with minimal stress and frustration, we must get organized! That's where Windows 7 comes in. Windows 7 supplies the framework—a basic file structure of libraries, drives, and some ready-made folders, which you can either use as is or create your own file- and folder-management system. You can organize the files within the folders—alphabetically or by size, type, date, and so on—and move, copy, and rename files or groups of files. If you want the people who share the computer with you to have access to certain files and folders, you can put those items in folders that are designed to be shared. You can change the appearance of the windows in which you view your documents and folders, and, depending on the information you need, you can view them in any of eight different views.

You can put the items you use every day on the computer's Desktop, just as you do on a real desktop, and, to gain immediate access to a document you're preparing, you can put a shortcut to it on the Desktop. You can take your files with you by copying them onto a removable memory device, and you can compress large files, either for storage or so that you can send them via e-mail. And you can use the handy toolbars to quickly navigate your way through the information on your computer.

# Windows Views

Although Windows 7 has eight view settings, there are actually just five major categories, one of which is a single category with four different sizes. The five major categories are Icons view, with the choice of four different sizes of icons; List view; Details view; Tiles view; and Content view. Additionally, you can choose an icon size setting anywhere between the four standard size settings. You'll probably want to experiment to see which view is best suited for your work and for the contents of your folders. For example, you might want to use Icons view in a folder that contains only a few files of different types, List view to see a vertical listing of files and folders, Details view when you're looking for files that were created on a specific date, Content view when you need as many details as possible, Tiles view when you're managing pictures, and Extra Large Icons view when you're reviewing the pictures. The eight views are described in detail on these two pages.

**Icons view:** The four icon sizes are Extra Large, Large, Medium, and Small. In most cases, it's only the size of the icon—not its content—that changes in any of these four settings. However, in Small Icons view, you'll see only the icons; in the other views, Windows 7 shows you a preview of the file—if it's available—as part of the icon. Each icon size has its purpose. For example, the Extra Large Icons setting is the best way to view pictures in detail, and to get a good view of the contents of a folder and its subfolders. It is, however, an inefficient use of space to have a file represented only by an icon. On the other hand, the Small Icons setting lets you view a large number of files but provides little detail about pictures, file contents, or folder contents. The icons are arranged in horizontal rows, and, if there are too many files to be shown in the window at one time, you simply scroll vertically to see the remaining files.

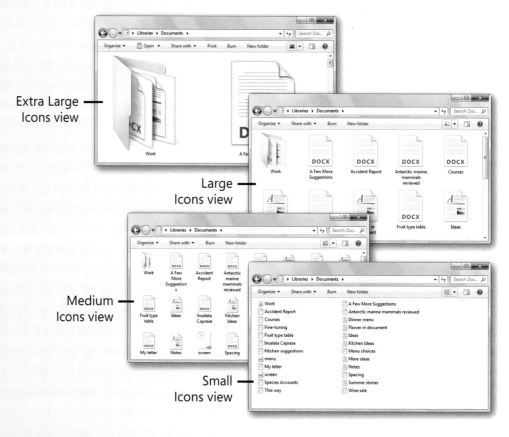

Extra Large Icons view

Large Icons view

Medium Icons view

Small Icons view

**List view:** This view displays small icons representing files and folders in a vertical listing that can snake through multiple columns. The name of the folder or file is listed next to the icon. If there are too many files to be shown in the window, you scroll horizontally to see the additional columns and the remaining files.

**Details view:** This view displays small icons in a single-column list that shows the name of the file or folder and includes details such as size, type, and date. The details shown depend on the types of files in the folder, and you can customize the details that are shown. If you can't see all the details, just scroll horizontally to see the additional details. If there are too many files to be shown in the window, you scroll vertically to see the remaining files.

**Tiles view:** This view displays medium-sized icons that include the name of the file or folder, the file type, and the file size. The files are arranged horizontally in as many columns as will fit within the window. If there are too many files to be shown in the window, you scroll vertically to see the remaining files.

**Content view:** This view displays each file or folder on a single line and includes information about the file that changes depending on the type of file. For example, a Word document might show author, tags, and date created; a video clip shows length and frame rate.

List vew

Details view

Tiles vew

Content view

After you've chosen the view you want, Windows 7 offers more options. In each view, you can arrange the way the files are sorted—for example, you can arrange the files in order by name, size, file type, or date. If you prefer, you can arrange the files in groups or include only items that fit specific parameters. If you're in a library, you can arrange the files by the name

of the folder they're in. You can also show different panes in the window—the Navigation pane to open other folders, the Details pane to show the *metadata* (such as title, tags, author, and size), and the Preview pane to show a preview, if available, of the selected item. These panes provide this information regardless of which view you're using.

# Changing the Window View

You can change the appearance of the windows that contain your files and folders so that the information is presented in the way that's most useful for you.

## Choose a View

1 In the window whose view you want to change, click the Views button to cycle through the views in order. (Only the Large Icons view is used for the Icons view in this instance.)

2 If you want to select a specific view, click the down arrow at the right of the Views button, and click the view you want.

3 If you want to create a custom size for icons, click the down arrow at the right of the Views button, and drag the slider to create the icon size you want.

**See Also**

"Windows Views" on pages 28–29 for information about all the different views.

"Customizing Your Folders" on pages 100–101 for information about changing the look and type of information displayed.

**Try This!**

Click in your folder window to select it. Hold down the Ctrl key and rotate the mouse wheel. Watch as all the views change in the same way they change when you use the slider on the Views button.

# Viewing File Information

There are numerous ways to view your files, folders, and libraries. In addition to changing your view of the files, the Preview and Details panes provide additional information so that you can identify whether you've located the file you want without having to open it first.

## Show the Information

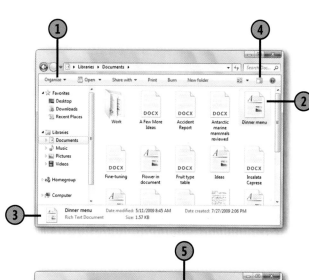

(1) Click Organize, point to Layout on the drop-down menu, and choose Details Pane, if it isn't already selected, from the submenu to display the Details pane.

(2) Click a file or folder.

(3) Read the information about the file or folder. The type of information shown varies depending on the type of file or folder you're looking at.

(4) Click the Show The Preview Pane button to display the Preview pane.

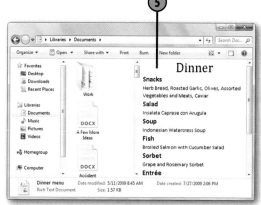

(5) View the preview of the file or the folder contents. (Note that not all files display a preview.) If the file is a sound, music, or video file, use the controls to play it. Click the Show The Preview Pane button again to hide the preview.

(6) Continue clicking files or folders and reviewing the material in the Details pane and/or the Preview pane until you've located the item you want.

**Tip**

If, when you click to show the Details or the Preview pane, you can't see it, the window is probably not large enough. Increase its size until you see the pane you want.

# Arranging Your Files

A single folder can contain a large number of files, so when you're looking for one particular file, it can be difficult to find, especially if you don't remember its name. When you combine the contents of two or more folders into a single library, you also can end up with an overwhelming number of files. Worse, if you need several files that are scattered throughout a folder or library, finding and selecting the ones you want can be quite time consuming. Fortunately, you can sort the information by any of the fields, group files by numerous categories, or filter the data so that only the information you want is displayed. In a library, the files are already arranged for you, but you can change the way they're grouped and sorted.

## Arrange Files in a Library

(1) In a library, if the Library pane isn't visible, click Organize, point to Layout on the drop-down menu, and choose Library Pane.

(2) In a library, click the button next to the Arrange By label. The name on the button shows you how the files are currently arranged.

(3) Click the way you want the files to be arranged.

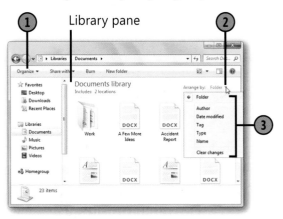

Library pane

## Sort by Field

(1) In either a library or a folder, select Details view if it isn't the current view, and click the field label you want to sort by.

(2) If you want to reverse the sort order, click the field a second time.

The tiny arrow above the field name indicates that the files are sorted by this field, and the arrow points in the direction of the sort.

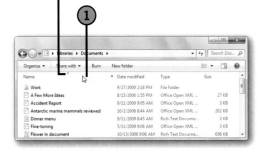

## Filter or Group

① Click the down arrow next to a field label.

② To show only selected files and folders, select the check boxes for the items to be displayed. If you're filtering by date, you can also specify a single date or a date range.

③ Click another field label, and select the appropriate check boxes if you want to include additional filtering.

④ Right-click a blank spot in the window, point to Group By on the shortcut menu that appears, and, on the submenu, click the item to be grouped by to display the files and folders in groups. In a library window, the Group By command is available only if the library has been arranged by folders.

⑤ To hide the content of a group, double-click the group name.

⑥ To display hidden content, double-click the group name.

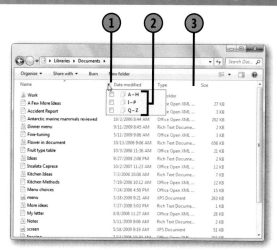

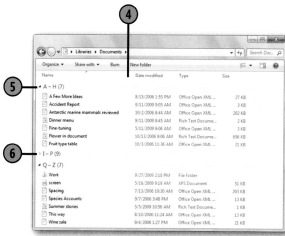

**Tip** ✓

The file arrangement that's listed depends on the type of library. When you select a new arrangement, the library selects the most appropriate view. You can, however, change the view to whichever one you want.

# Classifying Your Files

Before you know it, your computer can fill up with files—pictures, music, letters, worksheets, and much more. One method you can use to help keep track of these files—and to help you find the right ones later, when you need them—is to include additional information about the file. Depending on the type of file, this information can include author name, keywords, a rating, and more. A very powerful method you can use is to add tags to your files. A tag is a tool to classify a file by category, subject matter, or whatever you want. After your files are tagged, you can arrange them by their tags, so associated files can easily be grouped together. Although not all file formats support storing these extra details, called *metadata*, many common file formats do.

## Add More Information

① Locate the file you want to classify, and click to select it.

② Click in a field in the Details pane, and type the text you want for that field.

③ Click in another field, and enter any information you want. Continue clicking in fields and entering the text you want.

④ Press Enter or click Save when you've finished.

**Tip** ✓

Information in the Details pane varies by the type of document. For example, picture and music files have stars that you can click to rate the item, while a document might have a field for Current Status. To see all available fields, drag the upper Display pane border upward. You can't type information in some of the fields in the Details pane because these fields get their information automatically from Windows.

**See Also**

"Viewing File Information" on page 31 for information about displaying the Details pane if it isn't already displayed.

"Arranging Your Files" on pages 32–33 for information about sorting and grouping the files.

## Tag a File

① Locate and select the file to be tagged. To apply the tag or tags to multiple files, select all the files that will have the same tag or tags.

② In the Details pane, click the Tags field and start typing your text. If an existing tag you want to use appears, click the check box to complete the tag. To add another tag, type a semicolon, and then type or select the next tag.

③ When you've finished, click Save or press Enter to save the changes.

### Tip

To quickly identify the files in a library that don't have tags, choose Tags in the Arrange By list in the Library pane. Double-click the Unspecified group of files to see all the files without tags.

### See Also

"Viewing Photos with Windows Live Photo Gallery" on pages 164–165 for information about adding tags to pictures using Live Photo Gallery, and "Importing Photos from Your Camera or Removable Media" on page 171 for information about adding tags to pictures when you import them from a camera.

### Try This!

Open the Pictures Library and, holding down the Ctrl key, click the different picture files that you want to tag with the same tag. After you've selected the files, release the Ctrl key and click the Tag field in the Details pane. Type a tag, and then press Enter. Repeat for other pictures that you want to have a different tag. After you've tagged the pictures, click the Arrange By button in the Library pane, and choose Tag.

# Returning to a Folder or Library

Most of use just a few folders and libraries and return to them repeatedly. You can quickly access the most frequently visited ones with just a couple of mouse-clicks. If what you're looking for isn't in that list, you can see a more comprehensive list of the most recently visited folders or libraries.

## Return to a Folder or Library

① Right-click the Windows Explorer icon on the taskbar to display a Jump List containing your most frequently visited folders and libraries.

② Click the folder or library you want.

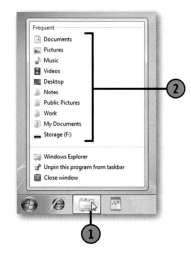

## Expand the List

① In the Navigation pane of Windows Explorer, click Recent Places in the Favorites list.

② Click the shortcut for the folder or the library you want.

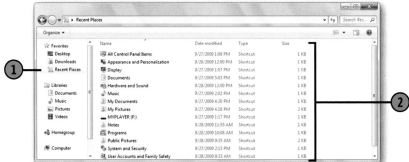

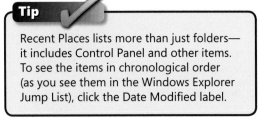

**Tip**

Recent Places lists more than just folders—it includes Control Panel and other items. To see the items in chronological order (as you see them in the Windows Explorer Jump List), click the Date Modified label.

# Creating Quick Access to a File or Folder

If you use a particular file or folder frequently, you can access it quickly by placing a shortcut to it on the Desktop, on the Start menu, or just about anywhere else you want. A shortcut to a document opens the document in its default program; a shortcut to a program file starts the program; a shortcut to a folder opens the folder in a window.

## Create a Shortcut to a File or Folder

1. Open the window that contains the file or folder for which you want to create a shortcut.

2. Right-click the file or folder, and choose Create Shortcut from the shortcut menu.

3. Drag the shortcut

   - Onto the Desktop.

   - Onto the Start button to "pin" it to the Start menu.

   - Onto the taskbar to pin it to its default program.

   - Onto a link in the Favorites list in the Navigation pane.

   - To any library or folder listed in the Navigation pane, or to any open folder.

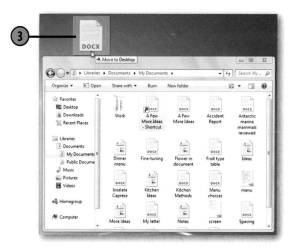

### See Also

"Using Jump Lists for Quick Access" on page 25 for information about quickly accessing files that you've used recently

"Adding Direct Access to a Folder or Library" on page 38 for information about placing a link in the Windows Explorer Jump List.

### Tip

To quickly create a shortcut on the Desktop, right-click the file or folder, point to Send To on the shortcut menu, and choose Desktop (Create Shortcut).

# Adding Direct Access to a Folder or Library

If you always want easy access to a folder or library, you can place it permanently in the Windows Explorer Jump List or on the Start menu. If you want access to the folder from an open Windows Explorer window, you can add a link to it in your Favorites list.

## Pin a Folder

① On the taskbar, right-click the Windows Explorer icon.

② Point to the folder you want pinned and click the Pin To This List button.

③ If the folder you want isn't listed, or if you want to add it to the Start menu, open Windows Explorer, locate the folder, and drag it onto the taskbar to pin it to Windows Explorer or onto the Start button to pin it to the Start menu.

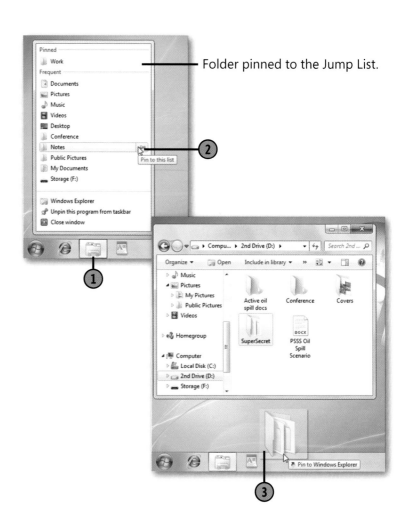

Folder pinned to the Jump List.

### Tip ✓

When you pin a folder to a Jump List or to the Start menu, the folder will remain in that list until you remove it. To remove a pinned item from a Jump List, point to the item and click the Unpin From This List button. To remove a pinned item from the Start menu, right-click the item and choose Remove It From This List.

### Tip ✓

Just as you can pin a folder or a library to the Windows Explorer Jump List, you can pin a file to a program's Jump List by opening the program's Jump List and clicking the listed file's Pin To This List button.

## Add a Link

1. Open Windows Explorer if it isn't already open. If the Navigation pane isn't displayed, click Organize, point to Layout on the drop-down menu, and choose Navigation Pane from the submenu.

2. Navigate to the location that contains the folder you want to link to.

3. Drag the folder onto the Favorite Links section of the Navigation pane.

4. If you want to change the order of the links, drag a link up or down into a new location. To place all the items in alphabetical order, right-click Favorites and choose Sort By Name from the shortcut menu that appears.

5. To remove a link, right-click it, and choose Remove Link from the shortcut menu.

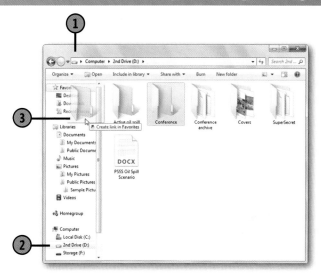

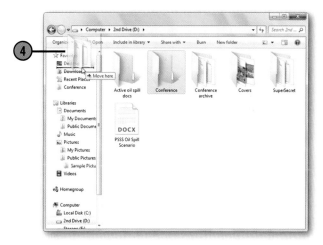

**Tip**

When you add a folder to the Favorites list, it will be shown in every window you open, provided the Navigation pane is shown. This means that regardless of where you've wandered off to, including roaming around in your network, you can return to that folder with just a click of the mouse. You can also add files to this folder by dragging them onto the folder name in the Favorites section.

# Organizing Your Files

If you have a limited number of files, you can easily keep them all in a single folder, such as the My Documents folder. However, if you have files that you want other people to have full access to, or files dealing with many different projects, you'll probably want to organize them by placing them in individual folders. If a file doesn't have a suitably descriptive name, you can change it to one that's more useful. If there's a group of related files, you can rename each file in the group with the same group name, followed by consecutive numbering—for example, *stories, stories(1), stories(2)*, and so on.

## Move, Copy, or Delete a File

**①** Open the window containing the file or files you want to move or copy.

**②** Select the file or files to be moved or copied.

**③** Hold down the right mouse button, and drag the item or items onto the destination folder in the Navigation pane.

**④** From the shortcut menu that appears, choose whether you want to move or to copy the item or items.

**⑤** To delete a file or a group of files, select the file or group of files, and press the Delete key.

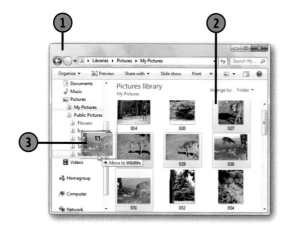

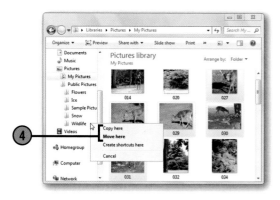

**See Also**

"Accessing Everything" on page 18 for information about displaying and using the Navigation pane.

"Sharing Files with Other Users" on page 44 for information about keeping your files private so that other people who have access to the computer can't open them.

## Rename a File or Folder or a Group of Files

**①** Select the file or folder or the group of files you want to rename, and press the F2 key; or right-click the first selected file of a group, and choose Rename from the shortcut menu.

**②** Type a new name, or click to position the insertion point and then edit the name. Press Enter when the name is correct.

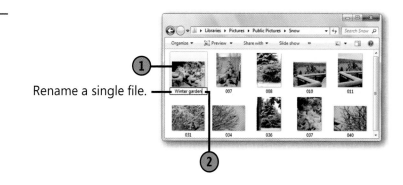

Rename a single file.

Rename a group of files.

The result of renaming a group of files

**Tip** ✔

To select a series of adjacent files, click the first file, hold down the Shift key, and click the last file in the group. To select non-adjacent files, hold down the Ctrl key as you click each file to be selected.

**Try This!** 🖱

Select a group of files or folders, and press Ctrl+C to copy them or Ctrl+X to cut them so that you can move them into a new location. Go to the new destination, and press Ctrl+V to paste the items into the new location. Now select a different file, press Alt+E, and, from the Edit menu, choose Copy To Folder or Move To Folder. Use the dialog box to copy or move the file.

# Recovering a Deleted Item

If you accidentally delete a file, a folder, or a shortcut from your computer's hard disk, you can quickly recover the item by either undoing your action immediately or restoring the deleted item from the Recycle Bin. The Recycle Bin holds all the files you've deleted from your hard disk(s) until you empty the bin or until it gets so full that the oldest files are deleted automatically. When you've deleted a folder, you have to restore the entire folder. You can't open a deleted folder in the Recycle Bin and restore selected files.

## Undo a Deletion

(1) Point to a blank spot on the Desktop or to a blank part of any folder window, and right-click.

(2) Choose Undo Delete from the shortcut menu.

**Caution**

You can't recover any files that you've deleted from a removable disk or device, so be careful! Once they're gone, they're gone forever.

## Restore an Item

(1) Double-click the Recycle Bin icon on the Desktop to open the Recycle Bin window.

(2) Select the item or items to be recovered.

(3) Click Restore This Item (or Restore The Selected Items if you've selected more than one item).

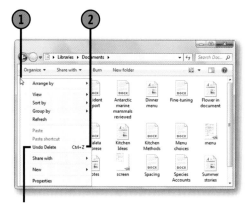

The command is available only if the deletion was your most recent action.

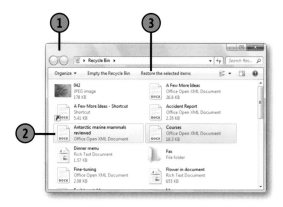

# Navigating with Toolbars

There are seven existing toolbars associated with the Windows taskbar, and they provide access to programs, folders, and documents as well as to Internet and intranet sites. You can also use the New Toolbar to create your own toolbars that link directly to the contents of folders. You probably won't see all the toolbars listed, however, because the Language Bar toolbar is shown only if you've chosen to display it in your Language settings, and the Tablet PC Input Panel requires the Tablet PC tools to be installed on your computer.

## Display a Toolbar

(1) Right-click a blank spot on the taskbar.

(2) Point to Toolbars on the shortcut menu, and choose the toolbar you want to display. (A toolbar with a check mark next to its name is one that's already displayed.) Use the table at the right to identify what each toolbar does.

(3) Double-click the toolbar if it isn't already expanded.

(4) If the toolbar doesn't expand, right-click a blank spot on the taskbar, choose Lock The Taskbar from the shortcut menu, and repeat step 3.

## The Taskbar's Toolbars

| Toolbar | Function |
| --- | --- |
| Address | Opens the item when you specify its address. The address can be the path and the file or folder name, a computer on the network, or even the Internet address of a Web page. |
| Desktop | Provides quick access to the icons, files, folders, and shortcuts on the Desktop. |
| Language Bar | Switches input languages if Windows has been configured to use more than one language. |
| Links | Shows the same links as those shown on the Internet Explorer Links toolbar. |
| New Toolbar | Creates a new toolbar that shows the contents of a folder you specify. |
| Tablet PC Input Panel | Displays the Tablet PC's Input Panel. |

# Sharing Files with Other Users

Each user of your computer has his or her individual set of folders in which to keep documents, music, and so on. Your private files and folders—My Documents and My Pictures, for example—are the ones that are located under your user name and that are normally accessible only by you when you're signed on to the computer, by someone with an Administrator account, or by members of your homegroup if you decided to share your libraries. However, if you want to grant the other people who use your computer full access to certain files, you can place those files in a Public folder.

## Share a File or Folder

1. Select the file or folder, or the group of files and/or folders, that's stored privately under your user name and that you want to share.

2. In the Navigation pane, expand the appropriate library to show the Public folder.

3. Do either of the following:

   - To share the only copy of the item (or items) with others, drag it to the Public folder to move it there.

   - To share a copy of the item (or items) with others, hold down the right mouse button, drag the item to the Public folder, and, from the shortcut menu that appears, choose to copy the file.

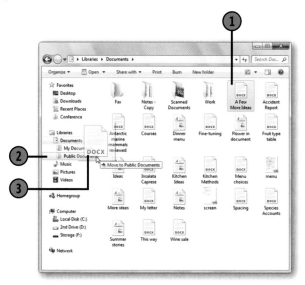

### See Also

"Sharing with Selected Users" on the facing page for information about specifying who can access a folder.

"Sharing with Your Homegroup on pages 250–251 and "Controlling Homegroup Sharing" on page 252 for information about sharing files with members of your homegroup network.

"Allowing Your Files to Be Shared" on page 254 for information about setting up network access to your Public folders and stipulating what changes can be made to the files.

# Sharing with Selected Users

If there are some items that you don't want to share with everyone who has access to your computer—whether they log directly on to your computer, connect over your network, or are members of your homegroup—you can specify which users can access the items, and whether they have the authority to change, copy, or delete the items.

## Share a File or Folder with Selected Users

**1** Open the folder that contains the file or folder you want to share, and select the item or items to be shared.

**2** Click Share With, and then choose Specific People from the drop-down list to start the File Sharing wizard.

**3** Select a person from the drop-down list with whom you want to share the item, and then click Add. Repeat for any other people you want to include.

**4** Click the down arrow for each individual to set the type of permission you're granting that person:

- Read to allow the person to open the file or the folder and any files in the folder, but not to save, rename, or delete that file or any files in the shared location

- Read/Write to allow the person to fully manage the file or folder contents, including saving, renaming, or deleting items

**5** Click Share. Use the wizard if you want to notify people via e-mail or other document that you've shared the item or items with them, and then click Done.

**6** If you want to stop sharing something with an individual, repeat steps 1 through 4, but choose Remove instead of Read or Read/Write.

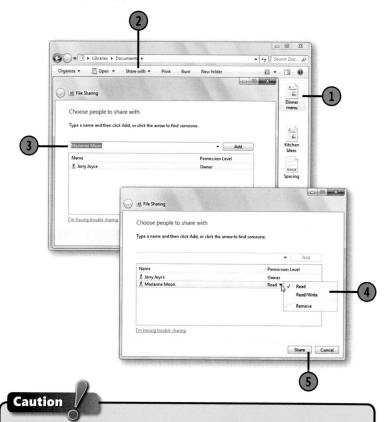

**Caution**

If you see an option that gives everyone access to your shared files or folders, don't select the check box unless you want to share your files or folders with everyone on your network, including those who don't normally have access to your computer. This option is available only if you don't use password-protected sharing.

# Copying Files to a CD or DVD

If you have a CD or DVD recorder (also called a burner) installed on, or attached to, your computer, you can copy your files to a CD or DVD for safe storage or distribution. When archiving, you can continue copying files to the disc until it's full. Files saved in this way, using the Live File format, are readable on Windows 7, Windows Vista, and Windows XP computers, but they won't be readable on most other computers or on CD and DVD players. When you're creating a disc for wide distribution or for use in CD or DVD players, you gather all the files for the disc and record them all at once, using the Mastered format.

## Archive Your Files

1. Place a blank, unformatted, recordable CD or DVD in the drive, and, when the AutoPlay dialog box appears, choose to burn files to disc to display the Burn A Disc dialog box.

2. Type a name for the disc, select the Like A USB Flash Drive option if it isn't already selected, and click Next. Wait for the disc to be formatted, and, when the AutoPlay dialog box appears, choose to open a folder to view the disc contents.

3. Add files to your disc folder that appears, either by dragging files into the window or by selecting them in Windows Explorer and clicking the Burn button. Delete any files that you don't want to keep on the disc.

4. When you've finished, choose Close Session, and wait for Windows to close the recording session. When the session has closed, the disc is readable on compatible computers.

5. Click Eject to remove the disc. To record more data or edit the contents on the disc, insert the disc again, and repeat steps 3 and 4.

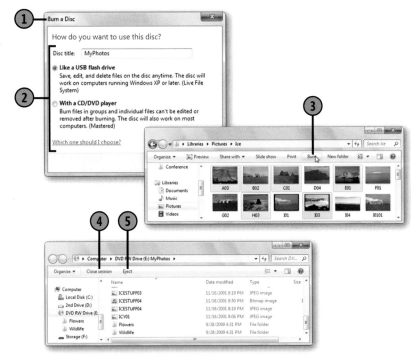

**Caution**

You must have a drive that can burn discs and use recordable discs. You can record CDs and DVDs using a DVD drive, but you can record only CDs when using a CD drive.

## Copy Files for Distribution

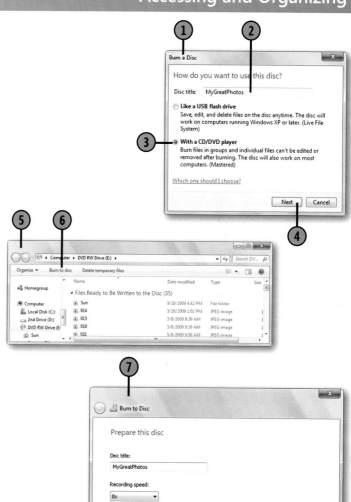

1. Place a blank, unformatted, recordable CD or DVD in the drive, and, when the AutoPlay dialog box appears, choose to burn files to disc to display the Burn A Disc dialog box.

2. Type a name for the disc.

3. Select the With A CD/DVD Player option, if it isn't already selected, to use the Mastered Format.

4. Click Next, and wait for the disc to be formatted.

5. Add files to your disc folder that appears, either by dragging files into the window or by selecting them in Windows Explorer and clicking the Burn button. In the disc-drive window, verify that all the items you want on the disc are present, and delete any items you don't want. Continue adding files until you're certain that all the items you want on the disc are listed.

6. Click Burn To Disc.

7. Step through the Burn To Disc wizard to

   • Confirm or change the disc name.

   • Specify the recording speed you want, and click Next.

   • Specify whether you want to make another disc using the same files.

8. Click Finish when you've finished, and remove and label your disc.

> **See Also**
>
> "Creating a VIdeo DVD" on page 194 for information about creating a video DVD disc for photos and videos.

# Compressing Files

Compressed folders are special folders that use compression software to decrease the sizes of the files they contain. Compressed folders are useful for reducing the file size of standard documents and programs, but they're invaluable when you're storing large graphics files such as bitmaps, or when you're transferring large files by e-mail.

## Create a Compressed Folder

1. Select the file or files to be copied to a compressed folder.

2. Right-click one of the selected files, point to Send To on the shortcut menu, and choose Compressed (Zipped) Folder from the submenu. Rename the compressed folder if necessary.

3. Drag any other files onto the Compressed Folder icon to copy those files to the compressed folder.

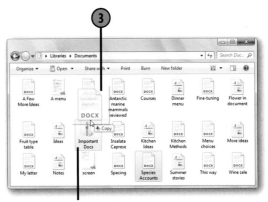

The zipped-folder icon identifies a compressed folder.

### Tip

Many file types, such as *.jpeg* pictures, are already compressed, so moving them to a compressed folder won't substantially reduce their size. However, using a compressed folder is still an excellent way to organize large files into a single file when you're transferring them.

### Caution

Compressed folders preserve the contents of most files, but it's possible that you could lose some data when you're using certain file formats. It's wise to test your file format in a compressed folder before you move valuable files into that folder.

# Use a Compressed File

**1** Double-click the compressed folder to open it.

**2** Double-click an item in the folder to open it in its associated program. If the item is a program, double-click it to run it. (Note, though, that not all files and programs will function properly from the compressed folder.)

**3** To decompress a single file, drag it (or copy and paste it) onto an uncompressed folder.

**4** To decompress all the files in the folder and copy them to another folder, click Extract All Files.

**5** In the Extract Compressed (Zipped) Files window, specify where you want the files to be extracted to.

**6** Click Extract.

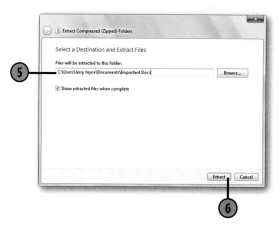

**Tip**

A compressed folder is compatible with any file-compression programs that support the ZIP file format.

**Try This!**

Compress a large file (or a group of files) by placing it in a compressed folder. Right-click the zipped-folder icon, point to Send To on the shortcut menu, and click Mail Recipient. Send the folder, which is now listed as a ZIP-type file, to the person who needs it. If the recipient's operating system isn't equipped with the compressed-folders feature, he or she will need to use a third-party compression program that uses ZIP-type compressed files to open the files.

# Organizing Library Folders

The libraries are great tools that enable you to access your files regardless of which folder they're in. However, you might want to organize your files by keeping certain items separated in their individual folders. To maintain easy access to those items, you can add folders to a library; to limit access, you can remove folders from a library. Additionally, you can create a new library for any type of material you want and then add folders to that library.

## Add a Folder to a Library

1. Open the folder you want to include in a library.

2. With no files selected, click Include In Library and, from the drop-down menu, choose the library you want to add the folder to.

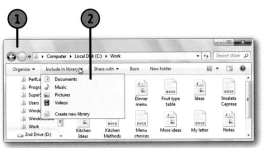

## Remove a Folder from a Library

1. In the library that contains the folder, click the Locations link in the Library pane.

2. In the Library Locations dialog box, select the folder you want to remove from the library.

3. Click Remove.

4. Click OK.

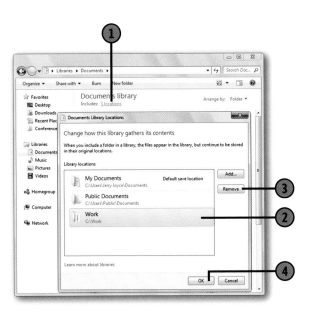

## Create a New Library

(1) Click Libraries in the Navigation pane.

(2) Click New Library.

(3) Type a name for the library.

(4) Double-click the new library to open it.

(5) In the new library's window, click Include A Folder.

(6) In the Include Folder In dialog box that appears, locate and then select the folder you want to include.

(7) Click Include Folder.

(8) Add any other folders you want to the library.

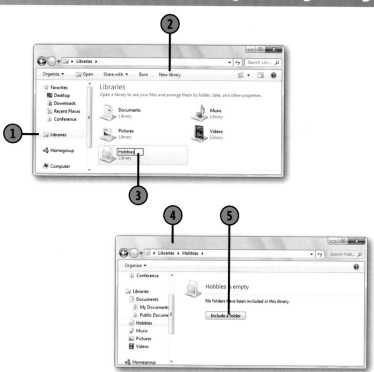

### See Also

"Sharing With Your Homegroup" on pages 250–251 for information about sharing your standard and custom libraries with members of your home network.

### Tip

To create a new library from an existing folder, navigate to the folder, click Include In Library, and choose Create New Library from the drop-down menu.

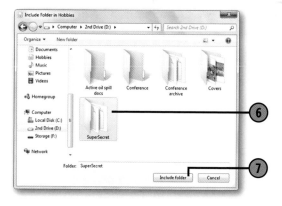

# Using a Removable Memory Device

The easiest way to take some of your files with you is to use a removable USB (Universal Serial Bus) memory device. There are many common names and brand names for these devices, but they all work in basically the same way: Plug the device into a USB port, copy information to or from it, and remove it when you've finished. Many people simply remove the device from the USB port when the file transfer is complete. Provided no data is being written to or from the device and there are no open files, you can do this without any loss of data. However, sooner or later you'll find that just as you start removing the device, some data is being written and you end up with some corrupted or deleted files.

## Use the Device

1. Plug the device into a free USB port. If Windows needs to install drivers for the device, wait for the installation to be complete.

2. If a window opens showing the contents of the device, use the window to manage the files on the device. If an AutoPlay dialog box appears, choose to open the folder. If the window doesn't open automatically, choose Computer from the Start menu, and double-click the drive for the device to open the window.

3. To copy files or folders from your computer to the device, select the items to copy, and right-click one of the selected items. On the shortcut menu that appears, point to Send To, and then click the device on the submenu.

4. When you've finished with the device and want to remove it, close any files or folders that are open in the device files.

5. Click the Safely Remove Hardware icon in the notification area of the taskbar, and click the device you want to remove. Wait for confirmation that the device can be safely removed.

# 4

# Running Programs and Gadgets

Getting to know the programs that come with Windows 7 is like moving into new living quarters. Just as your new abode has the basics—stove, refrigerator, and (dare we say it?) windows—the Windows 7 operating system comes with basic accessories and tools. Just as you add the accoutrements that transform empty rooms into a cozy home, you add programs to Windows 7 to utilize its full potential as you work and play.

But let's cover the basics first. We'll do some everyday tasks in WordPad: composing, saving, and printing a document; creating and editing text; copying items between documents that were created in different programs; and inserting characters such as © and é that don't exist on your keyboard. We'll look at Calculator, which is handy for figuring out basic arithmetic and some advanced and scientific calculations. We'll explore the Tablet PC tools, including the Input Panel for entering text with handwriting or the On-Screen Keyboard; onscreen Sticky Notes for typing quick notes; the Snipping Tool for copying just about anything on your computer; the Math Input Panel for writing mathematical formulas; and the Journal, where you can write and annotate to your heart's content. We'll show you the little Gadget programs you can run on your Desktop, and we'll discuss working at the command prompt and running MS-DOS programs.

# Using the Ribbon

WordPad and Paint, as well as many other programs you can add—including Windows Live Movie Maker and Microsoft Office 2007 and later programs—use the Ribbon and its different tabs instead of the standard menu structure to access the programs' commands and features. With the Ribbon, you can switch among the task-oriented tabs and see all the available options. Additionally, many items provide a live preview: You point to something on the Ribbon—a style or a font, for example—and see immediately how it affects the appearance of your document.

## Explore the Ribbon

**1** Open one of the programs that use the Ribbon.

**2** If you see the command tabs but the Ribbon is minimized, click a command tab to display the Ribbon temporarily, or double-click a tab to keep the Ribbon visible.

**3** Do any of the following:

- Click a button to execute a command.

- Click a down arrow to open a gallery, a drop-down menu, or a drop-down list.

- Click a Show Dialog Box button to open a dialog box that contains additional commands and options.

- Point to an item in a gallery to see its effect on the content of your document.

**4** Click another tab and explore those items.

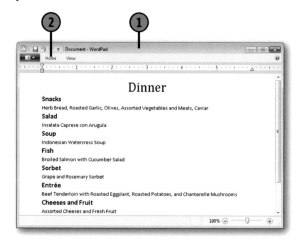

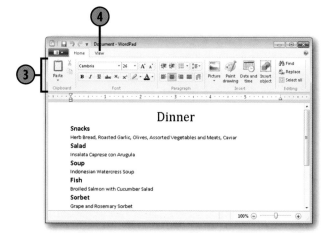

> **Tip**
>
> The Ribbon is composed of tabs and commands. When the Ribbon is minimized, you see only the tabs.

## Use the Quick Access Toolbar

1. Click a button on the Quick Access toolbar to execute an action.

2. Click the down arrow at the right of the Quick Access toolbar, and, on the Customize Quick Access Toolbar menu, click any unchecked command to add it to the Quick Access toolbar, or click a checked command to remove it from the toolbar.

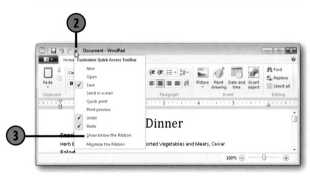

3. If you want the Quick Access toolbar to be located below the Ribbon instead of above it, open the Customize Quick Access Toolbar menu again, and click Show Below The Ribbon.

**Try This!**

With the Ribbon in its unhidden state, double-click the active tab to minimize the Ribbon, and then click any tab to display the Ribbon temporarily. Click in your document to minimize the Ribbon again. Double-click the active tab to have the Ribbon always displayed. Press Ctrl+F1 to hide the Ribbon, and press Ctrl+F1 again to have the Ribbon always displayed.

## Access More Commands

1. Click the program button.

2. Click a command to execute that command. If a command has a right-pointing arrow, a submenu appears with additional commands. Click a command on the submenu to execute the command.

3. Click one of the recently used files to open that file.

# Composing a Document

WordPad is a powerful little word processor that you can use to create documents in a variety of formats. In most cases, you'll want to create a document with formatting to achieve a well-designed, professional look. Save the document as you create it, and print it when you've finished.

## Create a Document

1. Click the Start button, type **wordpad** in the Search box of the Start menu, and choose WordPad from the menu to start the program. If WordPad is already running, click the WordPad button and choose New from the menu.

2. Type your text. Press Enter only when you want to start a new paragraph.

3. To edit the text, click in the document where you want to make the change. An insertion point indicates where your edit will be placed.

4. To insert additional text into a paragraph you've already typed, click where you want to insert the new text, and type it. If the text you want to insert is stored on the Clipboard, click the Paste button on the Home tab of the Ribbon (or press Ctrl+V) instead of typing the text.

5. To delete text, select it, and press Delete. To save the text for later use instead of deleting it, place it on the Clipboard by clicking the Cut button on the Home tab of the Ribbon (or pressing Ctrl+X). To replace text with different text, selected the existing text, and type the new text.

The WordPad button

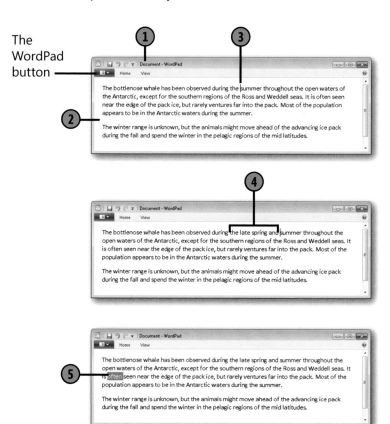

> **Tip**
>
> The Windows Clipboard is a temporary "holding area" for items you copy or cut; it holds only one item at a time.

# Format the Document

**①** If the ruler isn't displayed, click the View tab on the Ribbon, and select the Ruler check box. If the text wrap isn't set to wrap to the ruler, click Word Wrap, and choose Wrap To Ruler from the drop-down menu.

**②** Select the text to be formatted.

**③** On the Home tab, specify the font and font size. Apply bold, italic, underlined, or color emphasis as desired.

**④** Click in the paragraph you want to format, or select all the paragraphs to which you want to apply the same formatting.

**⑤** Use any of the buttons or lists in the Paragraph section of the Ribbon to modify the alignment of your text or set the line spacing, or use the Start A List button to create a bulleted or numbered list.

**⑥** Drag the indent markers to set the left, right, and first-line indents. Click in the ruler to set a tab stop.

**⑦** Click the Paragraph button to display the Paragraph dialog box if you want to set values for indents, line spacing, and tab positions.

**⑧** Save the document.

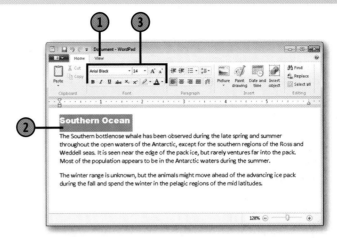

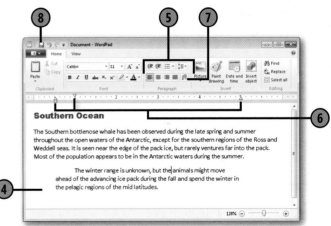

**Tip** ✓

The three formats that support formatting are Rich Text Format (RTF), which is the format used in earlier versions of WordPad and Word 97-2003 documents; Office Open XML Document, which is used in Word 2007 and later documents; and OpenDocument Text (ODT), which is used in several open-format programs. If you're planning to save your document as a Text Document, don't apply any formatting to it. If you do, all the formatting will be lost when you save the document.

**Try This!**

Select some text. Open the Font list on the Ribbon and point to different fonts. Note how your text changes. When you see a font you want, click it. Now open the Font Size list box and point to different font sizes. Click the size you want.

# Saving, Closing, and Opening a Document

After you've created a document, you'll probably want to save it for later use. When you've finished creating the document, close the program in which you created it so that the program isn't using space or taking power from your computer. When you're ready to work on your document again, you can easily restart the program and open the document directly from the running program.

## Save a Document

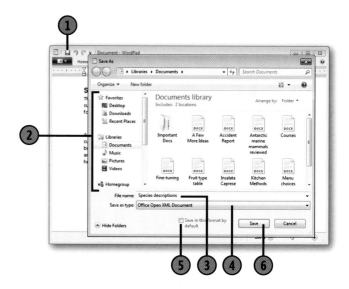

**①** Click the Save button on the toolbar, or, if the toolbar isn't visible, choose Save from either the Program menu (for programs that use the Ribbon) or the File menu.

**②** If you don't want to save the document to the default library or folder, specify a different location. If the libraries or folders aren't shown, click the Browse Folders button.

**③** Type a name for the document. The name can be up to 255 characters long (including any path and file extension); it can contain spaces but can't contain the * : < > | " \ or / characters. Note that long file names are often truncated by programs, so a descriptive short name is best.

**④** If you want to save the document in a different format from that of the default file format, select the format.

**⑤** Select this check box if you want to make the selected format the default format in which to save files.

**⑥** Click Save. As you work with the document, click Save frequently. In many programs, you can press Ctrl+S to quickly save a document. Windows will now save the file without displaying the Save As dialog box.

**Try This!**

Many programs can stay open for additional work even after you close the document you're working on. Open the Program or the File menu and look at the commands. If there's a Close command, click it to close the document without closing the program. If there's a New command but no Close command, choose New to see whether it closes the open document.

## Close a Document

**1** Click the Save button one last time to make sure you've saved all the changes in the document.

**2** Click the Close button to end the program.

## Open a Document

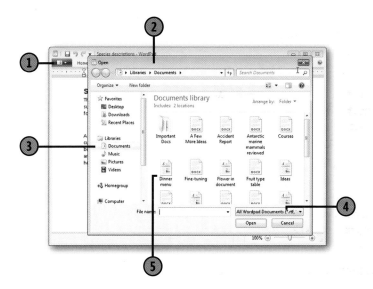

**1** With the program you want to use running, click the Program button or open the File menu, and click the document you want if it's displayed in the Recent list.

**2** If the document isn't listed, choose Open from either the Program menu (for programs that use the Ribbon) or the File menu to display the Open dialog box.

**3** If necessary, specify the location of the document you want.

**4** If necessary, specify the file type of the document you want to open. Only documents of the specified file type will be displayed in the list of files.

**5** Double-click the document to open it.

---

**Tip**

If you're unsure about which file you want, select a file and then click Show The Preview Pane to view the contents of the file. However, note that not all file types can be displayed in the Preview pane.

**See Also**

"Using Jump Lists for Quick Access" on page 25 for information about quickly opening a recently used document.

# Creating Easy Access to a Program

Many of us use one or two programs every day and sometimes open and close them several times a day. For such frequently used programs, you can attach—or *pin*—them to the taskbar or the Start menu. Then all you need to do to start a program is click it.

## Pin a Program to the Taskbar

**1** Start the program from the Start menu as you normally do.

**2** Right-click the program's icon and choose Pin This Program To Taskbar from the shortcut menu that appears. Use the program as you normally do, and when you've finished, close it.

**3** Click the program icon on the taskbar the next time you want to use the program.

## Pin a Program to the Start Menu

**1** Open the Start menu, locate the program, and right-click it.

**2** Choose Pin To Start Menu from the shortcut menu.

**3** Click the program near the top of the Start menu the next time you want to use it.

# Copying Material Between Documents

It's easy to copy material from a file that was created in one program to a file that was created in another program. The way you insert the material depends on what it is. If it's similar to and compatible with the receiving file—text that's being copied into a WordPad document, for example—you can usually insert it as is and then edit it in the receiving document's program. If the item is dissimilar—a sound clip, say, inserted into a WordPad document—either it's *encapsulated* (isolated) as an object and can be edited in the originating program only, or you simply are not able to paste that item into your document.

## Copy and Insert Material

① In the source file, select the material you want to copy.

② Click Copy on the Home tab of the Ribbon, or choose Copy from the Edit menu if there is no Ribbon (or press Ctrl+C). Windows places copied items on the Windows Clipboard. (You can copy only one item at a time, so always paste the Clipboard contents into your document before you copy anything else, or you'll lose whatever was on the Clipboard.)

③ Switch to the destination file.

④ Click where you want to insert the material.

⑤ Click the Paste button, or choose Paste from the Edit menu (or press Ctrl+V).

**Tip**

To insert the copied material in a different format, or as an icon if you're creating an online document, choose Paste Special from the Paste list on the Ribbon or from the Edit menu instead of choosing the Paste command. Not all programs have this option.

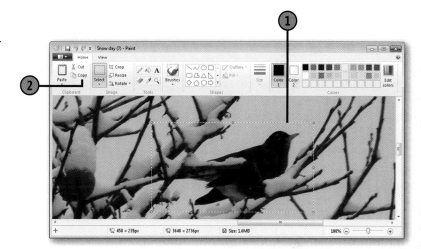

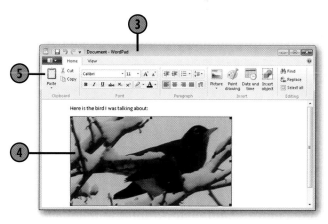

# Dialog Box Decisions

You're going to be seeing a lot of *dialog boxes* as you use Windows 7, and if you're not familiar with them now, you soon will be. Dialog boxes appear when Windows 7 or a program—WordPad, let's say—needs you to make one or more decisions about what you want to do. Sometimes all you have to do is click a Yes, a No, or an OK button; at other times, there'll be quite a few decisions to make in one dialog box. The Print dialog box, shown below, is typical of many dialog boxes and is one you'll probably be seeing frequently, so take a look at its parts and the way they work.

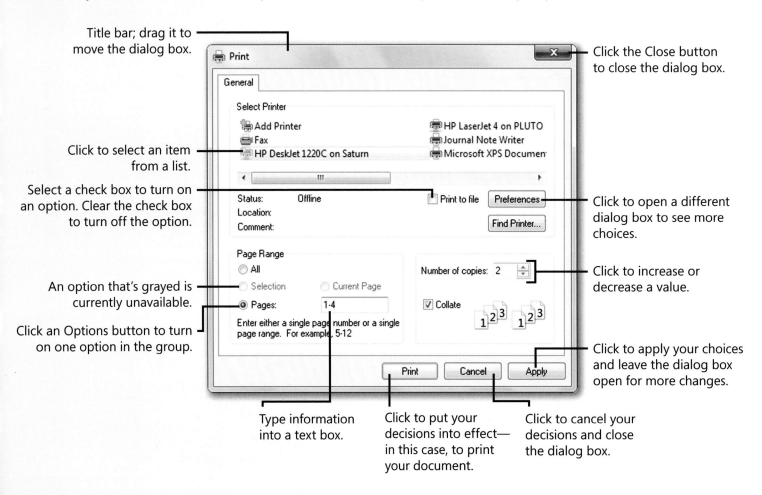

Title bar; drag it to move the dialog box.

Click the Close button to close the dialog box.

Click to select an item from a list.

Select a check box to turn on an option. Clear the check box to turn off the option.

Click to open a different dialog box to see more choices.

An option that's grayed is currently unavailable.

Click to increase or decrease a value.

Click an Options button to turn on one option in the group.

Click to apply your choices and leave the dialog box open for more changes.

Type information into a text box.

Click to put your decisions into effect—in this case, to print your document.

Click to cancel your decisions and close the dialog box.

# Inserting Special Characters

Windows 7 provides a special accessory program called Character Map that lets you insert into your programs those characters and symbols that aren't available on your keyboard.

Character Map displays all the characters that are available for each of the fonts on your computer.

## Find and Insert a Character

1. Start Character Map from the System Tools folder of the Start menu, or click the Start button, type **char** in the Search box of the Start menu, and choose Character Map from the menu to start the program.

2. Specify a font.

3. Double-click the character you want to insert. Double-click any other characters that you want to insert at the same time.

4. Click Copy to place the character or characters on the Clipboard.

5. Switch to your program, click where you want to insert the character or characters, and paste the character or characters from the Clipboard into your document. Format and edit the inserted text as desired.

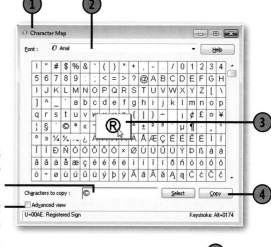

Displays the characters you've selected to be copied to the Clipboard.

Select this check box to use search features to locate a character.

Here are a couple of frequently used characters: © and ®.

**Tip**

Some programs, such as Microsoft Word, have their own tools for inserting special symbols. If the program you're using has this feature, try it first to see whether you prefer an alternative way of inserting symbols. The Character Map program, however, works in any program that lets you paste text from the Clipboard.

**Try This!**

In Character Map, select a character you insert frequently, and note the keyboard shortcut for the character in the bottom-right corner of the Character Map dialog box. Switch to the program into which you want to insert the character, hold down the Alt key, and use the numeric keypad, with NumLock turned on, to enter the numbers. Format the inserted character with a different font or font size if desired.

# Crunching Numbers

Calculator has two main modes—the basic configuration for standard number crunching, and an expanded configuration that includes specialized operations. The basic configuration includes a Standard calculator used for basic arithmetic operations, a Scientific calculator that includes more advanced operations including geometric and algebraic operations, a Programmer calculator to deal with bits, bytes, and such, and a Statistics calculator for basic statistical analysis.

## Use Calculator

1. Start Calculator from the Accessories folder on the Start menu, or click the Start button, type **calc** in the Search box of the Start menu, and choose Calculator from the menu to start the program. If the Standard calculator isn't shown, choose Standard from the Mode menu.

2. If you want a record of all your calculations, open the View menu and, if there is no check mark next to the History command, click History.

3. Use Calculator as you would any calculator, either by clicking the number buttons or by typing the numerals you want. Click or type the functions you want to use, and enter any additional numbers. Click Equal or press Enter when all numbers and functions have been entered.

4. If you want to copy your work, open the Edit menu and do either of the following:

   - Choose Copy to copy the current result.

   - Point to History, and choose Copy History to copy all your calculations.

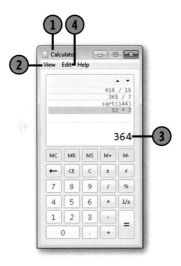

**Try This!**

With History turned on, enter a series of calculations. Use the up and down arrows to highlight the past calculations and see the results of the highlighted calculations. With one calculation highlighted, open the Edit menu, point to History, and choose Edit. Modify the calculation and press Enter.

## Make Advanced Calculations

 From the View menu, choose any of the advanced modes to calculate your values:

- Choose Scientific, select your numbering system, enter values, and use the function keys to calculate your values.

- Choose Programmer, and use the numbering systems, enter values, and use the functions to calculate values.

- Choose Statistics, and either enter your values, clicking Add after each value to create your data set, or choose Paste from the Edit menu to paste a data set that you had copied. Use the Dataset submenu on the Edit menu to copy, edit, or clear the data set. Use the functions to calculate your desired statistics on the existing data set.

**See Also**

"Making Specialized Calculations" on page 66 for information about using the expanded configuration of Calculator.

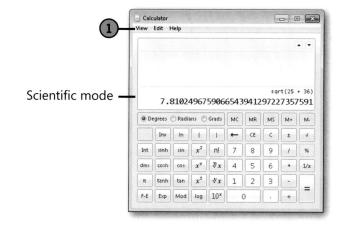

Scientific mode

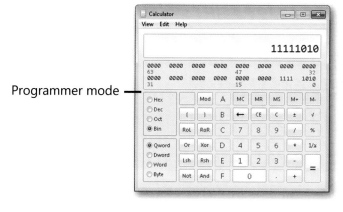

Programmer mode

Statistics mode

# Making Specialized Calculations

There are some special calculations we often need but that somehow end up being much more complex than they first seemed. For example, if you want to know what the date will be in 95 days or how many meters there are in 50 fathoms, you'd probably need to spend some time figuring out how to do the calculation. Fortunately, Calculator's expanded configuration makes these and many other calculations quite simple.

## Use the Specialized Calculations

① Open Calculator from the Start menu if it isn't already running.

② From the View menu, choose the type of calculation you want:

- Unit Conversion to convert a value from one unit to another

- Date Calculation to calculate the difference between dates or to add or subtract days from a date

- Worksheets, and then choose the type of worksheet from the submenu to make various types of calculations, such as monthly mortgage payments, gas mileage, and factors in a lease

③ Use the expanded area to select the type of calculation, and enter your values. After the values are entered, click Calculate if the button is available. If you want to copy the result, select it, and then choose Copy from the Edit menu.

④ To exit the expanded configuration, choose Basic from the View menu.

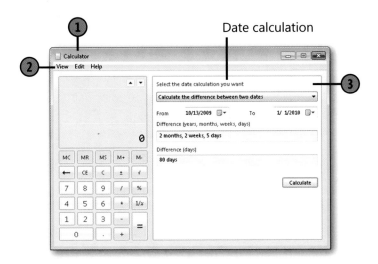

Date calculation

Unit conversion

# Writing Equations and Formulas

For the scientifically and technically minded, or the student being intimidated in Statistics class, being able to write an equation or a formula is often a necessity. However, such structures have always created major problems when they have to be entered on a computer. Fortunately, the Math

Input Panel lets you write your equation or formula and then converts it into type, using symbols, super- and subscripts, and more. You can then insert it into a program that supports Mathematical Markup Language, including Microsoft Word and several computational programs.

## Write an Equation

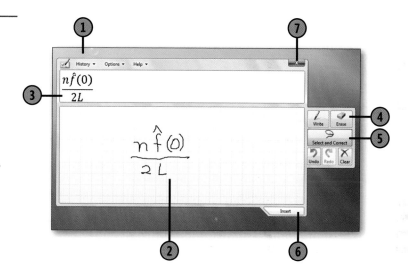

1. Make sure the program into which you want to insert your equation or formula is running. Click the Start button, type **math** in the Search box of the Start menu, and click Math Input Panel to start the Input Panel.

2. Use your writing tool, such as a stylus on a Tablet PC or digitizing pad, or the mouse with the left mouse button held down, to start writing your equation.

3. As you write, note how your writing is being interpreted.

4. If your writing isn't recognized, either click the Erase button and click the part not recognized, or click Undo to remove the latest part and try again.

5. If your writing is recognized as something other than what you intended, click the Select And Correct button, draw around the misrecognized piece, and, in the list that appears, select the correct item. If the entire equation or formula, or a large part of it, changes and isn't what you want, click the Select And Correct button, draw around the area, and, on the Correction menu, point to the most likely general correction and choose it from the submenu.

6. When you've completed the equation or formula, click in the document where you want it to be inserted, and click Insert.

7. Click Close.

**Tip**

Although this program is designed for use with a Tablet PC, you can use a digitizer pad, a touch-sensitive screen, or even a mouse to draw your equations. If you don't see the Math Input Panel on the Start menu, make sure that the Tablet PC features are turned on in Windows.

# Running Multiple Copies of One Program

You might want to have more than one file open in the same program—two different documents in WordPad, for example. If you open an additional existing file from a Jump List, the file will appear in a new copy of the program. But if you want to open a blank version of the program, you'll need to take extra steps. With multiple copies open, Windows gives you some very nice tools to figure out which copy you want to access. The thumbnails of open windows and the full-screen previews are available only when your computer is set to use the Aero Glass feature. If it's set to use a basic theme, such as the Windows 7 Basic theme, you'll see a list of open windows instead of previews when you point to the program icon.

## Open and Use Another Copy of a Program

① Right-click the program icon on the taskbar, and choose either of the following:

- The program's name to open the program with a blank file.

- The file you want open.

② Point to the program icon to see thumbnails of the open files.

③ Point to the thumbnail of the file you think you want to show in a full-screen preview.

④ If that isn't the file you want, point to a different thumbnail to see a full-screen preview of a different file.

⑤ To switch to the file you want, click the thumbnail for that file.

⑥ If you want to close a file without switching to it, point to the thumbnail and then click the Close button.

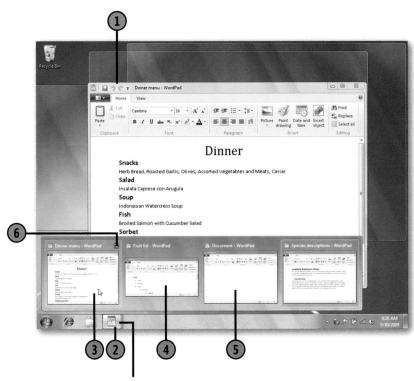

Overlapping icons indicate that more than one copy of the program is running.

# Copying Your Screen Content

You can use the Snipping Tool program to capture an image—or a snippet—of a Web page, or just about anything else on your computer screen. You can then e-mail the image, save it, or paste it into a file in another program.

## Snip an Image

① With the content you want to capture displayed on the screen, click the Start button, type **snip** in the Search box of the Start menu, and choose Snipping Tool from the menu to start the program.

② Click the down arrow next to the New button, and select the type of snip you want:

- Free Form Snip to capture any shape
- Rectangular Snip to capture a rectangular snip
- Window Snip to capture a program or a folder window
- Full-Screen Snip to capture everything on your screen

③ Capture your snip. For free-form and rectangular snips, drag out the shape with the mouse (while holding down the left mouse button) or a stylus or finger, depending on your system. For a window snip, click or tap anywhere in the window. The full-screen snip is captured automatically.

④ In the Snipping Tool window, use any of the tools to save, copy, send, or modify the snip.

⑤ Click New to capture another image, or click the Close button to close the Snipping Tool.

# Writing Your Text

The Tablet PC Input Panel isn't just for Tablet PCs anymore! You can enter text in a program by writing on the Input Panel using a pen-sensitive computer (such as a Tablet PC) or a touch-sensitive computer, or you can use a digitizing pad with a stylus or similar interface tool, or even just your mouse. The Input Panel has two writing modes—freehand style, in which you write as you would on paper, and character by character, in which you write one character at a time. However, these two modes are similar—you can even use the Character Pad to make corrections to your text when you use the Writing Pad. Whichever method you use to write your text, the program recognizes your writing and converts it into standard digital text. You can then insert the text into a document.

## Write Your Text

**1** Make sure that the program into which you want to insert your text is running. Then click the Start button, and either type **inp** in the Search box of the Start menu and then click Input Panel, or choose Tablet PC Input Panel from the Tablet PC submenu to start the program. If the Input Panel is already running but is minimized, click or tap the Input Panel tab.

**2** Click the Writing Pad button if it isn't already selected.

**3** Write your text.

**4** If your text isn't recognized correctly, click the incorrect word.

**5** Do either of the following:

- Click one of the alternative words.

- Rewrite the incorrect letter or letters.

**6** Click Close or click outside the word.

**7** Click Insert to insert the text into your program.

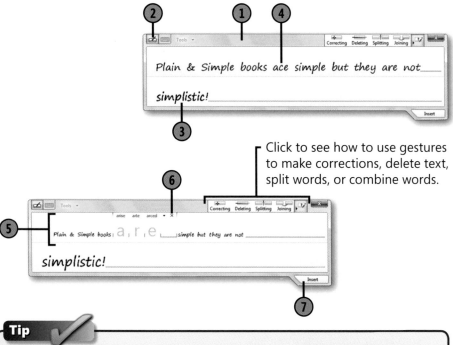

Click to see how to use gestures to make corrections, delete text, split words, or combine words.

**Tip**

With so many different input methods and types of hardware, we can't describe in exact detail all the ways you can use your equipment. For example, if you're using your mouse, hold down the left mouse button to write. If you're using a stylus or a finger, just write and tap to execute a mouse-click. You'll need to experiment to find the best way to use your input system with these Tablet PC tools.

## Add Other Elements

(1) With no written text in the Input Panel, use the navigation buttons to move the insertion point to the location where you want it in the program.

(2) Tap or click any of the following:

- The typographic element you want

- The editing keys to delete any content

- The Num button to display the Number pad, the Sym button to display the Symbols pad, or the Web button to display the Web Quick Keys pad, and then the item you want to insert into your document

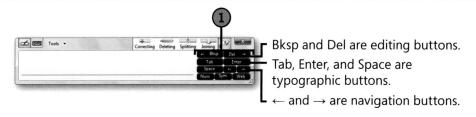

Bksp and Del are editing buttons.

Tab, Enter, and Space are typographic buttons.

← and → are navigation buttons.

Number pad

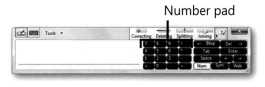

Symbols pad

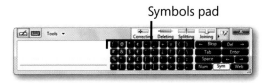

Web Quick Keys pad

**Tip**

If you click the Close button, the Input Panel moves off the Desktop but doesn't close. To use it again, click the edge of the Input Panel to restore it. To close the Input Panel, choose Exit from the Options menu.

**Tip**

To modify the Input Panel's location; to improve the handwriting recognition; or to change the way the Input Panel opens, edits existing text, and displays handwritten text, open the Tools menu before you write any text.

# Typing on Your Screen

The Touch Keyboard mode of the Tablet PC Input Panel lets you enter text directly onto your screen instead of using a physical keyboard. The content you enter appears in the document of your currently running program.

## Type Your Content

1. Make sure that the program into which you want to insert your text is running. Then click the Start button, and choose Tablet PC Input Panel from the Tablet PC submenu. If the Input Panel is already running but is minimized, click or tap the Input Panel tab.

2. Click the Touch Keyboard button.

3. Tap or click each character to enter it. If the correct word appears among any suggested words, click the word to insert it, and then continue typing the next word.

4. To modify the keyboard, tap or click a modifier key— for example, the Shift, Caps, or Fn (Function) key. Tap or click the key a second time to turn off the change.

5. To enter keyboard shortcuts, tap or click the Alt and/or the Ctrl key and then the assigned key. The Alt and/or Ctrl key will be turned off automatically when the keyboard shortcut is completed.

6. Tap or click the navigation and editing keys to use them just as you would on a standard keyboard, or use gestures to scroll in your document.

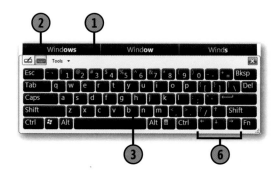

**See Also**

"Writing Your Text" on page 70 for information about changing settings for the Tablet PC Input Panel.

**Tip**

Windows 7 has another On-Screen Keyboard that isn't part of the Tablet PC Tools and that is available in all editions of Windows 7 as part of the Accessibility Options. To access this keyboard, click On-Screen Keyboard in the Ease Of Access folder on the Start menu.

# Writing Quick Notes

Just like those little sticky notes that clutter up your desk or parade around the edges of your computer screen, the Sticky Notes program provides a great way to quickly type a reminder, an idea, an address, or a phone number. There's an endless supply of these notes that you can scatter around the Desktop; you can change their colors to classify them, and you can make them vanish when you've finished with them.

## Write and Read Your Notes

(1) If Sticky Notes isn't already running, click the Start button, type **stic** in the Search box of the Start menu, and choose Sticky Notes from the menu to start the program.

(2) Type the text of your note. The note is saved automatically until you delete it.

(3) If you want to create another note, click New Note, and type your content.

(4) Drag the sticky note to where you want it.

(5) To change the color of a note, right-click it and choose the color you want from the shortcut menu. You can also use the shortcut menu to copy or delete selected text or to paste text from another location.

(6) Point to a note you no longer want, and click Delete.

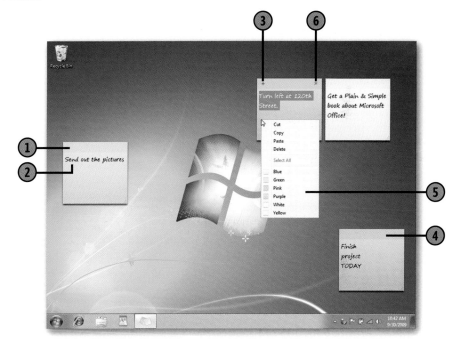

**Tip**

To temporarily hide your notes without deleting them, click the Sticky Notes icon on the taskbar to minimize all the notes. To hide the notes, even between sessions, right-click the Sticky Notes icon and choose Close Window from the shortcut menu. To see your notes again, choose Sticky Notes from the Start menu.

# Writing and Drawing Notes

The Windows Journal is an extremely versatile tool that provides an ideal palette on which you can assemble diverse types of information. Although it's primarily for writing notes and making quick sketches on a pen-sensitive or touch-sensitive computer, you can modify the content, move it around, and even convert your handwriting into text.

## Write and Draw

1. If the Journal isn't already running, click Windows Journal in the Tablet PC folder on the Start menu to start the program.

2. Write a title for the note using your stylus, your finger, or your mouse.

3. If you want to use a different pen color or shape, click and choose your options from the Pen drop-down menu. To make additional changes, choose Pen Settings, and make your selections in the Pen And Highlighter Settings dialog box.

4. Write the content of your note, and draw pictures using your stylus, touch, or mouse.

5. To highlight any material, click the Highlighter button and drag the highlight over the desired items. To use a different highlight color or width, click the down arrow next to the Highlighter button. To return to writing or drawing, click the Pen button again.

6. To delete content, click the Eraser button and drag the Eraser over the content you want to remove.

7. Click Save to save the note. Click Save periodically to save your most recent edits.

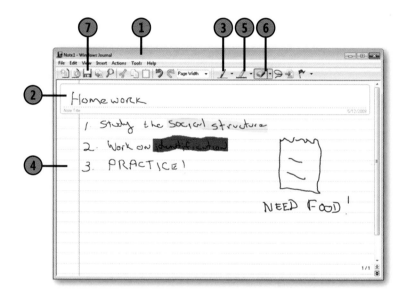

**Tip**

To always open a note with a specific template, pen color, or shape, or to design your default page using line spacing and a background picture, choose Options from the Tools menu, and make the settings you want.

**Tip**

To use a different background—for example, music staffs, graph paper, or a monthly calendar, among others—choose New Note From Template from the File menu, and select the background you want from the list in the Open dialog box.

## Modify and Use Your Content

**(1)** Click the Selection tool, and drag the selection around the material you want to change.

**(2)** To modify the content, do any of the following:

- Drag it to a new location.

- Drag a sizing box on the border of the selection rectangle to increase or decrease the size of the content.

- Click the Cut or the Copy button to move or copy the content to the Windows Clipboard.

- Choose Format Ink from the Edit menu to change the color and thickness of the ink or to apply bold or italic formatting to the selection.

- Choose Convert Selection To E-Mail from the Actions menu to convert writing to text and then send the text in an e-mail message.

- Choose Convert Handwriting To Text from the Actions menu to convert the writing to text, and then either copy the text to the Windows Clipboard or replace the selected writing with text.

- Point to Change Shape To on the Actions menu, and choose the shape you want the selected content to be converted to.

**(3)** Click the Pen button, and add more writing or drawings.

**(4)** Click any of the editing buttons to modify your document.

**(5)** Click Save.

**(6)** Click New Note to create a new note, or click the Close button to end your work in the Journal.

Cut selected content.
Copy selected content.
Paste material from the Clipboard.
Undo or redo your latest action.

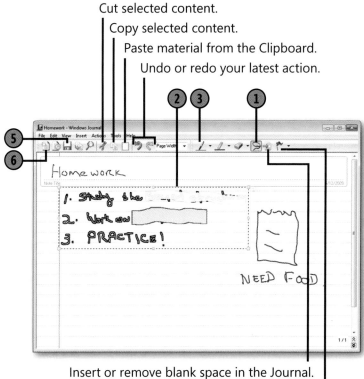

Insert or remove blank space in the Journal.
Add an identification flag.

**Tip**

When you choose to convert handwriting to text, a dialog box appears in which you can correct the handwriting-recognition results. If the results are so bad that the correct text isn't offered as an alternative, use your physical keyboard or an on-screen keyboard to enter the correct text.

# Annotating a Document

One of the most useful features of the Windows Journal is the ability it gives you to import a document from another program and then annotate the document with written notes, pictures, and highlights. This feature makes the Journal one of our favorite tools, whether or not we use a stylus for input.

There are two ways to import a document: Either the Journal automatically opens the document in its default program and then uses a special printer driver, or you open the document in its program and then use the printer driver to send the content of the document to the Journal.

## Make Your Comments

1. If the Journal isn't already running, click Windows Journal in the Tablet PC folder on the Start menu to start the program.

2. Click the Import button, select the file to be used, and click or tap the Import button in the Import dialog box. If you haven't already installed the Journal printer driver, do so when requested. If the Journal can't open the program for the type of file you want, open the file in its correct program, choose to print it with the Journal Note Printer, and save the print file as a note.

3. Use the Journal tools to annotate the document. You can't, however, modify the actual content of the document.

4. Save the original annotated note.

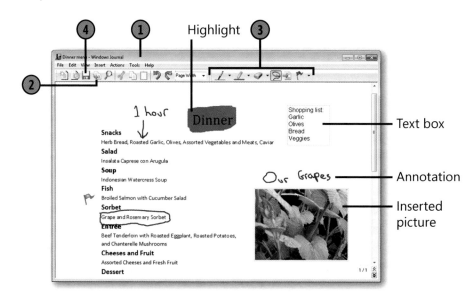

Highlight

Text box

Annotation

Inserted picture

**Tip**

To share your Journal note using an e-mail client installed on your computer, choose Send To Mail Recipient from the File menu to e-mail the note as a Journal file, a Web page, or a *tif* picture. You can also choose Export As from the File menu to create a Web page or a *tif* file that you can later distribute using Webmail or another method.

# Enlarging the Screen Content

When a computer screen is set to a high resolution, you can fit a lot of things on the screen, but sometimes some of those items are a bit difficult to see in detail. Windows is happy to help out with a tool that enlarges the screen content. You can select one of three views, depending on the way you want to work, and you can easily switch between views and even customize them.

## Magnify the Screen

1. Click the Start menu, type **mag** in the Search box of the Start menu, and choose Magnifier to start Magnifier.

2. Click the plus button to increase the magnification. Click the minus button to reduce the magnification.

3. If the Magnifier window changes into a magnifying glass, click the glass to restore the Magnifier window.

4. Click Views and choose any of the following:

   - Full Screen to enlarge the entire screen content.

   - Lens to move an enlarged field around and magnify a section, as you would with a normal magnifying glass.

   - Docked to use a window at the top of the screen to view the enlarged area.

   - Preview Full Screen to see a quick view of the unmagnified screen with the magnified area highlighted. This setting is available only when you're using Full Screen view.

5. Click Close when you've finished.

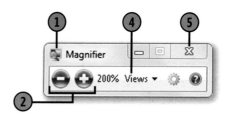

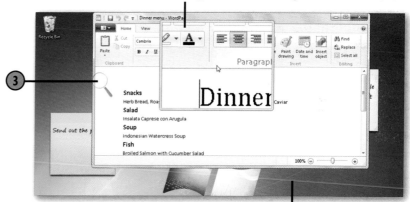

Magnified view using Lens view

Normal view of the Windows Desktop

**See Also**

"Enlarging Text" on page 87 for information about changing the size of text on the screen.

**Tip**

If your computer doesn't support the Aero Glass feature, or if you're using a basic theme, such as the Widows 7 Basic theme, your only view option is Docked.

# Controlling Your Gadgets

Gadgets are nice little programs that sit quietly on your Desktop doing their own specific thing, usually without your having to do much to make them work.

## Control a Gadget

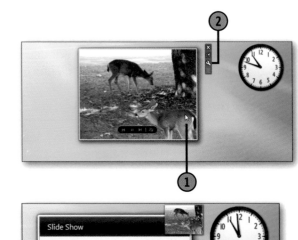

1. Point to the gadget you want to control so that the controls appear.

2. Click the Options button.

3. In the gadget's dialog box, make whatever settings you want, and then click OK.

4. Point to a gadget and control it using any controls that appear.

5. To move a gadget anywhere on the Desktop, point to the gadget's handle and drag the gadget into the position you want.

**Tip**

Each gadget is an individual program that works in its own way. Therefore, the controls for using it, as well as its options, are different for each gadget.

**Try This!**

Right-click a gadget, point to Opacity on the shortcut menu that appears, and choose an opacity percentage from the submenu that appears.

## Add or Delete Gadgets

① Right-click the Desktop, and choose Gadgets from the shortcut menu to display the Gadgets Gallery window.

② Click Show Details to display the details for each gadget you select.

③ Click a gadget, and review the details about the item.

④ Click Get More Gadgets Online to see and download other gadgets from the Web.

⑤ Double-click any other gadgets you want to add, including those that you downloaded.

⑥ Close the Gadgets window when you've finished.

⑦ To remove a gadget, point to it and click the Delete button. The gadget is deleted from the Desktop, but the file remains stored on your computer in case you want to restore it.

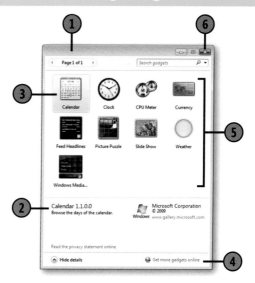

# Running Commands

In Windows 7, the command prompt is the place where you can execute *command-line* instructions. Most of the commands are the old standard MS-DOS commands, some are enhancements of the MS-DOS commands, and others are commands unique to Windows 7. When you need to work from the command prompt, you can open a command-prompt window and execute all your tasks there, including using the basic commands, starting a program, and even starting a program in a new window. Note that the command prompt is a powerful weapon that can disrupt your system, delete files, and create general havoc. Don't execute commands unless you know what they're designed for.

## Run a Command

① Open a command-prompt window by choosing Command Prompt from the Accessories folder of the Start menu.

② At the prompt, type a command, including any *switches* and *extra parameters,* and press Enter.

③ Enter any additional commands you want to run.

## The Top 10 Command-Prompt Commands

| Command | Function |
| --- | --- |
| cd | Switches to the specified folder (or directory). |
| cls | Clears the screen. |
| copy | Copies the specified files or folders. |
| dir | Shows the contents of the current directory. |
| exit | Ends the session. |
| ipconfig | Displays network connection information. |
| ping | Tests network connection using IP address. |
| path | Displays or sets the path the command searches. |
| prompt | Changes the information displayed at the prompt. |
| rename | Renames the specified file or files if the wildcard characters ? or * are used. |

**Tip**

Many commands have switches that allow the use of extra parameters, giving you greater control of the command. A switch is the part of the command with the forward slash (/) followed by a letter, a number, or some other instruction. A parameter is an additional instruction you provide, such as the file name or the drive letter.

## Find a Command

① At the command prompt, type **help** and press Enter.

② Review the list of commands.

③ If the information scrolls off the screen, use the scroll bar or the scroll arrows so that you can see the entire list.

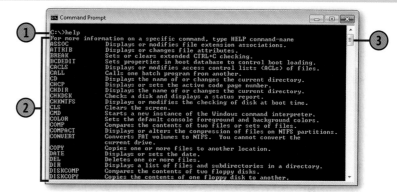

**Tip**

To change some of the settings for the Command Prompt window—the font, the cursor size, or the colors, for example—right-click the window's title bar, and choose Properties from the shortcut menu.

**Try This!**

At the command prompt, type **help > dosref.txt** and press Enter. Use Notepad or WordPad to open the file *dosref.txt* that's stored on your hard disk (it's the folder that was active when you typed the command). The > symbol redirected the output from the screen to the file. You now have a reference for the commands, which you can easily print out.

## Get Information About a Command

① Type a command followed by a space and **/?** and then press Enter to get information about the command.

② Read the information.

# Running Older Programs

Most programs work well with Windows 7. Some older ones, however, are designed exclusively for earlier versions of Windows and won't work properly in Windows 7. In most cases, Windows 7 will try to run a program that doesn't work, using settings that should allow the program to run while at the same time protecting your system. However, in a few cases, you might need to change settings to get the program to work correctly.

## Set the Compatibility

1. Locate the program you want to run, either on the Start menu or in a folder window.

2. Right-click the program, and choose Properties from the shortcut menu to display the program's Properties dialog box.

3. On the Compatibility tab, select this check box to run the program in Compatibility mode.

4. Specify the version of Windows for which the program was designed.

5. Select the check boxes for applying the appropriate restrictions to the display based on the program's documentation and updated notes from the manufacturer.

6. Select this check box if the program needs to access restricted content and you're sure the program will do no harm to your computer.

7. Click OK, and try running the program. If it still doesn't run, open the Properties dialog box again and change the settings. Continue experimenting until you get the program to work or until you're convinced the program can't run on your computer. (If changing the Compatibility mode or the display settings doesn't fix the problem, check with the manufacturer for updated drivers or other fixes.)

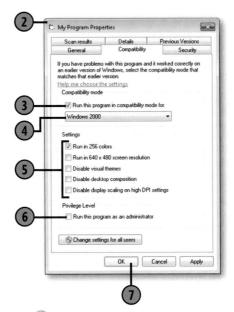

## Caution

Running programs that weren't designed for recent versions of Windows can cause problems—for example, a program might start working and then lock up. Windows 7 will usually close the stopped program for you, but if it doesn't, click the Close button. If that doesn't work, right-click a blank spot on the taskbar, and choose Start Task Manager from the shortcut menu. On the Applications tab of the Task Manager dialog box, click the offending program, and then click End Task.

# 5 Personalizing

You can customize just about everything on your computer to make it look and work exactly the way you want. It's fun to experiment with the various themes, and to try out the cool transparent look in windows, the taskbar, the Start menu, and other parts of Windows 7. You can create a slide show for your Desktop background and for your screen saver. You can change the size and color of almost everything; set items to open with one click instead of two; and rearrange or hide the taskbar, toolbars, Start menu, and Desktop items. You can even customize your little friend the mouse.

You can use a single window in which to open all your folders, or use a separate window for each folder; and you can choose the details—date, author, and so on—that you want to be shown in your folder windows. If you sometimes work in a different language, you can switch the layout of your keyboard to that language, and you can add clocks to check the time in other cities or countries. If you have problems with your vision, hearing, or manual dexterity—or if you just want to try a different way of working—the Ease Of Access Center presents an array of alternative tools you can try. You can also control just how much information you share with Microsoft, and you can control when and how you update your computer's software.

# Changing the Overall Look

The visual and auditory interface elements of Windows 7—colors, Desktop background, icons, sounds, screen savers, mouse pointers, and so on—are all part of a *theme*.

Windows 7 comes with a few themes. Other themes are available for download, and you can also create your own theme by modifying an existing one.

## Change the Theme

1. Click the Start button, type **pers** in the Search box of the Start menu, and choose Personalization from the menu to open the Personalization window.

2. Select a different theme.

3. If you don't see a theme you like, click Get More Themes Online, find a theme you like, and download it.

4. Preview the theme. If you don't like it, choose a different theme.

5. When you have the theme you want, close the window.

**See Also**

"Using Alternative Ways of Working" on page 104 for information about using Ease Of Access options for increasing the contrast of items on your screen.

**Tip**

A theme affects more than just visual appearance, sounds, and screen saver; it also affects some basic features. For example, if you use a theme that doesn't support the Aero Glass feature, you'll have limited color choices and no transparency in your windows; additionally, a feature such as Aero Peek, which allows you to quickly see the Desktop, won't work. If you find that some features aren't working, try applying one of the unmodified Aero themes.

## Modify the Theme

1. If the Personalization window isn't already open, right-click a blank spot on the Desktop, and choose Personalize to open the Personalization window.

2. Select the theme that looks the most like what you want.

3. Click the items that you want to modify, select your changes, and save them.

4. Select an option to modify the mouse pointers and/or the Desktop icons.

5. Click Save Theme.

6. In the Save Theme As dialog box, type a name for the theme, and click Save.

7. Close the Personalization window when you've finished.

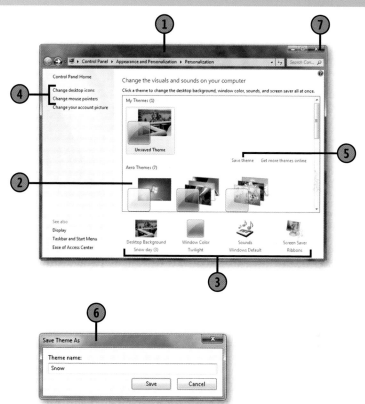

**Tip** ✓

To delete a custom theme, first make sure it's not the active theme, and then right-click the theme. From the shortcut menu that appears, choose Delete Theme.

**Tip** ✓

If you want Windows 7 to look like Windows XP or an earlier version of Windows, choose the Windows Classic theme.

**See Also** ▶

"Changing the Window Color" on page 86, "Setting Your Desktop Background" on page 88, "Using a Screen Saver" on page 91, and "Creating a Sound Theme" on pages 204–205 for information about modifying the main features of a theme.

# Changing the Window Color

Although the themes provide a choice of colors, you can easily specify a new color. You can also set windows to be partially transparent and can even tweak the color intensity. To keep your changes if you later want to switch themes, you should save your changes as a new theme.

## Change the Color

**1** If the Personalization window isn't already open, right-click a blank spot on the Desktop, and choose Personalize to open the Personalization window. Click Window Color to open the Window Color And Appearance window.

**2** Click the color you want.

**3** If you want the transparent effect in the title bar, taskbar, and other locations, select the Enable Transparency check box; clear the check box if you don't want the effect.

**4** Drag the slider to adjust the color intensity, and note the changes in the window borders.

**5** If you don't like any of the preset colors, click the Show Color Mixer option and adjust the hue, saturation, and brightness to define your own color.

**6** Click Save Changes.

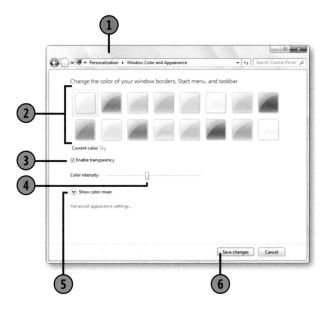

**See Also**

"Customizing Individual Window Elements" on page 94 for information about modifying individual items.

**Tip**

If your computer isn't capable of displaying the Aero Glass features, and/or if you selected one of the Basic And High Contrast Themes, you can't enable transparency or modify the color intensity. Instead, when you click Window Color, the Window Color And Appearance dialog box appears, and you'll be able to use it to modify some color and appearance settings.

# Enlarging Text

If you find the text on the screen just a bit too small for easy reading, you can set your computer to always show all the type on the screen in the size you want.

## Enlarge the Font

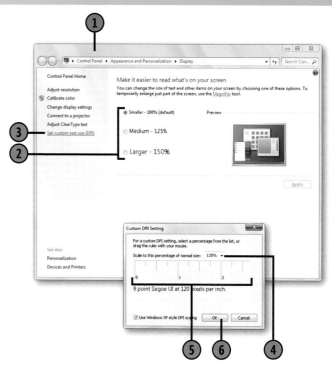

(1) Click the Start button, type **display** in the Search box of the Start menu, and choose Display from the menu to open the Display window.

(2) Select the type size you want.

(3) If you don't see the size you want, click Set Custom Text Size (DPI) to display the Custom DPI Setting dialog box.

(4) Select the size you want from the drop-down list.

(5) If you don't see the size you want, drag the ruler to set a size up to 500%.

(6) Click OK.

(7) Click Apply.

(8) Choose to log off now to close all your programs and then log on to apply the changes, or choose Log Off Later to keep the text size the same until the next time you log on.

**See Also**

See "Enlarging the Screen Content" on page 77 for information about using the Magnifier to temporarily enlarge everything on the screen.

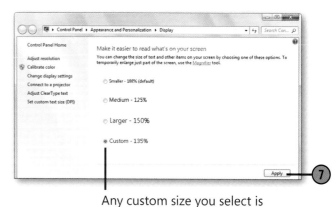

Any custom size you select is added to the Display window.

# Setting Your Desktop Background

One of the ways you can personalize your computer is to choose an image you like for the background of your Desktop. The image can be a single color, a pattern, or your favorite picture or photograph. You can also choose to display your pictures as a background slide show.

## Set the Background

**(1)** If the Personalization window isn't already open, right-click a blank spot on the Desktop, and choose Personalize from the shortcut menu. Click Desktop Background to display the Desktop Background window.

**(2)** Select the type and/or location of the image you want.

**(3)** Click Browse if you want to locate and use a picture from a location not in the list.

**(4)** If an image is selected that you don't want to use, or if multiple images are selected, click Clear All.

**(5)** Select any item for your Desktop background.

**(6)** Specify how you want to display the image:

- Fill to display it so that it covers the entire Desktop, cropping part of the picture if it doesn't fit

- Fit to scale it so that the entire image is displayed, even if there are blank edges

- Stretch to fill the screen with the full image, even if the image is distorted

- Tile to show it at its standard size and repeated to fill the screen

- Center with it at its normal size with a colored background that fills the rest of the screen

**(7)** Click Save Changes and, in the Personalization window, save the modified theme.

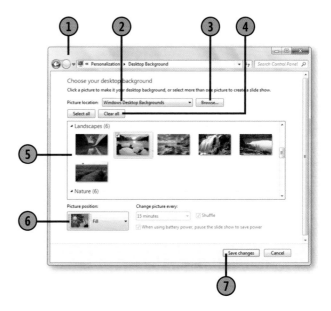

**Tip**

Point to the Show Desktop button at the right edge of the taskbar to preview your selected background.

## Create a Background Slide Show

(1) Click Desktop Background in the Personalization window, and choose the type and source of your images.

(2) If you don't want to use a selected image, point to it and click the check mark to clear the image, or click Clear All to deselect all the images.

(3) Point to each image you want to use and click the check box to select the image, or click Select All to include all the images at this location.

(4) Specify how you want the images to appear on the screen.

(5) Specify how often you want the images to change.

(6) Select this check box if you want the images to appear in a random order. Clear the check box if you want the images to appear in the order in which they appear in the window.

(7) If you're using a laptop, check this box to disable the slide show when using battery power, or clear it if you want to see your slide show despite the drain on the battery.

(8) Click Save Changes and, in the Personalization window, save the modified theme.

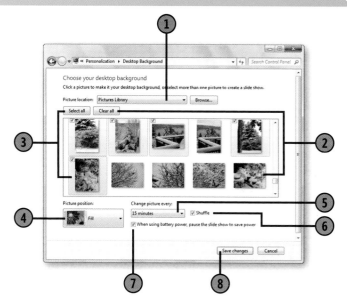

### See Also

"Classifying Your Files" on pages 34–35 for information about adding ratings, tags, and other information to your photos and other files.

### Try This!

In your Pictures Library, select one or more of your favorite photos. In the Details pane, click the fourth or fifth star to create a high ranking for these photos, and then click Save. Repeat the process for other photos you like. Now, in the Desktop Background window, click Picture Location, and choose Top Rated Photos from the drop-down list. Click Save Changes, save the modified theme, and enjoy your favorite photos as your background slide show.

# Customizing the Desktop Icons

You can display all the standard Desktop icons, hide them, or show only the ones you want. You can also change the image for each icon, adjust its size, and then arrange the icons however you want to see them on your Desktop.

## Select and Modify the Icons

1. Click the Start button, type **pers** in the Search box of the Start menu, and choose Personalization from the menu to display the Personalization window.

2. Click Change Desktop Icons to display the Desktop Icon Settings dialog box.

3. Select the icons you want to be shown on the Desktop.

4. To change the appearance of an icon, select it, click Change Icon, and, in the Change Icon dialog box that appears, click the image you want to replace the image of the selected icon. Click OK.

5. If you don't want the icons to change when you apply a theme, clear this check box. If you want the icons to change and to be consistent with the theme, select the check box.

6. Click OK.

7. Right-click a blank spot on the Desktop, point to View, and specify

   - The size you want for the icons.

   - The alignment you want.

   - Whether you want the icons to be shown on the Desktop or hidden.

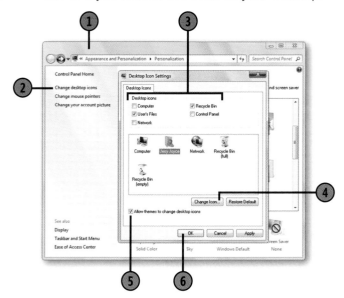

# Using a Screen Saver

A screen saver can provide a nice little respite from your work, as well as some privacy. If you work with other people, you might not want them to read your screen, albeit unintentionally, any time your computer is unattended. To prevent anyone from using your computer—but still allow

network access to it—when you're away from your desk, use the password option. You'll need to sign in to Windows 7 using your password when you get back to work. Note that the screen-saver setting is applied only to your current theme, so you can have different screen savers for different themes.

## Choose a Screen Saver

1. Click the Start button, type **pers** in the Search box of the Start menu, choose Personalization from the menu, and then click Screen Saver in the Personalization window to display the Screen Saver Settings dialog box.

2. Select a screen saver in the Screen Saver list.

3. Click Settings.

4. Specify the options you want for the screen saver. (Some have no options; those that do have their own unique settings.) Click Save when you've finished.

5. Click Preview to see the screen saver in full-screen view. Move your mouse to end the preview.

6. Specify the length of time you want your computer to be inactive before the screen saver starts.

7. Select this check box to require you to log on so that you can get back to work.

8. Click OK.

**Tip**

If you have Windows Live Photo Gallery installed and chose that option from the Screen Saver list, you can include videos as part of the screen saver.

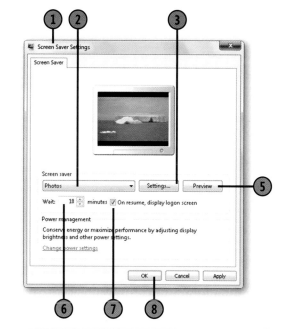

# Customizing Your Mouse

You're probably on pretty friendly terms with your mouse, but haven't you sometimes wished that you could build a better mouse? If your mouse's occasional disobedience is a source of frustration, you can lay down the law and tell that critter how to behave, and then you'll live together happily ever after.

## Set the Buttons

1 Click the Start button, type **mou** in the Search box of the Start menu, and choose Mouse from the menu to display the Mouse Properties dialog box.

2 On the Buttons tab, select this check box to switch the functions of the left and right mouse buttons.

3 Move the slider to set the speed at which you need to double-click for Windows to recognize your double-click. Double-click the folder icon as a test to see whether the setting is correct for your clicking speed.

4 Select this check box if you want to be able to select content or drag the mouse without having to hold down the mouse button. With the check box selected, the Click-Lock feature is activated when you hold down the mouse button for a short time and is then deactivated when you click the mouse button. Use the Settings button to set the length of time the mouse button needs to be held down to activate ClickLock.

5 Click Apply.

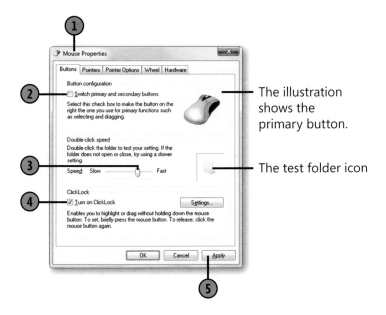

The illustration shows the primary button.

The test folder icon

**See Also**

"Managing Pen Settings" on page 333, "Managing Navigational and Editing Flicks" on pages 334–335, and "Managing Touch Settings" on pages 336–337 for information about customizing pen and touch input as alternatives to using the mouse.

**Try This!**

On the Pointers tab, select a pointer, click Browse, click the alternate pointer, and click Open. Repeat for any other pointer you want to change. When you've finished, click Save As, type a name for your custom scheme, and click OK.

## Set the Mouse Pointer

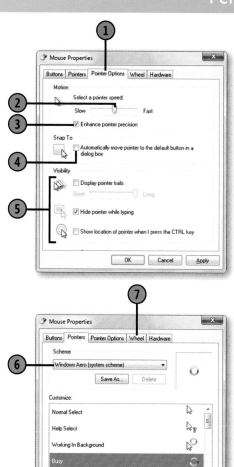

**(1)** Click the Pointer Options tab.

**(2)** Use the slider to set the speed at which you want the mouse pointer to move. Move your mouse to see how the setting affects its speed.

**(3)** Select this check box if you want to increase the precision of the pointer when you move short distances.

**(4)** Select this check box if you want the mouse to automatically move to the default button in a dialog box to facilitate quick selection of the button.

**(5)** Select or clear the check boxes in the Visibility section to customize the way the mouse pointer appears:

- Display Pointer Trails to increase the mouse pointer's visibility by temporarily showing its path.

- Hide Pointer While Typing if you find the mouse pointer's visibility annoying or distracting when you're typing and not using the mouse.

- Show Location Of Pointer When I Press The CTRL Key to show an animation that locates the pointer on your screen

**(6)** On the Pointers tab, choose a theme to change the overall appearance of the mouse.

**(7)** Use the options on the Wheel tab to specify how far you want the window to scroll when you scroll or tilt the wheel.

**(8)** Select or clear the check boxes to show a shadow under the pointer and to specify whether to allow themes to change your mouse-pointer scheme.

**(9)** Click OK when you've finished.

# Customizing Individual Window Elements

If you're using a basic or a high-contrast theme, you can customize the color, font, and size of individual items, either for the ultimate in individuality or simply to make items easier to see. If you're using one of the Aero themes, you can make a few changes, but the theme overrides many of your customizations.

## Change Individual Items

**(1)** Click the Start button, type **pers** in the Search box of the Start menu, and choose Personalization from the menu to display the Personalization window.

**(2)** Click the theme you want to modify.

**(3)** Click Window Color. For an Aero theme, click Advanced Appearance Settings in the Window Color And Appearance window.

**(4)** In the Window Color And Appearance dialog box that appears, select the item you want to customize.

**(5)** Change any settings. Only the appropriate settings are available for the item you selected.

**(6)** Click Apply to see the effect of your change. Repeat steps 4 through 6 to change other items you want to customize.

**(7)** Click OK, and then save the theme. If you're modifying an Aero theme, click Save Changes in the Window Color And Appearance window before you save the theme.

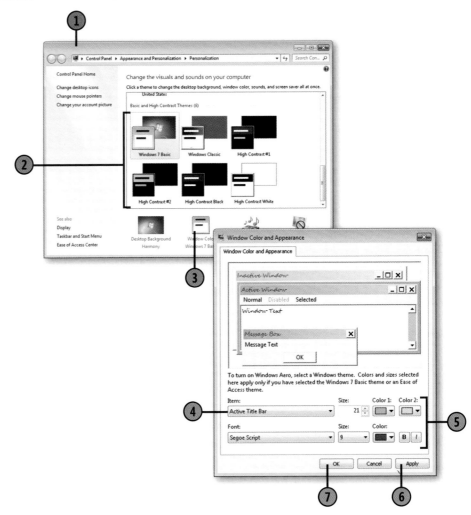

# Controlling the User Account Control

The User Account Control is the dialog box that appears when Windows asks you for permission to do something. It is a very powerful security tool that helps protect you from malicious programs that try to take over your computer and from accidental changes you might make that can disrupt the workings of Windows. However, depending on what you're doing, the control can become very annoying, popping up every time you want to do something. Fortunately, you can adjust which actions cause the control to appear.

## Set the Notification Level

① Click the Action Center icon in the notification area of the taskbar, and click Open Action Center in the window that appears. In the Action Center window, click Change User Account Control Settings to display the User Account Control Settings window.

② Drag the Notification slider to set the level of notification you want. Use the descriptions to decide which setting is best for you.

③ Click OK, and confirm the change. If you're not logged on as an Administrator, provide Administrator credentials, and then confirm the change.

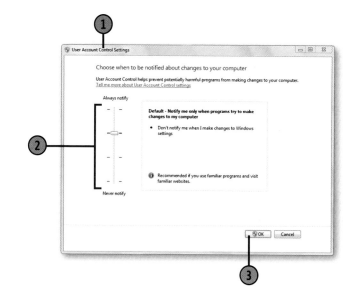

**Caution**

Do not set the User Account Control to its lowest setting unless you're certain you have no virus or other malicious programs on your computer and that you're either disconnected from the Internet or connected to a secure network. Use this setting only temporarily, and only if you need to run a program that isn't compatible with the User Account Control.

**See Also**

"Restricting User Rights" on pages 298–299 and "Know Your Rights" on page 300 for information about assigning users different levels of access.

"Maintaining High Security" on page 311 for information about using the User Account Control and other tools to keep your computer secure.

# Customizing the Taskbar

The taskbar is a really handy navigation device, and you can make it even more useful by customizing it to your work habits. You can specify which items you want to be displayed on the taskbar and how you want them displayed, and you can even hide the taskbar when you aren't using it and then make it reappear when you need it.

## Customize the Taskbar

① Click the Start button, type **taskb** in the Search box of the Start menu, and choose Taskbar And Start Menu from the menu to display the Taskbar And Start Menu Properties dialog box.

② Select this check box to prevent the taskbar from being moved to a new location or to prevent the taskbar and the toolbars from being resized.

③ Select this check box to hide the taskbar when you're not using it. The taskbar will reappear when you move the mouse to whichever edge of the screen contains the taskbar.

④ Select this check box to show small icons on the taskbar.

⑤ Click and select from the drop-down list the location where you want the taskbar.

⑥ Click and select the way you want similar items to be displayed and what to do when the taskbar is crowded.

⑦ Select this check box to make all windows transparent when you move the mouse to the Show Desktop button at the right end of the taskbar.

⑧ Click Apply if you've made any changes.

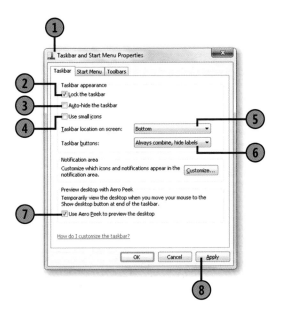

**Tip**

You can quickly lock or unlock the taskbar by right-clicking it and choosing Lock The Taskbar from the shortcut menu. You can also display the Taskbar And Start Menu Properties dialog box by right-clicking the taskbar and choosing Properties from the shortcut menu.

## Customize the Notification Area of the Taskbar

**1** On the Taskbar tab of the Taskbar And Start Menu Properties dialog box, click the Customize button to display the Notification Area Icons window.

**2** Click the Behaviors button for the icon you want to modify, and select the setting you want.

**3** Repeat for any other icons you want to change.

**4** Select this check box if you want to have all icons and notifications appear in the notification area of the taskbar.

**5** Click this link to display the System Icons window.

**6** Click the Behaviors button to modify the setting for the system icon you want to show or hide. Choose to have the icon shown (On) or hidden (Off). Repeat for any other system icons you want to turn on or off.

**7** Click OK.

**8** Click OK, and then click OK in the Taskbar And Start Menu Properties dialog box.

**Tip**

Whenever you need to access a hidden icon, just click the Show Hidden Icons button on the left side of the notification area of the taskbar.

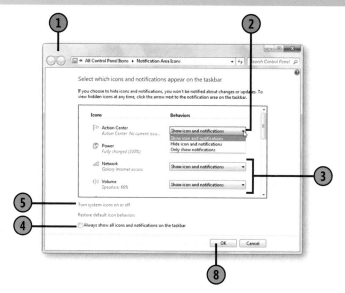

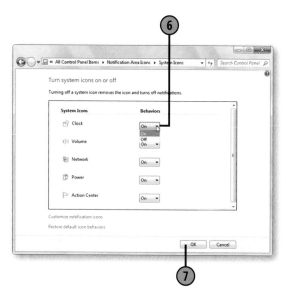

# Moving the Taskbar

The taskbar normally resides at the bottom of your computer's Desktop. However, you can move the taskbar to any side of the Desktop and then resize it to work best at that location.

If you're using multiple monitors, especially if you're giving a presentation, you can also move the taskbar onto one of the monitors so that it won't be visible during your presentation.

## Move and Resize the Taskbar

(1) Point to a blank spot on the taskbar, and drag the taskbar to the side of the Desktop where you want it. If the taskbar doesn't move, right-click it and, if the Lock The Taskbar command has a check mark next to it, click the command to unlock the taskbar. When the taskbar is unlocked, you can drag it to the new location.

(2) Place the mouse pointer on the inner edge of the taskbar until the pointer turns into a two-headed arrow, and then drag the border to change the width of the taskbar.

> **Tip**
>
> If you're using multiple monitors, you can move the taskbar to any side of your primary monitor, but you can't move it onto any other monitor.

> **Tip**
>
> You can enlarge the taskbar but you can't make it smaller than its default size. To make the taskbar smaller, right-click it, choose Properties from the shortcut menu, and, on the Taskbar tab of the Taskbar And Start Menu Properties dialog box, select the Use Small Icons check box. Click OK.

> **See Also**
>
> "Customize the Taskbar" on page 96 for information about selecting a position for the taskbar without dragging it with the mouse,
>
> "Setting Up Multiple Monitors" on pages 330–331 for information about using multiple monitors.

# Customizing the Start Menu

The Start menu is your main resource for organizing your programs and files and getting your work done in Windows. You can customize the Start menu in several ways: You can set which action is the default for the power button, you can choose whether your recently used programs and files are displayed on the Start menu, and you can select which items are shown as submenus or as links, or are not shown at all.

## Set the Power Button and Privacy Defaults

① Click the Start button, type **start** in the Search box of the Start menu, and choose Taskbar And Start Menu from the menu to display the Taskbar And Start Menu Properties dialog box.

② On the Start Menu tab, click the Power Button Action button, and select the default action from the drop-down list.

③ Select or clear the check box to show or hide the list of recently used programs on the Start menu.

④ Select or clear the check box to show or hide on both the Start menu and the taskbar the list of items that you've recently opened.

⑤ Click Customize to display the Customize Start Menu dialog box.

⑥ For items that are in folders, specify whether you want an item displayed as a link or as a menu, or not displayed. For other items, select the options you want.

⑦ Specify how many recently used programs you want to be displayed, and how many items are displayed in the Jump Lists.

⑧ Click if you want to remove all custom settings.

⑨ Click OK, and then click OK again to close the Taskbar And Start Menu Properties dialog box.

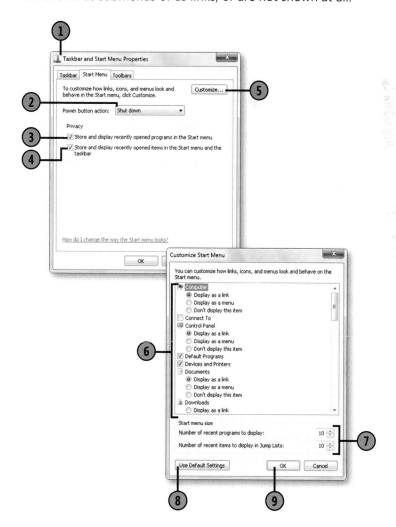

# Customizing Windows Explorer

Working in Windows 7 means that you work with Windows Explorer to access your libraries and folders, as well as your drives and network locations. To adapt Windows Explorer to your working style, you can customize it so that it looks and works in exactly the way you want. You can choose whether to use a single window or multiple windows when you're browsing various locations, whether to use a single-click or a double-click to open items, and which items you want to be shown and which you want to be hidden.

## Change the Way Windows Explorer Works

1. In a folder that you want to modify, click Organize, and choose Folder And Search Options from the drop-down menu to display the Folder Options dialog box.

2. On the General tab, specify whether you want all your folders to open in the same window (that is, to replace the window's current content), or whether you want to use a separate window for each folder that you open.

3. Click the first option if you want to click only once to open an item in a folder. Click the second option if you want to double-click to open an item. If you chose the first option, specify how you want the icon text to be underlined.

4. Select the first check box if you want to show all folders, including your personal folders, in the Navigation pane. Select the second check box if you want the Navigation pane to expand to show all the subfolders that are at the same level as the one you select in the folder window.

5. Click the View tab.

6. Select the check boxes for the options you want, and clear the check boxes for the options you don't want.

7. Click OK.

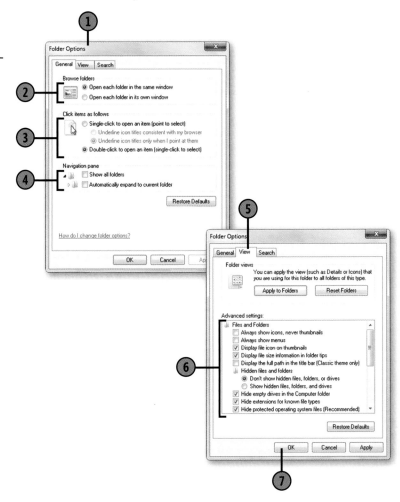

# Change the Content That's Shown

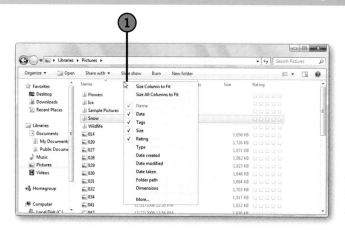

**1** In Details view, right-click the descriptive label, or detail, of one of the columns in the folder window (Name, for example), and, on the shortcut menu that appears, click an unchecked item to display that label if it isn't shown, or click a checked item to hide that label. If you don't see the item you want, click More.

**2** In the Choose Details dialog box, select the check boxes for the labels, or details, that you want to be shown in the folder window, and clear the check boxes for the details that don't need to be shown.

**3** Use the appropriate buttons to change the order of the currently selected label or to show or hide it.

**4** Specify the width in pixels of the column for the selected label.

**5** Click OK when you've finished.

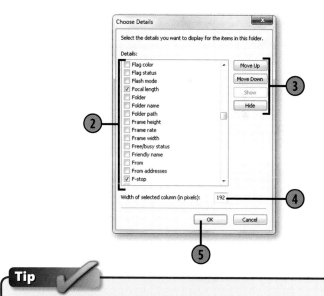

---

**Tip**

The items shown by default in Details view are based on the type of content that's contained in the library or folder. In most cases, Windows correctly detects the content and optimizes the window for that content. However, if the items shown in Details view, as well as the items shown on the toolbar, are not appropriate for the content, you can change the type of content the window is optimized for. For a library, right-click it, choose Properties from the shortcut menu, select the type of content the window should be optimized for, and click OK. For a folder that isn't part of a library, right-click the folder, choose Properties from the shortcut menu, and, on the Customize tab, select the type of content the window should be optimized for, and then click OK.

**Tip**

When you change the content shown in Details view for a library, the change will also be made in any folder that's part of that library.

# Changing Your Account Picture

When you set up your account, you have a selection of pictures to choose from to use next to your name. The picture you choose is important because not only does it appear when you log on to Windows 7 and at the top of the Start menu, but you can also use it in your Contacts folder, on your business cards, and in other programs. If you don't like the current picture, or if it has no relevance to your personality—and if you have a picture that's just right—you can change the picture.

## Change Your Picture

1. Click the Start button to open the Start menu, click your account picture at the top of the menu, and, in the User Accounts window that appears, click Change Your Picture to display the Change Your Picture window.

2. Click a picture you want to use.

3. If you don't like any of the pictures, click Browse For More Pictures, locate and select the picture you want, and click Open. The picture is changed, and the Change Your Picture window is closed.

4. If you selected one of the provided pictures, click Change Picture to change your picture and close the Change Your Picture window.

5. In the User Accounts window and/or on the Start menu, verify that you can see the picture you want.

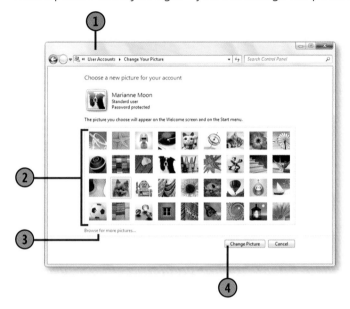

# Setting the Way a Removable Storage Device Starts

When you insert a CD, a DVD, a USB media device, or any other removable media device, Windows detects the type of content—music, pictures, or a movie, for example. You can set Windows to perform a specific action for each media type and/or device.

## Set the AutoPlay

① Click the Start button, type **autoplay** in the Search box of the Start menu, and choose AutoPlay from the menu to display the AutoPlay window.

② If you want some action to take place when you insert or attach a media type or media device, select this check box. If you want the action only for the media types and devices for which you set the default action, clear the check box.

③ For a media type or device for which you want to set the default action, choose the action you want to take:

- An action using a program or a Windows feature

- Open Folder To View Files Using Windows Explorer to view files

- Take No Action for Windows to do nothing

- Ask Me Every Time to display the AutoPlay dialog box showing available actions

④ Repeat step 3 for other media types or devices.

⑤ Click Save.

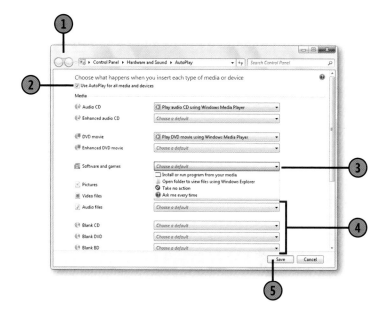

**Tip**

The AutoPlay actions listed for each type of media will differ depending on which programs or features you've installed.

# Using Alternative Ways of Working

If you have any difficulties when you're working with your computer, the Ease Of Access Center provides easy steps you can use to set up your computer with alternative tools and settings that will make the work easiest for you.

## Set the Options

① Click the Start button, type **access** in the Search box of the Start menu, and choose Ease Of Access Center; or choose Ease Of Access Center from the Ease Of Access submenu of the Start menu to display the Ease Of Access Center window.

② Select these check boxes if you want the contents of this section read aloud and want to have each of the tools highlighted in order.

③ If you want to use any of the listed tools to improve the view, to have the window's contents read to you, or to use the On-Screen Keyboard for alternative input, click the tool or press the Spacebar to select the highlighted tool.

④ Select the scenario that best fits the way you want to adjust the system.

⑤ Select the item or items you want to use.

⑥ If necessary, for each item, select an option or click an item to make additional settings.

⑦ Click OK when you've finished.

⑧ Select any other scenario that fits your needs, and repeat steps 5 through 7.

⑨ Close the Ease Of Access Center window.

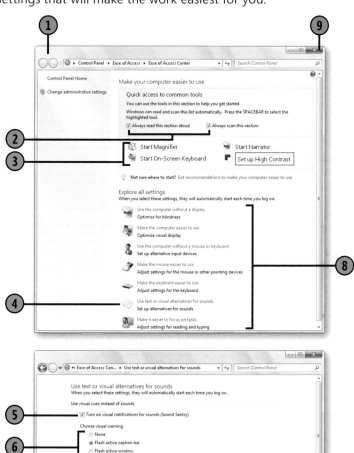

# Working Alternatives

Windows 7 provides several tools and settings that let you change the way you enter information into, or receive information from, the computer. These tools and settings—although designed primarily for people who experience difficulty when typing, using the mouse, seeing details on the screen, concentrating, or hearing sounds—can be used by anyone who'd like to try different ways of working on the computer. For example, you can use the keyboard to execute mouse actions, or use the mouse or another pointing device for keyboard input.

You can access these tools and settings from the Ease of Access Center; or, by choosing the Let Windows Suggest Settings in the Ease Of Access section of the Control Panel, you can walk through a five-step wizard that tries to identify the best settings for your needs. You can also access six tools and settings (Narrator, Magnifier, High Contrast, On-Screen Keyboard, StickyKeys, and FilterKeys) from the Logon screen when you sign in by clicking the Ease Of Access button or by pressing the Windows key+U key combination to display the Ease Of Access Center window.

## Alternative Tools

Windows 7 provides four major tools to help you do your work:

**Narrator:** Reads aloud the text on your screen.

**Magnifier:** Enlarges the active section of your screen.

**On-Screen Keyboard:** Displays a keyboard on your screen; you then use the mouse or another pointing device to type your text.

**Speech Recognition:** Recognizes your voice commands and standard dictation commands.

## Alternative Settings

Windows 7 provides numerous settings that help you work, some of which change the way Windows works and others that adjust the look of your screen. The most common settings are listed below.

**StickyKeys:** Sets key combinations with the Alt, Ctrl, and Shift keys to be pressable one key at a time.

**FilterKeys:** Ignores repeated characters or too-rapid key presses.

**ToggleKeys:** Makes different sounds when you turn the Caps Lock, Num Lock, or Scroll Lock key on or off.

**SoundSentry:** Flashes a specified screen component when the system beeps.

**High Contrast Themes:** Creates high contrast between elements on the screen by modifying the colors of the Desktop and the windows. There are several high-contrast themes to choose from to create the type of contrast you want.

**MouseKeys:** Sets the numeric keypad to control mouse movements.

You can also adjust the general Windows environment by changing the size and color of the mouse pointer, and you can execute mouse actions by pointing (hovering) instead of clicking. You can underline access and shortcut keys and can set the duration for which notification dialog boxes that appear from the notification area of the taskbar are shown. Other settings depend on whether a program or a file supports those features—turning off unnecessary animations, for example, or removing backgrounds, showing text captions for spoken dialog, or providing audio descriptions of actions in videos.

# Working in a Different Part of the World

If you're working in, or producing documents for use in, a region or country other than the one for which your computer was configured, you can change the default region and have Windows 7 adjust the numbering format, the type of currency, and the time-and-date schemes used by your programs. If you're working in a different language, you can switch the layout of your keyboard to conform to that language.

## Change the Default Region

1 Click the Start button, type **region** in the Search box of the Start menu, and choose Region And Language from the menu to display the Region And Language dialog box.

2 On the Formats tab, select the regional language you want to use.

3 Inspect the sample formats to make sure they're displayed as you want. If you want a different format, click the format and choose a new format from the drop-down list.

4 If you want to make additional changes to the formats, click Additional Settings, make your changes on the Numbers, Currency, Time, or Date tabs of the Customize Regional Options dialog box, and click OK.

5 On the Location tab, select the country or region in which you'll actually be doing your work.

6 Click Apply.

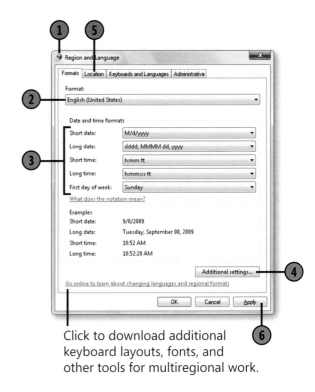

Click to download additional keyboard layouts, fonts, and other tools for multiregional work.

**See Also**

"Add Keyboard and Language Support" on the facing page for information about adding languages.

**Tip**

If you want to use more than one regional setting on your computer, you can add additional languages. When you switch the input language using the Language bar or a keyboard shortcut, the regional settings also change.

# Add Keyboard and Language Support

1. On the Keyboards And Languages tab of the Region And Language dialog box, click the Change Keyboards button to display the Text Services And Input Languages dialog box.

2. Select the language you want as the default input language.

3. Click the Add button to display the Add Input Language dialog box.

4. Click the plus sign next to the language you want, and then click the plus sign next to Keyboard to see a list of keyboards.

5. Select the keyboard layout you want. Click Show More if you want to display a list of all available keyboard layouts.

6. Click OK.

7. On the Language Bar tab, specify the way you want the Language bar to be displayed.

8. On the Advanced Key Settings tab, configure keyboard shortcuts that you can use to switch between languages.

9. Click OK, and then click OK again in the Region And Language dialog box.

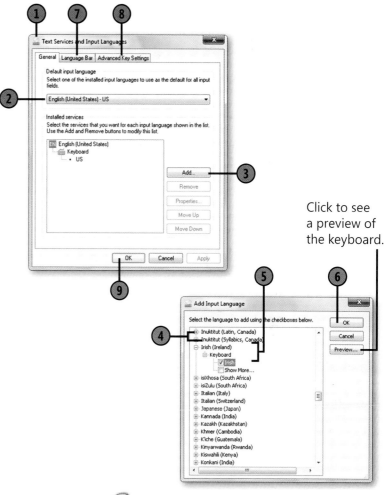

Click to see a preview of the keyboard.

**Tip**
To quickly switch between languages, click the Language icon on the Language bar and choose the language you want from the drop-down list; or use the keyboard shortcut you set on the Advanced Key Settings tab.

**Tip**
To add a special keyboard, such as a left- or right-handed Dvorak keyboard, select the language you're using, expand the list of keyboards, and select the keyboard you want to use.

# Adding Time Zone Clocks

If you want to keep track of what time it is in a different city or country, you can add a clock set to that particular time zone to the clock that's already on the taskbar. You can add up to two clocks for different time zones. However, note that the clocks, like the calendar, are there solely for your information and can't be used to change the time or the time zone.

## Create the Clocks

1. Click the Start button, type **time** in the Search box of the Start menu, and choose Date And Time from the menu to display the Date And Time dialog box.

2. On the Additional Clocks tab, select this check box to show an additional clock.

3. Select the time zone you want.

4. Enter a short, descriptive name for the new clock.

5. Select this check box, and repeat steps 2 through 4 if you want to add another clock.

6. Click OK.

7. To see the clocks, click the clock on the taskbar.

8. Click anywhere outside the window to close it.

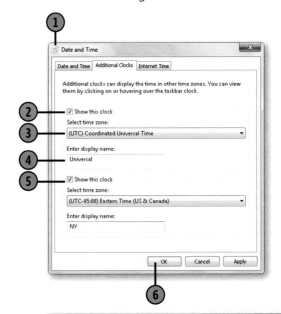

**Tip**

To quickly see the clock times, point to the clock on the task-bar to show a small window with the time in digital format for each clock.

# Controlling Updates

Updating your computer is very important, both to keep it running at its best and to help maintain security. Windows 7 uses Windows Update to make it easy to keep current with all the updates and fixes. However, automatic updates and

their frequent needs for restarting the computer can be very annoying. If you find that the way updates are conducted interferes with the way you work, you can modify the way the updates are installed.

## Modify Windows Update

1. Click the Start button, type **upd** in the Search box of the Start menu, and choose Windows Update from the menu to open the Windows Update window.

2. Click Change Settings.

3. Specify whether you want updates

    • Installed automatically.

    • Downloaded but not installed until you say so.

    • Checked for, but not downloaded and installed until you say so.

    • Not checked.

4. If you chose to have updates installed automatically, choose a day and time when the computer will be on but when you won't be working. If the computer is sleeping or is turned off at the time for the updates, the updates will occur the next time you awaken or turn on the computer—probably not a good time to have the computer download, install, and possibly restart.

5. Select or clear the check boxes for receiving other types of updates, for indicating who can install them, and for specifying whether you use Microsoft Update to receive updates for other Microsoft products.

6. Click OK.

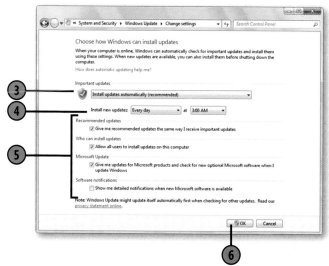

# Customizing the Action Center Messages

The Action Center is a great resource that accumulates all your alerts and issues in one place. Although this handy center helps you keep your computer healthy and up to date, there are notifications that you just don't want to be bothered with. You can easily set up the Action Center so that it notifies you of only the things you need to know about.

## Select the Type of Action Center Messages

1. Click the Action Center icon in the notification area of the taskbar, and click Open Action Center in the window that appears. In the Action Center window, click Change Action Center Settings to display the Change Action Center Settings window.

2. In the Security Messages section, clear the check boxes for any security-related messages you don't want to receive, and select the check boxes for any items you want to add to your messages.

3. In the Maintenance Messages section, select or clear the check boxes for the items you do or don't want to receive messages for.

4. Click OK.

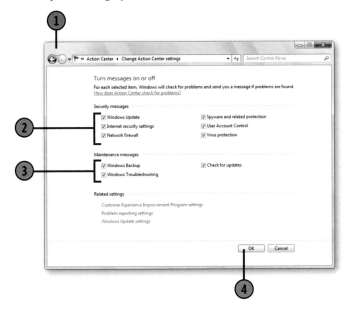

### See Also

"Customize the Notification Area of the Taskbar" on page 97 for information about displaying or hiding the Action Center icon and notifications.

"Monitoring Your Security Settings" on page 301 for information about using the Action Center.

### Tip

If the Action Center icon isn't displayed, open the Start menu, type **action** in the Search box, and click Action Center.

# Controlling Information Gathering

In certain circumstances, your computer system sends information to Microsoft about the way you use your computer and about the way the hardware is operating. This information is sent without identifying you or your computer and is intended to help improve operations, but if you don't feel comfortable providing these details, you can control this data gathering to maintain the level of privacy you want.

## Control Sending Profiles

1. Click the Start button, type **exper** in the Search box of the Start menu, and choose Change Customer Experience Improvement Program Settings from the menu to display the Customer Experience Improvement Program dialog box.

2. Click to open in your browser the current privacy statement from Microsoft that explains what data is collected and how it's used.

3. Specify whether or not you want to participate in the program.

4. Click Save Changes.

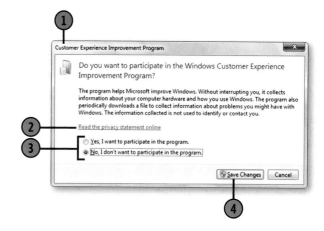

**Tip**

Some computer manufacturers use similar types of programs to gather information on the performance of their equipment. Check the documentation that came with your computer or from the manufacturer's Web site to determine whether and what type of information is collected, to read about the manufacturer's privacy policy, and to learn how to stop the information gathering if you so desire.

**See Also**

"Browsing in Private" on pages 132–133 and "Keeping Your Information Private" on page 134 for tips on how to prevent information from being collected when you're on the Internet.

# Controlling Problem Reporting

If you have a problem with software on your computer, Windows 7 can report the problem to a service. Once it has been reported, the service looks for a solution to the problem and, if one is known, reports it to you. However, in collecting the data, your Internet address (IP address) is recorded, and other information, including some contained in memory, might be collected. Although Microsoft doesn't use this information to identify you, you can change the settings for this reporting if you want. You can also exclude reporting from specific programs so that you can make sure your super-secret work stays that way.

## Control Problem Information

① Click the Action Center icon in the notification area of the taskbar, and click Open Action Center in the window that appears. In the Action Center window, click Change Action Center Settings, and then click the Problem Reporting Settings link to display the Problem Reporting Settings window.

② Select the option you want for checking for solutions to problems.

③ Click OK.

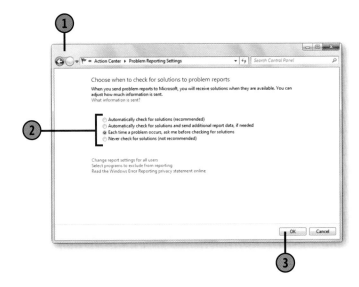

 **Tip**

When you change the setting that lets you check for solutions to problems, you're making the changes for your account only. To make the changes for all accounts on the computer (provided you have Administrator permission), click the Change Report Settings For All Users link, and, in the Problem Reporting dialog box that appears, make the changes for everyone.

## Control Individual Program Reports

**1** In the Problem Reporting Settings window, click the Select Programs To Exclude From Reporting link to display the Advanced Problem Reporting Settings window.

**2** Click Add.

**3** Locate and select the program you want to exclude from reporting, and click Open in the Problem Reporting window.

**4** Repeat steps 2 and 3 for any other programs to be excluded.

**5** Click OK when you've finished, click OK twice more to close the windows, and then close the Action Center window.

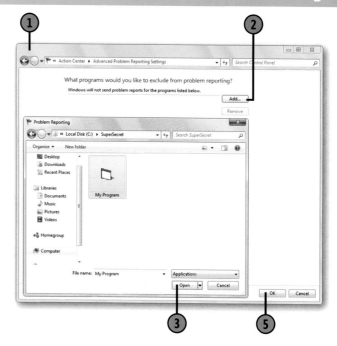

**Caution**

If you disable error reporting or exclude too many programs, you might end up with serious problems on your computer. Error reporting often occurs when a program stops working. If you don't find out what the problem is, the problem might continue to occur, and you could end up losing your work when that program crashes or causes other programs to crash. Diagnosing the problem without error reporting is often difficult, as it can involve seemingly unrelated causes such as incompatible drivers.

**Tip**

Even with the error-reporting program turned on, not all problems will be solved. Some problems are impossible to diagnose remotely, especially if there might be some problems with the hardware. Also, not all program publishers participate in the error-reporting program.

# Sharing Your Customizations

Now that you've personalized your computer, why not personalize someone else's computer? You can do so by creating your own theme and including your customizations of the background, window colors, sounds, screen saver, mouse pointers, Desktop icons, and so on. You do this by creating a theme and then saving it as a *theme pack*. The theme pack is a single file that contains all the settings you made, plus any additional resource files, such as background images. When you share this file with friends or colleagues who are running Windows 7 on their computers, all they need to do is double-click the file, and all your creative work will be at their disposal.

## Share Your Theme

**1** Right-click a blank spot on the Desktop, and choose Personalize to display the Personalization window.

**2** Create your personal theme, modifying as many elements as you want, and then save the theme.

**3** Right-click the theme and choose Save Theme For Sharing. In the Save Theme Pack As dialog box, name and save the theme-pack file.

**4** Share your theme with others by transferring the theme-pack file to them. Tell them to double-click the file if they want to install the theme on their computers.

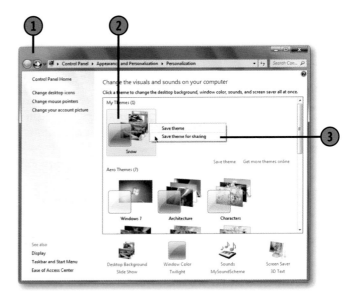

> **Tip** ✓
>
> You can save a theme or a theme pack, provided the theme is the current theme on your computer. If you see the command to delete the theme when you right-click it, it isn't the active theme. Click the theme to make it the current theme, and then right-click it to save it.

> **Caution** !
>
> The theme-pack file contains any pictures that you've included, so if the theme incorporates a large slide show of high-resolution photos, the theme-pack file will be very large. Try using a few lower-resolution photos to reduce the file size.

# 6

# Exploring the Internet

Whether you call it the Internet, the Net, or the Web, and whether you use it for business, homework, research, communicating, or shopping, the Web is probably already your window on the world. Your interface with the Web is your *Web browser*. There are numerous Web browsers available, and the browser that in many places comes with Windows 7 is Microsoft Internet Explorer 8. Internet Explorer is designed specifically for the world of the Web; it provides powerful features to make your explorations as easy and as safe as possible.

When you start Internet Explorer, it takes you to your *home page* (or *home pages*)—usually a page (or a group of pages) that displays information you want to see every day. However, if you want to change your home page or pages to another page or group of pages, you can do so with a couple of mouse-clicks. You can keep several Web pages open, each on its own *tab,* and you can switch back and forth among them. If there's a page or a group of pages you want to revisit, you can add it to your Favorites list, and Internet Explorer will create a shortcut to it for you. You can save a Web page and send it to others, or copy part of the page and use it in a document. You can also subscribe to part of a Web page and to online feeds to see new content on a Web site—updated news, schedules, or blog entries, for example.

# What's Where in Internet Explorer?

Although you can use the Web browser of your choice in Windows, you might want to try the new and improved version of Internet Explorer 8 that in many places comes with Windows 7; it's powerful, useful, and friendly. If you don't care for its streamlined look, you can display the classic menus by clicking the Tools button or pressing the Alt key.

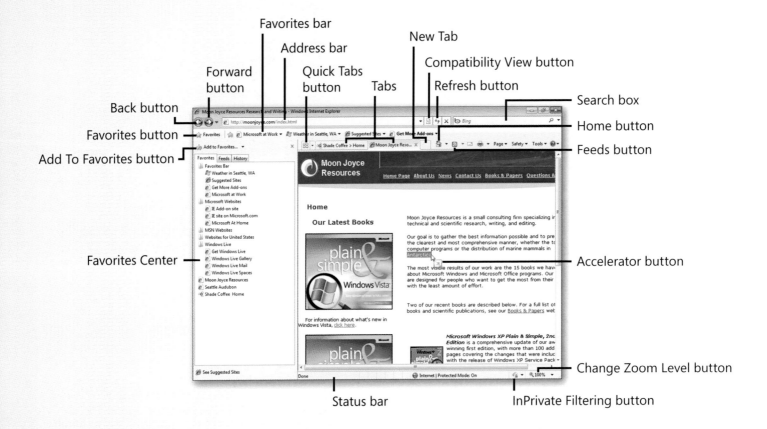

Favorites bar

Address bar

New Tab

Forward button

Quick Tabs button

Tabs

Compatibility View button

Refresh button

Search box

Back button

Favorites button

Home button

Add To Favorites button

Feeds button

Favorites Center

Accelerator button

Change Zoom Level button

Status bar

InPrivate Filtering button

# Finding a Web Page

You do most of your navigation on the Internet using the *hyperlinks* (also called *links* or *jumps*) that are located on Web pages and in search results. When you click a link, an Internet address is sent to your Web browser, which looks for the Web site and then displays the requested page. After you've located a Web page, you can explore further if you want. It's a bit like looking up a word in a dictionary and then looking up another word to expand your understanding of the first one.

## Explore

 Connect to the Internet if you're not already connected, and start Internet Explorer if it isn't already running.

Grouped tabs

 From your current page, do any of the following:

- Click in the Search box, start typing search words or a search phrase, and click the most relevant suggested search words or phrase. If no appropriate suggestion is offered, type your entire search phrase, and then press Enter to display a listing of search results on a new tab.

- Click a relevant link on the page to go to a new page or site.

- Hold down the Ctrl key and click a link to open the Web page on a new tab, keeping the existing Web page open and grouping the tabs.

- Click the Forward or the Back button to return to a previously visited site.

- Click the tab for an open Web page to view that page again.

- Open the Address bar drop-down list to specify and jump to a previously visited site, or type a new address to go to that site. Click the New Tab button first if you want the page to open on a new tab without replacing the existing page.

Use a link to jump to another page.

**Tip**

If you start Internet Explorer from the Start menu or from the taskbar, Internet Explorer goes to the page you've designated as your home page. If you start Internet Explorer by clicking a link, choosing a menu command, clicking search results, or using an Internet address, Internet Explorer goes to that specific page and bypasses your home page.

# Going to a Specific Web Page

If someone has given you an Internet address that isn't in one of the usual forms—for example, a hyperlink in an online document, in an e-mail message, or on another Web page—you can easily specify the address. You don't even need to go to your default home page but can simply jump to the destination. To do so, you use the Address bar in Internet Explorer, on the Windows taskbar, or in any folder window.

## Specify an Address

1. Click the current address on the Address bar to select the entire address.

2. Start typing the address you want to use to replace the currently selected address. (You don't need to type the *http://* part of the address.)

3. If the name of the Web page appears, click it.

4. If the correct Web page doesn't appear, finish typing the name, and then click the Go button or press Enter to go to the site. If you want the site to open on a new tab, hold down the Alt key when you click Go or press Enter.

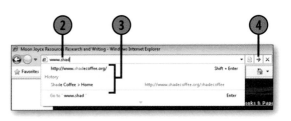

**Try This!**

In a document, a message, or the source of the Web-page address, select the address, and press Ctrl+C to copy it. In Internet Explorer, click in the Address bar to select the existing address, and press Ctrl+V to paste in the new address. Press Enter to go to that page.

**Tip**

If no proposed addresses ever appear as you type an address, in Internet Explorer choose Internet Options from the Tools menu, click Settings in the AutoComplete section of the Content tab, and select the Address Bar check box and the check boxes for the features you want. Click OK twice, and then try typing the address again.

# Opening Multiple Web Pages

If you've ever wanted to jump back and forth among two or more Web pages, the tabs in Internet Explorer make it simple.

Just open the Web pages on their own tabs, and they'll remain there until you close the page.

## Specify the Web Page

1. In Internet Explorer, click New Tab.

2. Start typing the address of the Web site you want. If the address is displayed in a drop-down list, click the address. If it doesn't appear, type the entire address, and then press Enter.

**See Also**

"Returning to Your Favorite Sites" on pages 122–123 for information about opening Web pages on their own tabs.

"Printing Web Pages" on page 221 for information about printing Web pages.

## Use a Link

1. Hold down the Ctrl key and click the link.

2. Click the newly opened tab to view it.

**Try This!**

In Internet Explorer, search for something on the Internet. On the Search Results page that appears, hold down the Ctrl key as you click a result. View the information. Switch back to the Search Results page, hold down the Ctrl key, and click another result. Continue opening new tabs for results and closing tabs that aren't relevant to your search.

# Viewing Multiple Web Pages

A very useful feature in Internet Explorer 8 is the ability it gives you to keep multiple Web pages open at the same time, each on its own tab. That way, you can leave a page open, open another page, and then easily and quickly move among pages.

## View Different Web Pages

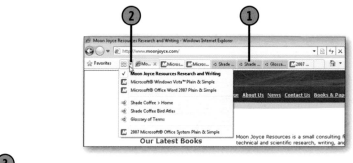

① In Internet Explorer, click a tab to view that Web page, or hold down the Ctrl key and press Tab to move through the different tabs.

② Click the Tabs List button to see a list of all the open Web pages. Click the Web-page name to switch to that tab.

③ Click the Quick Tabs button if you want to view all the open Web pages.

④ Click a Web-page thumbnail to switch to the tab for that Web page.

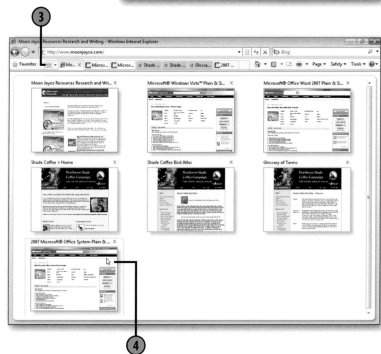

> **Tip** ✓
>
> If the Web page doesn't look the way you expect it to, click the Compatibility View button or choose Compatibility View from the Tools menu. The Compatibility View command on the Tools menu and the Compatibility View button on the Favorites bar are available only if Internet Explorer determines that the Web page might not be fully compatible with Internet Explorer's features.

## Control Your Tabs

**1** With multiple Web pages open, right-click a tab, and, on the shortcut menu that appears, do any of the following:

- Choose Close Tab to close the Web page and the tab that you clicked.

- Choose Close This Tab Group if the Web page is part of a tab group and you want to close all the Web pages in the group.

- Choose Close Other Tabs to close all the other Web pages and tabs except for the one you right-clicked.

- Choose Ungroup This Tab if the Web page is part of a tab group and you no longer want it to be part of that group.

- Choose Reopen Closed Tab to reopen the last Web page you closed in the session.

- Point to Recently Closed Tabs, and either choose the Web page that you closed in this session to reopen it, or choose Open All Closed Tabs to open all the Web pages that you closed in this session.

**2** Drag a tab to a new location if you want to re-order the tabs for easy access to related Web pages.

**3** Right-click a blank spot at the right of the tabs, point to Customize on the shortcut menu, and choose how you want the labels to appear on the tabs.

Tab group

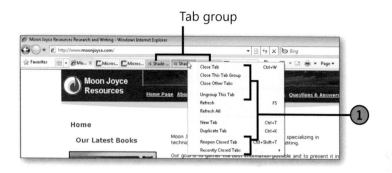

**Tip**

Internet Explorer creates a Tab group when you open a new tab from the Web site you're currently viewing. Tab groups are always placed together for easy viewing and are color coded for easy reference.

# Returning to Your Favorite Sites

When you've found a good source of information or entertainment, you won't need to waste a lot of time searching for that site the next time you want to visit it. You can simply add the site to your Favorites Center or Favorites bar, and Internet Explorer will obligingly create a link to the site for you.

## Save a Location

1. Go to the site whose location you want to save.

2. To save the location on the Favorites bar, click the Add To Favorites Bar button. If the Favorites bar isn't displayed, click the Tools button, point to Toolbars, and click Favorites Bar.

3. To add the site to your Favorites Center, click the Favorites button if the Favorites Center isn't already open, and then click the Add To Favorites button.

4. In the Add A Favorite dialog box that appears, type a name for the site, or use the proposed name if there is one.

5. If you want to place the link in an existing folder, select the folder.

6. If you want to place the link in a new folder, click New Folder, type a name for the folder, select a location for it, and click Create.

7. Click Add.

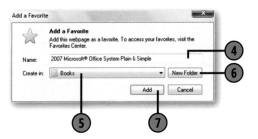

**See Also**

"Browsing in Private" on pages 132–133 for information about exploring sites without having your history and other information collected.

**Tip**

To add the Web pages that are open on all tabs as a group to your Favorites list, in the Favorites Center click the down arrow at the right of the Add To Favorites button, and choose Add Current Tabs To Favorites. You can then specify a folder and location in which to place all the Web-page links.

## Return to a Location

**1** If the Web page is on the Favorites bar, click it.

**2** If the Web page isn't on the Favorites bar, click the Favorites button, and, in the Favorites Center pane, click the Favorites tab if it isn't already clicked.

**3** If the link to the Web page you want to return to is visible, click the link.

**4** If the Web-page link is contained in a folder and isn't visible, click the folder to display its contents.

**5** If you want to open one of the Web pages listed, click the link.

**6** To open the Web page on a new tab, point to the link, and click the Open In New Tab button.

**7** If you want to open all the Web pages in the folder on their own tabs, point to the folder, and click the Open In A Tab Group button.

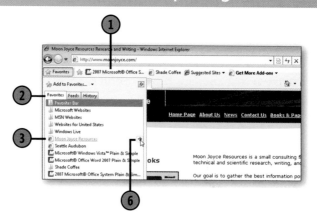

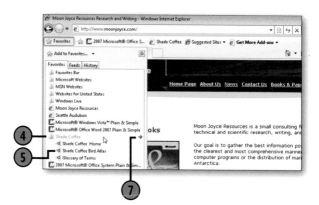

# Setting Your Home Page or Pages

When you start Internet Explorer, you automatically go directly to your home page—a page that you might have customized or that contains the links and services you want. You can also set several pages as part of your home-page tab set. If you'd rather use a different home page, or if you want to reset the home page after a service or a program has changed it, you can designate a new home page with just a couple of mouse-clicks.

## Set Your Home Page or Pages

① Use Internet Explorer to go to the page you want to use as your home page. If you want to designate additional pages as a new home-page tab set, open the other pages on their own tabs.

② Click the Home button down arrow, and choose Add Or Change Home Page from the drop-down menu.

③ In the Add Or Change Home Page dialog box, select the option you want.

④ Click Yes.

The current page will be your only home page.

The current page will be added to any other home pages and displayed on its own tab.

All the pages on the different tabs will become your new home-page tab set.

**Tip** ✓
Web-page content changes frequently, so what you see on some of the Web pages shown in this book might look a bit different from what you see when you access those same pages on line.

**Tip** ✓
To remove a page from your home-page tab set, click the Home button down arrow, point to Remove on the drop-down menu, and, on the submenu that appears, click the Web-page address you want to remove.

# Finding Related Web Sites

Suggested Sites is a Web service from Microsoft that uses your browsing history and search terms to determine which sites

you visit the most and then suggests other sites that might contain related information.

## See Other Sites

① Open Internet Explorer if it isn't already open. If the Favorites bar isn't displayed, click a blank spot at the right of the tabs, and then click Favorites Bar on the drop-down menu to display the Favorites bar.

② Click Suggested Sites. If Suggested Sites isn't already turned on, click the Tools menu and choose Suggested Sites from the drop-down menu. In the Suggested Sites dialog box that appears, click Yes to turn on Suggested Sites.

③ If Suggested Sites is already turned on, click any of the suggested sites you want to visit.

④ If you no longer want to send your information to the Web service, click the Tools menu in Internet Explorer, and click Suggested Sites to turn off this feature.

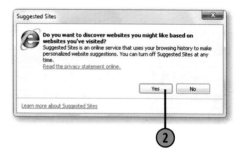

**Tip** ✓

Suggested Sites is an online service that uses your browsing history to suggest appropriate sites you might want to visit. To accomplish this, your browsing history is periodically sent to Microsoft, you can turn off this feature. If you don't want your browsing history available to Microsoft, you can turn off this feature.

# Finding Information on the Internet

To search for a specific item on the Internet—a list of sources where you can buy other *Plain & Simple* books, for example, or the menu and locator map for that new restaurant you want to try—you can search from almost anywhere in Windows 7.

When the results are displayed, you can jump to the page that contains the information you're looking for, and, if it's not what you want, you can try another page.

## Search for an Item

**1** In Internet Explorer, click the Search Options button, and select a search service if you want to use one other than your default service. If the service you want isn't listed, click Find More Providers, and then select the one you want from the Web page that appears.

**2** Click in the Search box, and start typing the search text. If you see a suggestion that matches the search text you want, click it, or hold down the Ctrl key when you click it to open the search results on a new tab. If you don't see an appropriate suggestion, finish typing the search text, and press Enter to start the search. If you want the results to appear on a new tab, press Alt+Enter instead.

**3** Click a link on the Search Results page.

**4** If you want to find the search text on your current Web page, click in the Search box, type your search text, and then click Find.

**5** Use the Find bar to find individual instances of the text, to highlight all instances of the text, or to modify your search.

**6** Close the Find bar when you've finished.

Click to see results from one of your other search providers.

# Viewing One Section of a Page

A new feature in Internet Explorer 8 gives you the ability to subscribe to a section—or *slice*—of a Web page. After you've subscribed, you'll be able to see updated information for only that slice of the Web page. Of course, the Web page must be designed to support this feature, which is really only useful for information that changes frequently.

## Subscribe to a Web Slice

1. In Internet Explorer, go to the Web site that contains the slice you want. The Feeds button will show a green icon if there are Web slices available.

2. Click the button at the right of the Feeds button. (This button is available only when there are available Web slices or RSS feeds on that Web site.)

3. Click the Web slice you want.

4. Verify the information about the Web slice, and then click Add To Favorites Bar.

5. To view the Web slice and see any updated information, click the button on the Favorites bar.

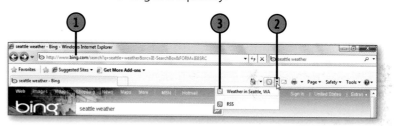

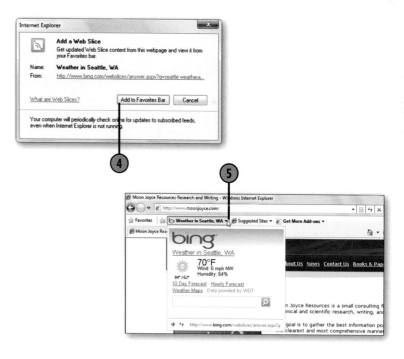

**Tip** ✓

If you've added so many Web slices or other items to the Favorites bar that they don't all fit, right-click one of the items, and point to Customize Title Widths on the shortcut menu that appears. Then choose either Short Titles or Icons Only from the submenu to shrink the button width for each item.

# Reading RSS Feeds

RSS feeds provide information—often from news Web sites or *blogs* (Web logs)—that's available for a one-time download or by subscription. When you subscribe, updated information is periodically sent to your computer. And, okay, here's yet another abbreviation to add to your list: RSS stands for Really Simple Syndication.

## Get Your Feed

① In Internet Explorer, go to the Web site that has the RSS feed you want.

② Click the button at the right of the Feeds button. The button is available only when there are available RSS feeds or Web slices on that site. RSS feeds are indicated by an orange icon; Web slices have a green icon.

③ Click the RSS feed you want.

④ On the Web page that appears, review the page to make sure you want to subscribe to this feed, and, if so, click to subscribe to the RSS feed or feeds that you want.

⑤ In the Subscribe To This Feed dialog box that appears, make any changes you want to the name or location of the RSS feed.

⑥ Click Subscribe.

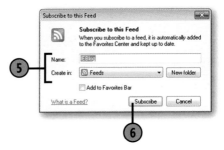

**See Also**

"Viewing One Section of a Page" on page 127 for information about subscribing to Web slices.

**Tip**

Not all Web sites that provide RSS feeds use the same methodology, so sometimes the RSS button won't be available. In those cases, follow the directions on the Web site to subscribe to the RSS feed.

## Read Your Feed

**①** Click the Favorites button to display the Favorites Center.

**②** Click the Feeds tab if it isn't already selected.

**③** Click the feed you want to view.

**④** Use the Search In Feed box or other tools to find the material you want in the feed.

**⑤** Read the information.

The Refresh This Feed button

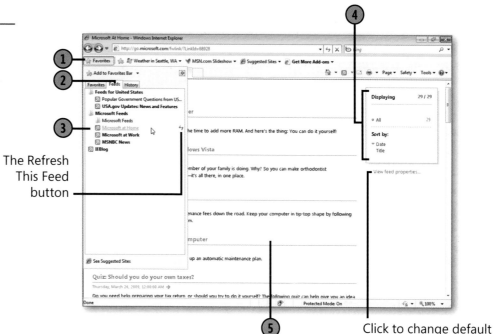

Click to change default settings, including how frequently your feeds will be updated.

### Try This!

Open the Favorites Center and click the Feeds tab. Point to an RSS feed and click the Refresh This Feed button. Now click the feed. Note that only the latest information is shown.

### Tip

If you added the RSS feed to your Favorites bar, you can click the down arrow at the right of the feed's button on the Favorites bar to see a list of the most recent feeds. To add to the Favorites bar after you've added the feed to your Favorites Center, open the Favorites Center, right-click the feed on the Feeds tab, and choose Add To Favorites Bar.

### Tip

Internet Explorer is only one of many different RSS readers. You can also use an RSS gadget on your Desktop or in a different program. The list of RSS feeds you subscribe to in Internet Explorer should be available in any other RSS feed readers you use.

# Controlling Pop-Up Windows

Argh! Doesn't it drive you crazy when you go to a Web site, only to face a relentless barrage of pop-up windows that try to sell you a bunch of stuff you don't want? With Windows 7, you can tell Internet Explorer to whack those pop-up windows. However, if there are certain pop-up windows you want to look at, you can tell Internet Explorer to display them.

## Set the Pop-Up Blocker

1. In Internet Explorer, click the Tools button, point to Pop-Up Blocker on the drop-down menu, and click Pop-Up Blocker Settings to display the Pop-Up Blocker Settings dialog box. If the Pop-Up Blocker Settings command is grayed (unavailable), first choose Turn On Pop-Up Blocker from the submenu.

2. If you want to allow pop-ups from a specific Web site, start typing the name of the site, and, if the full address of the site is suggested, click it. If the site isn't suggested, type its full address.

3. Click Add.

4. Select the notification options you want.

5. Select the level of filtering you want:

   - High to block all pop-ups

   - Medium to block pop-ups, except when you click a link to open a pop-up window or when the Web site you're visiting is in the Internet Explorer Local Intranet or the Trusted Sites security zone

   - Low to allow most pop-ups

6. Click Close.

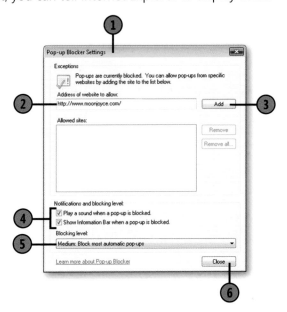

**Tip**

Visit a site before you add it to the Allowed Sites list to verify that it's the correct site. That way, when you start typing the address of a Web site to put it in your Allowed list, the Auto-Complete list appears with recently visited sites, so you can just click the site you want and thereby avoid misspellings.

## Control the Pop-Up Windows

**1** On a Web site where a pop-up has been blocked, click the Information bar.

**2** Specify the action you want from the menu:

- Temporarily Allow Pop-Ups to allow pop-ups from this Web site during this one visit

- Always Allow Pop-Ups From This Site to add this site to your list of exceptions and to always permit pop-ups from this site

- Settings to turn off the Pop-Up Blocker, to hide the Information bar, to manually add the addresses of sites that you'll allow to show pop-ups, or to change the filtering level (High, Medium, or Low) of pop-ups

- Information Bar Help to find out even more details about working with the Information bar

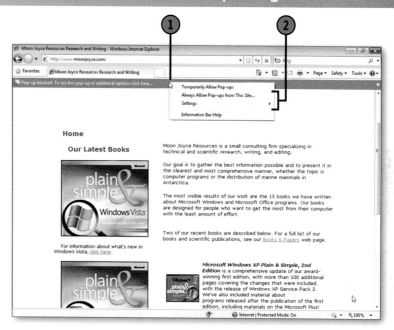

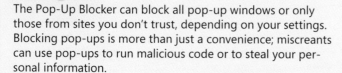

**See Also**

"Maintaining High Security" on page 311 for information about protecting yourself and your computer from scams known as *phishing*.

**Tip**

The Pop-Up Blocker can block all pop-up windows or only those from sites you don't trust, depending on your settings. Blocking pop-ups is more than just a convenience; miscreants can use pop-ups to run malicious code or to steal your personal information.

**Caution**

The Information bar appears whenever a security problem is encountered—when a Web page tries to download a file or an ActiveX control, for example. To maintain security, make sure the Information bar isn't turned off, and pay attention to the messages it contains.

# Browsing in Private

When you roam around the Internet, your computer records certain information, including the sites you visit. If you don't want to reveal your activities to anyone who has access to your computer, you can eliminate this history by setting Internet Explorer so that it won't keep a list of the Web sites you visit. For even more privacy, you can use InPrivate Browsing, in which your computer doesn't record your viewing history, doesn't keep cookies or temporary Internet files, and doesn't store any passwords. There is, however, a cost for this privacy, including being unable to use your History list to return to a site, being unable to store some customization settings, being unable to use quick logins, and having some page views slowed down.

## Forget Your History

1. In Internet Explorer, click the Safety menu, and choose Delete Browsing History from the drop-down list to display the Delete Browsing History dialog box.

2. Select this check box if you want information for the Web sites you've added to your Favorites list to be preserved, or clear the check box if you want this information cleared along with all other Web sites.

3. Select the check boxes for the items you want to delete, and clear any selected check boxes for the items you want to keep.

4. Click Delete.

5. If you want these items deleted automatically each time you close Internet Explorer, click the Tools menu, choose Internet Options from the drop-down menu to display the Internet Options dialog box, and, on the General tab, select this check box.

6. Click OK.

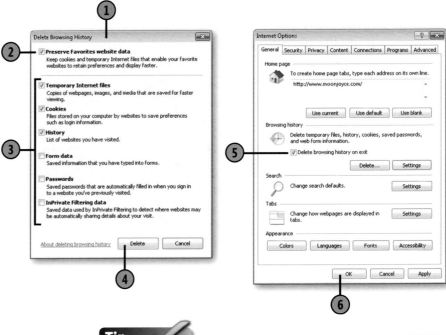

---

**Tip**

To keep Internet Explorer from recording the sites you visit but still allow it to keep other material such as cookies and temporary files, on the Internet Options tab in the Browsing History section, click Settings, set Days To Keep Pages In History to zero, and then click OK twice.

## Turn On Private Browsing

1. With Internet Explorer running, click the Safety menu, and choose InPrivate from the drop-down list to open a new browser window.

2. In the new window that uses the InPrivate features, type the address of the Web site you want to visit, or use the Search feature to find and then go to the Web site.

3. Browse pages and open new tabs as you normally do. Each tab will use the InPrivate settings.

4. Click Close when you've finished to close the Internet Explorer window with the InPrivate settings and to return to the original Internet Explorer window with your normal Web-browser settings.

When InPrivate Browsing is turned on, you will see this indicator

To confirm that you're using InPrivate settings, check that the InPrivate label appears.

---

**Tip**

You can quickly open the Delete Browsing History dialog box by pressing the key combination Ctrl+Shift+Del. You can open a window for InPrivate browsing by pressing Ctrl+Shift+P or by opening a new tab and clicking the Browse With InPrivate link.

**See Also**

"Keeping Your Information Private" on page 134 for information about preventing Web sites from profiling your activities.

**Caution**

Deleting the History list or using InPrivate browsing won't keep your browsing habits hidden from the tracking software that's frequently used on corporate networks. These efforts also won't hide your activities from a professional review of your computer's hard disks. Be aware too that some tracking software—including software such as Windows Live Family Safety that's part of the parental controls—can disable InPrivate browsing.

# Keeping Your Information Private

Many Web sites use outside services to provide some of their content. In some instances, providers can track you whenever you visit Web sites that use their services. So, for widely distributed services, providers can, over time, create a profile of some of your viewing activities. When you use InPrivate Filtering, some of these information-gathering programs on Web sites are blocked. Although this filtering can protect your privacy, it might also stop you from being able to see all the content on a Web page.

## Block Information Gathering

**1** With Internet Explorer running, click the Safety menu, and click InPrivate Filtering on the drop-down menu if there isn't already a check mark next to it.

**2** If the content you want to view is blocked, click the down arrow at the right of the InPrivate Filtering button, and then click Off. To restore blocking, click the down arrow again, and choose Automatically Block from the list.

**3** To block content from specific providers, click Safety and, on the drop-down menu, click InPrivate Filtering Settings to display the InPrivate Filtering Settings dialog box.

**4** Select this option.

**5** Select a provider you want to allow or block.

**6** Click the Allow or the Block button to control the provider's tracking of your activities.

**7** Repeat steps 5 and 6 for the other providers.

**8** Click OK.

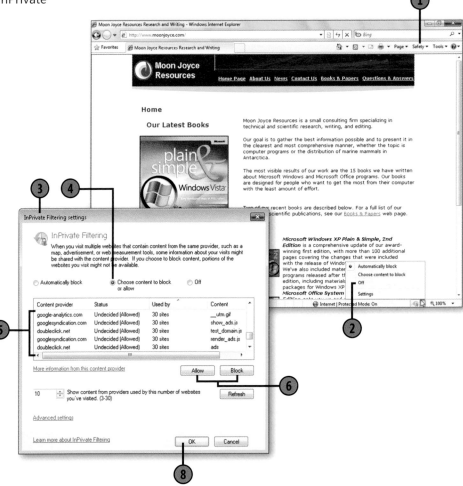

# Managing Add-Ons

Internet Explorer uses add-ons to expand its functionality. Some of these add-ons are from Microsoft, but many are from other suppliers, and you'll find that the add-ons can be either very useful or very annoying. Fortunately, it's easy to see the add-ons, to find out more about them, and then to disable or remove them if you don't want to keep them.

## Manage the Add-Ons

① In Internet Explorer, click the Tools menu, and choose Manage Add-Ons from the drop-down menu to display the Manage Add-Ons dialog box.

② Select the type of add-on you want to manage.

③ Click the add-on to be managed.

④ Use the information provided to learn more about the item. The information and the links vary depending on the type of add-on selected.

⑤ Use the buttons to remove or disable the add-on. The buttons available depend on the type of add-on selected.

⑥ Choose a different type of add-on to be managed, select it, and take whatever actions you want.

⑦ Click Close when you've finished.

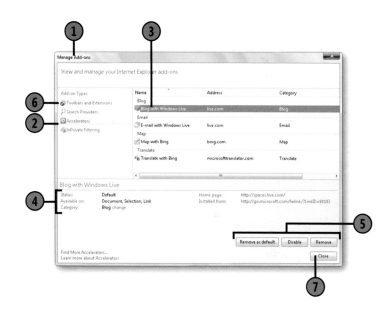

# Transferring Your Settings

If you use more than one computer or more than one type of browser to explore the Internet, you don't need to duplicate your list of favorite Web sites, nor do you need to duplicate the registrations, sign-ins, and customizations for Web sites that usually keep that information stored as "cookies" (small data files) on your computer. Instead, you can export your list of favorite sites and cookies from one computer or program and import them into another computer.

## Save the Information

① With Internet Explorer running, on the computer that contains the items you want to transfer, choose Import And Export from the File menu to start the Import/Export Settings wizard. If the menus aren't displayed, press the Alt key to display them.

② Step through the wizard, specifying

- That you want to export your settings.

- The type of items you want to export.

- The Favorites folder you want to export. Select Subfolders if you want to export only a subset of your Favorites.

- The locations and file names for each of the items being exported.

③ Transfer the files to a location that the other computer can access, such as a shared folder or removable storage—a disc or a USB storage device, for example.

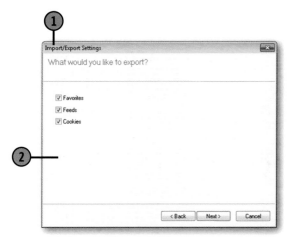

You can export all your favorites or just those contained in a folder.

**Tip**

If you have more than one Internet browser on your computer, you can use the Import/Export Settings wizard to transfer Favorites (bookmarks) and cookie information directly among the browsers.

## Transfer the Information

**①** With Internet Explorer running, on the computer to which you want to transfer the information, choose Import And Export from the File menu to start the Import/Export Settings wizard. If the menus aren't displayed, press the Alt key.

**②** Step through the wizard, specifying

- Which items you want to import.

- The names and locations of the files that contain the information you previously exported.

- The destination folder for your favorites and, if you're importing them, the feeds.

**③** Click Import to import the information you specified, and then click Finish to close the wizard.

You can add the imported favorites to your Favorites list or place them in an existing folder.

**Tip**

When you press the Alt key to display the menus, they're displayed only temporarily; they'll hide again after you've used a menu command or executed another action such as clicking a tab. To display the menus all the time, click the Tools button, point to Toolbars on the drop-down menu, and choose Menu Bar from the submenu.

# Saving a Web Page

If a Web page contains important information that you know you'll want to refer to in the future, you can save the page on your computer. That way, even if the online Web page changes, you'll still have the original information. The way in which you save the page, however, affects which information will be available when you open it. After you've saved the Web page, you can send it to your friends and colleagues if you want.

## Save a Web Page

① Start Internet Explorer if it isn't already running, and connect to the Internet if you aren't already connected. Go to the Web page you want to save.

② Click the Page menu, and choose Save As from the drop-down menu to display the Save Webpage dialog box.

③ Type a name for the file, or use the proposed name. Choose a destination if you want to save the file in a different location.

④ Click Save As Type, and, from the drop-down list, specify how you want to save the Web page:

- Webpage Complete to save the formatted text and layout and to place all the linked resources, such as pictures, in a separate folder

- Web Archive, Single File to create a single archive file that contains all the elements of the Web page

- Webpage, HTML Only to save the formatted text and layout but none of the linked items, such as pictures

- Text File to save only the text

⑤ Click Save.

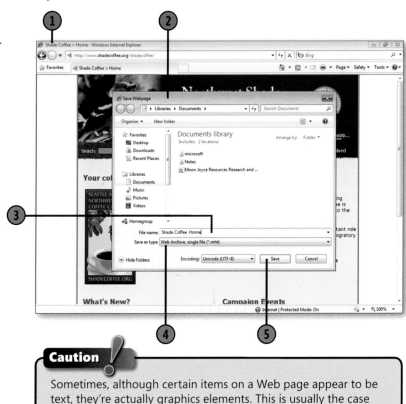

### Caution

Sometimes, although certain items on a Web page appear to be text, they're actually graphics elements. This is usually the case when the designer of the page or the site wanted to include some special formatting that couldn't be done with the usual HTML formatting. If you save the page as either Web Page HTML Only, or Text File, the information that contains the special formatting won't be saved.

# Copying Material from a Web Page

Sometimes, although you might want to save one or two items from a Web page, you have no use for the entire page. It's a simple matter to save only the parts of the page you want.

## Save a Picture

**1** Right-click the picture, and choose Save Picture As from the shortcut menu.

**2** In the Save Picture dialog box that appears, save the picture in the library or folder and in the format you want, using a descriptive file name.

**Caution**

When you copy material from a Web page, make sure that you're not violating any copyrights.

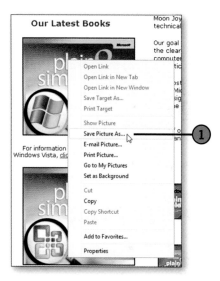

## Save Some Text

**1** Click at the beginning of the text you want to copy. You won't see an insertion point, but Internet Explorer is smart—it knows where you clicked.

**2** Drag the mouse over the text you want to copy.

**3** Press Ctrl+C to copy the text.

**4** Switch to a word processing program such as WordPad, paste the text (press Ctrl+V), and save the document.

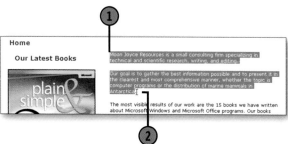

**See Also**

"Copying Your Screen Content" on page 69 for information about copying an image of a Web page.

# Using Accelerators for Quick Actions

Accelerators are links to online services that can speed up some of your routine tasks while you're browsing. Internet Explorer comes with a few accelerators, and you can download additional ones.

## Use an Accelerator

**1** In Internet Explorer, select the word or content that you want to use.

**2** Click the Accelerator button, which appears when you make your selection.

**3** On the menu that appears, click the accelerator you want to use. If you don't see the accelerator you want, point to All Accelerators, and then choose the accelerator you want from the submenu.

**4** If you don't see the accelerator you want on the submenu, click Find More Accelerators, and then use the Internet Explorer 8 Add-Ons Gallery to find, download, and install the accelerator you want.

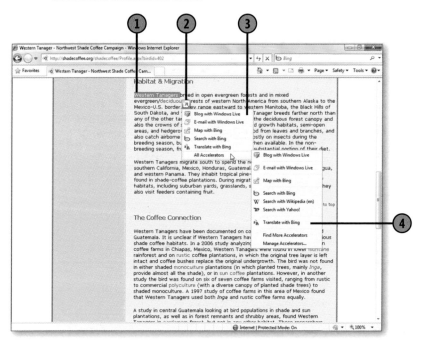

**See Also**

"Managing Add-Ons" on page 135 for information about controlling accelerators and other add-ons.

**Tip** ✓

The accelerators listed to search using various search services are based on the search providers you've set up. If you want additional search accelerators, click the down arrow at the right of the Search box, and click Find More Providers. If you have too many search providers listed, click Manage Search Providers instead of Find More Providers to delete the providers you don't use.

# 7 Playing Games

As the saying goes, "All work and no play makes Jack—or Jacqueline—a dull boy (or girl)!" Because we know that you, our readers, are anything but dull, this section of the book is all about playing games and having fun!

Whether you want to take a few minutes to work off some energy with a quick game of Minesweeper or FreeCell, lose yourself for an hour or two in a game of Solitaire, or invite a friend or colleague to join you in a game of Chess Titans, Windows 7 is ready to play! If you're a devotee of the traditional mah-jongg game, there's an intriguing one-player version called Mahjong Titans that you'll want to try. And if you want to match your skills with people around the world, there are some games that you can play over the Internet.

There are also some games that small children can play, either by themselves or with your help. They'll be learning about colors and shapes as they create fantastic confections in the Comfy Cakes game, strengthening their visual memory as they match tile patterns in the Purble Pairs game, and playing a guessing game in Purble Shop. Our young tester got the hang of all three games with a minimum of assistance from us, and she enthusiastically challenged herself by increasing the difficulty level. So, without further ado...let the games begin!

# Playing Your Games

Windows 7 comes with a few games, but if you want, you can easily install more. To access and control them, the Games Explorer gathers all the games and the information about them into one window. From that window, you can see the rating for the game, how well it will run on your system, and how well you've done playing the game. If you have problems playing a game or getting updated information about it, you can tweak your settings. And if you're concerned about youngsters accessing the wrong types of games or playing too late into the evening, you can set parental controls to limit their access.

## Play a Game

1. Choose Games from the Start menu to display the Games Explorer window. If Games isn't listed on the Start menu, type **games** in the Search box of the Start menu, and choose Games Explorer from the menu.

2. Select a game.

3. Use the tabs to read the age rating, the performance ratings that are required and recommended for the game, the rating of your computer, and, if you've played the game before, your statistics. (Note that this information isn't available for all games.)

4. If you don't see any games you want to play, click to go on line to play online games, download trial versions of games, or purchase additional games.

5. Double-click a game to start playing it.

**Tip**

Microsoft Blackboard, Microsoft Garden Pond, and Microsoft Rebound are three games that are available in the Microsoft Touch Pack, an add-on that's designed to work with computers that have multi-touch capabilities.

## Control the Games

**①** In the Games Explorer window, click Options to display the Set Up Game Updates And Options dialog box.

**②** Specify whether you want to check for updates and news.

**③** Select this check box if you want to download art and information about installed games from the Internet.

**④** Select this check box if you want to keep statistics on your game playing.

**⑤** Click the Clear Information button if you want to clear the past statistics.

**⑥** Click OK.

**⑦** If you need to adjust any of your computer's hardware or firewall settings, click the Tools menu, and select the item you want to change.

**⑧** Click the Parental Controls button to set up or change any parental controls to restrict the games that you'll allow to be played on this computer, based on their ratings and the time of day.

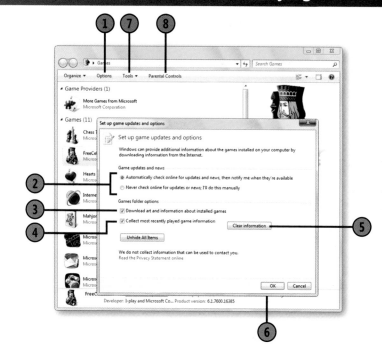

### Tip

To prevent an installed game from being shown in the Games Explorer window, right-click the game, and choose Hide This Game. To have all hidden games shown, click Options, and, in the Set Up Game Updates And Options dialog box, click Unhide All Items.

### See Also

"Limiting Access to the Computer" on page 306, "Restricting Time on the Computer" on page 307, "Restricting Access to Games" on page 308, "Restricting Access to Programs" on page 309, and "Restricting Internet Content" on page 310 for information about setting up parental controls.

# Playing Chess Titans

Chess Titans is a great way to learn about chess and practice your game. You can play against the computer or against an actual human opponent; in the latter case, you and your opponent have to take turns using the same computer. When you play against the computer, you can choose the level of difficulty you want. You use the same rules and strategies in Chess Titans as you do when you're playing on a regular chessboard.

## Play Chess Titans

**1** Click Games on the Start menu, and then double-click Chess Titans in the Games Explorer window to start the game. By default, you'll play the game against the computer.

**2** If you want to play against a human, choose New Game Against Human from the Game menu.

**3** Click the chess piece you want to move.

**4** Click the square into which you want to move the piece. (Squares into which you can legally move your piece are highlighted.)

**5** Wait for either the computer or your human opponent to move.

**6** Repeat steps 2 through 4 until a King is in check. If your King is in check, move a piece to remove the King from check, if possible.

**7** Continue playing until a King is checkmated or until someone quits by choosing Resign from the Game menu.

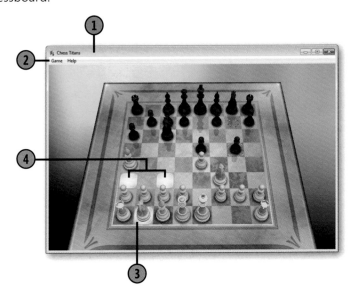

**Tip**

To change the appearance of the game pieces and the board, press the F7 key, and make your selections in the Change Appearance dialog box.

**Tip**

To change the level of difficulty when you're playing against the computer, choose Options from the Game menu. In the Options dialog box, you can also change your designation (white or black), whether tips are displayed, and how you view the board.

# Playing FreeCell

FreeCell—a modified version of Solitaire—is a game you play by yourself. The entire deck is dealt, and, as in Solitaire, you arrange the cards by stacking them in descending order, alternating the red and black cards. Unlike the way you play Solitaire, the sequence of cards can begin anywhere in the stack. You can move a single card onto another card to add to the sequence of cards, or into one of the free cells at the top, or into a blank column after the column has been emptied of cards. You win the game by stacking all the cards by suit in ascending order from Ace through King.

## Play FreeCell

① Click Games on the Start menu, and then double-click FreeCell in the Games Explorer window to start the game.

② When possible, move an Ace to the top of the window, and stack the cards by suit in ascending order (FreeCell might do this for you automatically).

③ Click to select the card or cards you want to move.

④ Either drag the card or cards to where you want them, or click another card to move the selected card or cards on top of it. (The cards must be stacked in alternating colors in descending numeric order.)

⑤ Continue stacking the cards, including moving cards into or out of a free cell. You can also move one card or a series of cards into an empty column.

⑥ Repeat steps 2 through 5 until all the cards are stacked by suit.

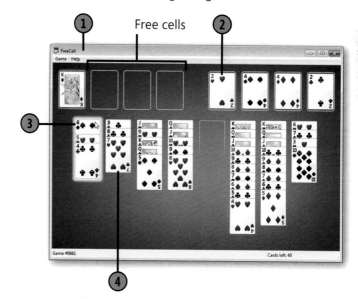

Free cells

 **Tip**

To replay a specific game, note the game number on the status bar. When you're ready to replay the game, choose Select Game from the Game menu, enter the game number, and click OK.

 **Tip**

Try to free the Ace cards early in the game, and to keep as many free cells and empty columns as possible.

 **Tip**

If there are enough available free cells, you can move an entire series of cards from one column into another.

# Playing Hearts

You play Hearts against three hands controlled by the computer. The objective is to score the *fewest* points. For each trick you win, you receive 1 point for each heart and 13 points for the Queen of Spades. You must use the same suit that's played first unless you're void of that suit. You take the trick if you've played the highest card of the suit being played.

## Play Hearts

(1) Click Games on the Start menu, and then double-click Hearts in the Games Explorer window to start the game.

(2) Click the three cards to be passed, and click the Pass button.

(3) If you have the Two of Clubs, play it to start the game. If you don't have the Two of Clubs, it's played automatically. When it's your turn, click the card you want to play. Continue playing until the hand is completed.

(4) At the completion of each hand, note the score, and click Play Next Hand. Continue playing hands until the first player scores 100 or more points. The lowest score wins.

**Tip**

Another scoring option is to "shoot the moon," wherein you collect all the points in one hand. If you succeed, each of the other players receives 26 points, and you receive 0 (zero) points for the hand.

**Tip**

You pass the first hand to the left, the second hand to the right, and the third hand across. On the fourth hand, you don't pass any cards.

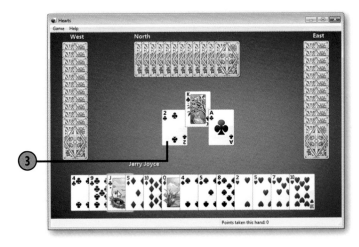

The Pass button

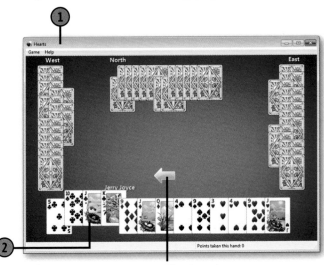

# Playing Mahjong Titans

Mahjong Titans is a single-player version of the traditional mah-jongg game. The object is to remove all the tiles by selecting matching tiles that are free to be removed. To be free, they must have either their left or their right side unimpeded by another tile. The tiles have both classes and numbers, except for the special tiles depicting flowers, dragons, seasons, and winds. The tiles must match exactly, except for the seasons and flowers tiles; any season tile can match any other season tile, and any flower tile can match any other flower tile.

## Play Mahjong Titans

① Click Games on the Start menu, choose Mahjong Titans from the Games Explorer window, and select the game pattern you want to play to start the game.

② Locate two matching free tiles, click the first tile, and then click the second tile.

③ If you're stuck, do either of the following, and then click the highlighted matching pair of tiles:

• Press the H key to have the game highlight a matching pair.

• Right-click a tile, and, if a match is free, the matching tile will be highlighted.

④ Continue clicking free matching tiles until all the tiles are removed (you win) or until there are no more available matches (you lose). To get bonus points, remove tiles of the same class and/or the same class and number in consecutive turns, or remove sets of seasons or sets of flowers in consecutive turns.

**Tip**

If you find it difficult to judge the height of each stack of tiles, try changing the appearance of the tiles and the background by pressing the F7 key.

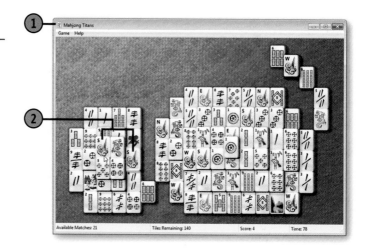

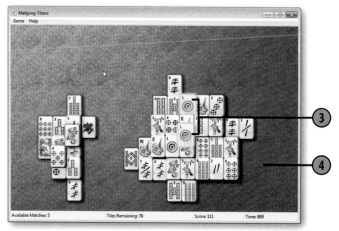

# Playing Minesweeper

Minesweeper is a game that you play against the computer. The goal is to uncover, in the shortest possible time, all the squares that don't contain mines. If you uncover a square that contains a mine, you lose. The key is to use the numbers in the uncovered squares to determine which adjacent squares contain the mines.

## Play Minesweeper

① Click Games on the Start menu, and then double-click Minesweeper in the Games Explorer window to start the game. If this is the first time you've played this game, click the difficulty level you want to try.

② Click a square to uncover it and to uncover any adjacent squares that don't have mines next to them. You might need to click more squares before you can use the numbers of adjacent squares to determine mine locations.

③ Right-click to mark a square that you believe contains a mine. If you're not sure, right-click the square a second time to mark it as a possible mine. Right-click the square a third time to remove the mark.

④ Click a square that you believe doesn't contain a mine. Continue finding unmined squares and marking squares that contain mines until you've revealed all the unmined squares.

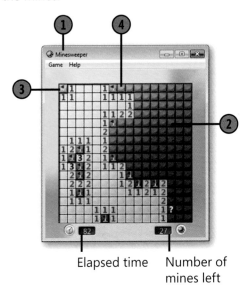

Elapsed time   Number of mines left

**Tip** ✓

The number in a square represents the total number of mines in adjacent squares—directly above, below, diagonal to, or at the left or right of the numbered square. Use several exposed numbers to figure out where the mines are.

**Tip** ✓

If the game is too easy or too difficult, choose a different level of difficulty for the game from the Game menu. The greater the level of difficulty, the more squares and mines the game contains.

# Playing Solitaire

Solitaire is a classic card game that, as its name implies, you play by yourself. The object is to reveal all the cards that are turned face down and eventually to arrange all the cards in four piles, with each pile being a single suit stacked in ascending order from Ace through King.

## Play Solitaire

1. Click Games on the Start menu, and then double-click Solitaire in the Games Explorer window to start the game.

2. Use the mouse to drag one card on top of another card. (The cards must be stacked in descending numeric order, alternating the red and black cards.)

3. Drag any Ace cards into the top row. If there are any other cards of that suit in the pile, stack them in ascending numeric order.

4. Move an entire series of cards onto a card to continue the series.

5. If you can't make a play, click the stack to turn the cards over. Drag the top card on top of a face-up card if the top card has the correct number and suit.

6. If all the cards have been moved from a row, move a King, if one is available, and any cards that are stacked on it, into the empty spot.

7. Continue moving the cards until you've moved all the cards stacked by suit on top of the Aces.

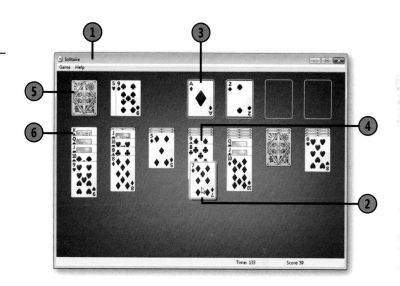

**Tip**

If you can't see a play, press the H key to see a suggested move.

**Tip**

To change the way a game is played—the number of cards drawn at one time, whether or not the game is timed, or the method of scoring—choose Options from the Game menu. To change the pattern of the card backs, choose Change Appearance from the Game menu.

# Playing Purble Place

Here's a game for the younger set. It's designed to teach colors and shapes, and perhaps hook kids very early on computers—in the unlikely event that they're not hooked already! Purble Place contains three games: Comfy Cakes, in which you (or a child) assemble a cake to match the shape, color, and patterns of the specified design; Purble Pairs, in which you turn over two tiles at a time and try to match symbols; and Purble Shop, in which you add eyes, nose, mouth, and other accoutrements to a figure, and then try to guess which features are on the mystery Purble behind the curtain.

## Play Comfy Cakes

1. Click Games on the Start menu, and then double-click Purble Place in the Games Explorer window. Click the Comfy Cakes Factory, or choose it from the Game menu, to start the Comfy Cakes game. If this is the first time you're playing, choose the level of difficulty you want from the Select Difficulty dialog box that appears.

2. Look at the cake you're trying to create.

3. Click the correct pan shape.

4. As the cake moves along the assembly line, click the correct ingredients, and then move forward or backward to add ingredients and layers. To create a second layer, add a cake pan on top of the existing layer.

5. If a piece of cake paper enters the assembly line, start creating another cake while you're still working on the first one.

6. Move the completed cake to the end of the assembly line for packaging and credit for completing a cake.

7. Continue assembling cakes until you've either completed the cake order or made three incorrect cakes.

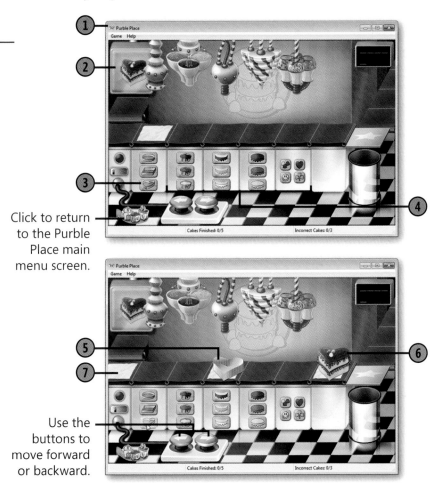

Click to return to the Purble Place main menu screen.

Use the buttons to move forward or backward.

## Play Purble Shop

1. In the Purble Place main menu window, click Purble Shop, or choose it from the Game menu, and, if asked, specify the level of difficulty you want.

2. Click an item from each shelf. (The number of shelves changes with the level of difficulty.)

3. Click the Check button to see whether your selection matches the Purble behind the curtain.

4. For items that aren't correct, select different features, and click the Check button. Continue selecting features until you've selected all the correct features for the mystery Purble, or until you've run out of guesses.

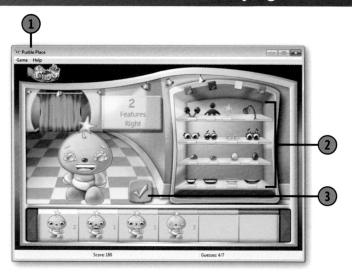

## Play Purble Pairs

1. In the Purble Place main menu window, click Purble School, or choose Purble Pairs from the Game menu, and, if asked, specify the level of difficulty you want.

2. Click one tile and then a second tile. If the tiles don't match, remember the location of each.

3. Click a tile, and, using your memory, click a tile that matches.

4. If you want to take a quick look at all the items on the tiles, click a Sneak Peek token. Then continue trying to match two tiles until all the tiles have been matched.

Time remaining

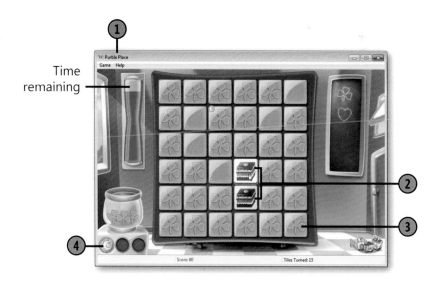

# Playing Spider Solitaire

Spider Solitaire is yet another version of Solitaire. Unlike the objective of other Solitaire games, the objective of Spider Solitaire is to stack the cards by suit in one column in descending order. When a series from King to Ace is complete, the cards are removed. The level of difficulty is determined by how many suits are used (one, two, or four).

## Play Spider Solitaire

1. Click Games on the Start menu, and then double-click Spider Solitaire in the Games Explorer window to start the game. If this is the first time you've played this game, click the difficulty level you want to use.

2. Use the mouse to drag one card on top of another card. You can stack the cards in descending numeric order regardless of suit, but it's best to stack by suit.

3. Drag a group of sequential cards of the same suit onto another card. (Only cards of the same suit can be moved as a group.)

4. If there's an empty column, move a card or a sequence of cards into the column.

5. If no moves are available, click the stacked cards to deal another round. (You can't deal if there's an empty column.) Continue playing until all the cards have been removed, or until all the cards have been dealt and there are no longer any moves available.

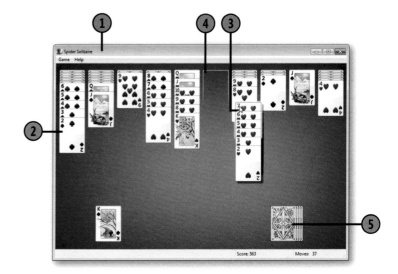

**Tip**
To display possible moves, press the M key. Press it again to see another possible move.

**Tip**
To change the difficulty level of the game, choose Options from the Game menu.

# Playing Games over the Internet

If you're ready for some real human competition, Windows 7 provides three games—Backgammon, Checkers, and Spades—that are designed to be played against other players over the Internet. When you start a game and are connected to the Internet, the game server will try to find players matched to your skill level and language.

## Play a Game

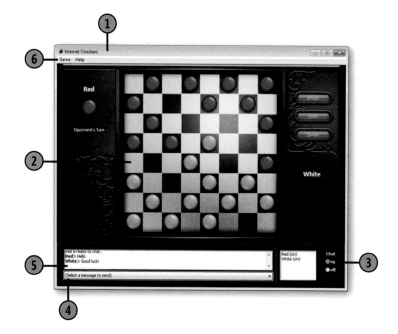

**1** Click Games on the Start menu, and then double-click one of the Internet games in the Games Explorer window to open the game. Read the introductory screen and the privacy statement. Click Play to start the game. Wait for the game server to locate a player or players, and start the game.

**2** Play the game as you would normally, responding to any prompts that appear.

**3** If you want to chat with your opponent or opponents, select the Chat On button.

**4** Click the down arrow and select one of the messages from the list to send that message.

**5** Read any messages from an opponent.

**6** At the conclusion of the game, use the Game menu to start a new game with a different opponent, to change your skill level or the appearance of the game board, or to quit the game.

# Playing Microsoft Touch Pack Games

Microsoft Touch Pack is an add-on group of programs specifically designed for computers that are running Windows 7 and that have multi-touch capabilities. Many new computers with multi-touch input will come with the Touch Pack installed, and it will be available as an add-on from Microsoft. The Touch Pack has three games that use and highlight the computer's multi-touch capabilities.

## Play the Touch Games

① Tap Games on the Start menu, and then double-tap the Touch Pack game you want.

- **Microsoft Blackboard** is a game of physics, in which you drag and rotate objects on a virtual blackboard to build a machine that moves balloons, balls, or other objects safely from their starting positions to the light bulb. You must successfully complete a level before you can advance to the next level. There are fifty levels, each more difficult than the previous one.

- **Microsoft Garden Pond** is a game in which you steer floating origami boats around a garden pond by touching the pond and creating ripples that move the boats. You must then avoid setting your boats on fire (unless that's what you really want to do!) by trying not to let them touch the floating candles. If a boat is ignited, you can douse the flames with a flick motion. You can play against a set time or against an opponent.

- **Microsoft Rebound** is game with a futuristic theme played on an electrified court for a set time. You drag a pair of electrified orbs around to hit and propel a ball or multiple balls around the court, both defending your goal and trying to send the ball into your opponent's goal. You can compete against the computer or against an opponent. Each match continues until you reach the time limit.

② Click Play, select your level or game type, and, for Garden Pond or Rebound, whether you want to play as a single player or against an opponent. Enjoy the games!

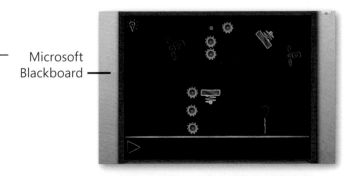
Microsoft Blackboard

Microsoft Garden Pond

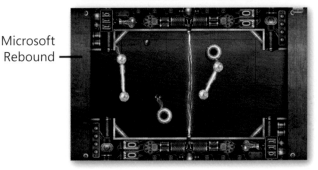
Microsoft Rebound

# 8 Working with Pictures

We all love our photographs—those treasured pictures that record significant events in our lives, and the candid shots of people, pets, and places. Windows 7 provides several tools to organize and view your digital photos. You can use a wizard to move your digital camera pictures onto your computer, and then use the Pictures Library to manage them or view them individually or in a slide show. And, of course, one of the things we love to do with our pictures is share them with other people.

You have several options when it comes to viewing and working with your photos. There's Windows Photo Viewer to view, rotate, or zoom in or out of your pictures, to send them off to be printed, or to create video discs. There's Windows Media Center to display a dramatic slide show on your computer or TV. And there's Windows Live Photo Gallery—an add-on you use to view, organize, edit, create online photo albums, make an animated slide show on a DVD, and stitch together a series of pictures to create a panoramic photo of an idyllic pastoral scene or a spectacular cityscape. You can also use Windows Paint to open an existing photo and add text, edit the photo pixel by pixel, or copy just the parts of it you want. With Paint, you can also create your own drawings or edit existing ones, using Paint's tools to create the special effects you want.

# Viewing Your Photos

Windows 7 Pictures Library provides a variety of ways to view your photos and other pictures so that you can decide which ones to keep, copy, print, or send to friends. The Pictures Library provides easy access to the Windows Photo Viewer, which provides you with additional control for viewing and modifying your pictures.

## View Your Photos

**1** In the Pictures Library, click the down arrow at the right of the Views button, and select an icon size large enough so that you can see a good preview of your photo.

**2** Click a photo that you want to see in detail.

**3** Do any of the following:

- Click the Show The Preview Pane button, view the photo, and then click the button again to close the Preview pane.

- Double-click the photo to view it in the default program that's been set for previewing your photos.

- Click the Preview button to view the photo in the default program.

- Click the down arrow at the right of the Preview button, and choose the program in which you want to view the photo.

- Select all the photos you want to view, or select only one photo to be able to step through each photo in the Pictures Library, and then click the Slide Show button to view the photos as a slide show. Press Esc to end the slide show.

Preview button

Slide Show button

Show The Preview Pane button

Preview pane

## Use the Viewer

① Select the photo you want to view. Click the down arrow at the right of the Preview button, and choose Windows Photo Viewer to display the selected photo in Windows Photo Viewer.

② Click the Change Display Size button and, using the slider that appears, adjust the magnification of the photo. If the photo is too large to fit in the window, point to the photo and drag it to display the part of it you want to see.

③ Click to switch views between fitting the photo to the window and displaying it at its full size.

④ Click to see the previous or the next photo, or click the center button to play a slide show.

⑤ Click to rotate the photo clockwise or counterclockwise to view it in the correct orientation.

⑥ Click to delete the photo.

⑦ Close the viewer when you've finished.

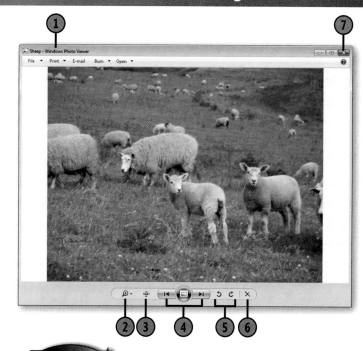

**Tip**

To change the order of the slides or the speed of the slide show, and to specify whether the slide show runs continuously, right-click anywhere in the slide show, and choose the action you want from the shortcut menu.

**See Also**

"Viewing Photos with Windows Media Center" on pages 162–163 for information about viewing your photos and photo slide shows using Windows Media Center.

"Viewing Photos with Windows Live Photo Gallery" on pages 164–165 for information about viewing your photos, and "Viewing a Custom Photo Slide Show" on page 168 for information about viewing and customizing a slide show using Windows Live Photo Gallery.

"Printing Your Photographs" on page 220 for information about printing your photos.

"Setting Your Default Programs" on pages 274–275 for information about setting the program that opens by default for a specific type of file.

# So Many Photo Tools!

Windows 7 comes with numerous tools for working with your photos, and you can download even more. With so many tools, most of them offering different features, we started to feel a bit overwhelmed ourselves. So here's a quick and useful summary of all those tools—what to expect from them, and when you should use them.

**Pictures Library** is the most basic of the tools for viewing photos, but it's also a powerful tool for organizing photos, including viewing and modifying their properties in the Details pane. When you add tags, ratings, and other relevant information, you can set up a classification system that you can use to determine how your photos are sorted and which of them are displayed by any of the other programs. In the Pictures Library you can view large thumbnails of your pictures by setting the view to either large or extra-large icons. Click the Show The Preview Pane button, and you get to see an even larger preview of the selected photo. Details about using the library, setting which folders are included in the library, changing the view, viewing and modifying properties, and adding tags to create a custom classification system are all discussed throughout section 3 of this book. In the Pictures Library, you can specify with whom you want to share individual photos, view the photos in a separate viewer or program, print the photos, and run a simple full-screen slide show of your photos.

As is the case with other libraries and folder windows, you can manipulate the Pictures Library by using gestures, including panning, on pen-based and multi-touch-capable computers. Panning is a gesture-based method of scrolling in the window. On a multi-touch-capable computer, you can also use gestures to change the size of the icons.

**Windows Photo Viewer** is a utility program you can use to view your photos with a little more control than you have in the Pictures Library. You can easily zoom in and out of a photo, adjust the orientation by rotating it, make a copy of it, and step through all the photos in your library. You can run the same slide show that you can also run in the Pictures Library. Windows Photo Viewer also gives you access to tools that help you share your photos with other people. From the viewer, you can easily e-mail your photos to friends, burn a video disc containing a custom slide show, or send the photos out to a commercial printer to order prints.

Windows Photo Viewer also has multi-touch features for a multi-touch-capable computer. Using multi-touch gestures, you can rotate a photo and change its size. You can also use gestures to view the previous or the next photo.

**Windows Paint** is a fairly simple program that you can use to modify a photo. Paint isn't designed specifically for photo editing, but it can be useful for copying a portion of the photo, adding text or designs, and even changing the file format.

**Windows Media Center** is a program designed for playing and viewing videos, television programs, and other multimedia, including your photo collection. Depending on the way you have Media Center configured, you can view the material on a computer or—if your computer either is directly connected to a TV or uses an extender for the connection—on your TV. With Media Center, you can view individual photos or display them in dynamic slide shows. Media Center uses the same photo collection that you have in your Pictures Library. We discuss using Media Center for viewing multimedia in section 9 of this book.

**Windows Media Player** is another program designed for playing and viewing multimedia. Like Media Center, it uses the contents of your Pictures Library, but you can customize your playlist to select the photos you want to be included. Media Player steps through the photos one at a time, either in order or using a shuffle mode. You can also use Media Player to show your photos on other computers and other compatible devices, such as an electronic photo frame or a portable media player. We discuss more details about Media Player in section 9 of this book.

**Windows Live Photo Gallery** is a program that doesn't come with Windows 7, but you can easily download it for free. It gives you viewing, organizing, and editing tools, and it's designed specifically to work with Windows. The viewer in Photo Gallery is similar to the Windows Photo Viewer, except that it contains tools for editing photos, including a powerful Auto Adjust feature that can straighten a crooked or tilted photo and adjust its exposure and color. You can also use Photo Gallery to crop pictures, eliminate "red eye," and add special effects.

The Gallery part of Windows Live Photo Gallery is a powerful tool that you can use to organize your photos by many different categories, including date, tags, rating, type, person, and so on. Photo Gallery also gives you the ability to create online photo albums, send your photos to a Web site or a blog post, create panoramic photos, and display a slide show that you can customize using themes and various other settings.

Throughout this book, we discuss other features in Windows 7 that enhance the use and sharing of your photos. In section 5, for example, we talk about using a slide show of your photos as the background for your Desktop and as a screen saver. You can also use your photos as a slide-show screen saver when you're using Windows Media Center. If your home network is set up with a homegroup, you can share your photo library with members of the homegroup. You can also easily burn your photos onto a CD or a DVD to share with friends or colleagues, or simply to create a safe repository for the files.

As if all these weren't enough choices, there are numerous other programs out there that can help you organize, view, edit, and share your photos. For example, if you have a multi-touch computer, you might already have the Windows Touch Pack, which includes Microsoft Surface Collage—a program for creating a collage by using multi-touch gestures to move, resize, rotate, and overlap photos on a background. With a little exploration (and some degree of patience!) you'll find a program or a combination of programs that you're comfortable with and that can help you do exactly what you want with your photos. Then, every so often, just sit back and enjoy them!

# Creating a Multimedia Slide Show

A great way to display your photographs is to create a slide show on a DVD. You can enliven the photos with panning and zooming, and you can even add a musical soundtrack and videos to animate your show.

## Assemble a DVD Slide Show

**①** Click the Start button, type **dvd** in the Search box of the Start menu, and choose Windows DVD Maker from the menu to start Windows DVD Maker. If the introductory Turn Your Digital Memories Into A DVD page appears, choose not to show the page again, and then click Choose Photos And Videos to start creating your DVD.

**②** Click Add Items.

**③** In the Add Items To DVD dialog box that appears, locate and select the photos you want, and then click Add.

**④** Click a photo, and use the Move Up or Move Down button to position the photo. If you see a folder instead of all the photos, double-click the folder to open it. Continue selecting and arranging the photos until they're in the order you want.

**⑤** Type a name for the slide show.

**⑥** Click Options if you want to customize when the DVD menu appears or change the screen's aspect ratio for wide-screen viewing.

**⑦** Click Next.

**See Also**

"Creating a Video DVD" on page 194 for additional information about using Windows DVD Maker.

## Create the Slide Show

**①** Select the menu style you want.

**②** Click the Menu Text button or the Customize Menu button if you want to modify the menu or add background video or audio to it.

**③** Click Slide Show to display the Change Your Slide Show Settings page.

**④** Click Add Music to add music files for the audio background.

**⑤** Select the options you want for the slide show.

**⑥** Click Change Slide Show.

**⑦** Click Preview to view your slide show, and then click OK.

**⑧** With a recordable DVD in the DVD drive, click Burn to create your DVD slide show.

**Tip**

To save the project if you're not going to complete it in one session, click the File button, and choose Save.

**Tip**

You can start Windows DVD Maker from Windows Photo Viewer by clicking the Burn button and choosing Video DVD from the drop-down menu. You can also start DVD Maker from Windows Live Photo Gallery. In Gallery view, select your photos, click Make, and choose Burn A DVD from the drop-down menu to start Windows DVD Maker.

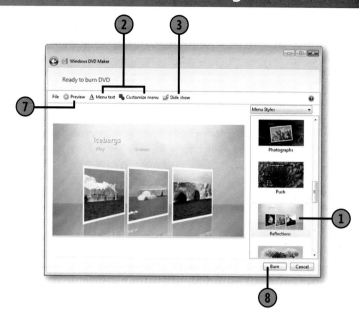

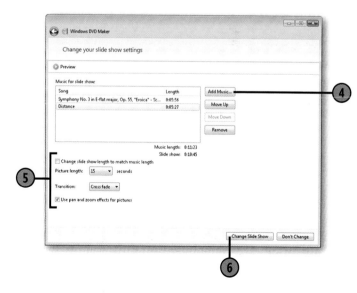

# Viewing Photos with Windows Media Center

If you already use Media Center for watching or recording television shows, listening to music, or other activities, you can enjoy viewing your photos using the same setup. You can also use it exclusively for viewing your photos individually or as a slide show on a large screen and in high resolution.

## View Individual Photos

**1** With Windows Media Center running, choose Pictures+Videos from the main menu, and then click Pictures Library.

**2** Specify how you want the photos to be organized.

**3** If the photos you want to show are in a group, click the group to display the contents, and then click the photo you want to view.

**4** Do either of the following:

- Click the Next or the Previous button to go to the next or the previous photo.

- Click Play to view all the photos in the group, using a slide show that animates the photos with panning and zooming effects. You can still use the Next or the Previous button to move through the slides manually.

**5** Click the Back button until you've returned to the Pictures Library, or click the Start menu button to return to the Start menu.

Main menu button

Back button

Previous button

Next button

Play button

## Create and Play a Slide Show

**1** In the Pictures Library, click Slide Shows, and then click Create Slide Show to start the Slide Show wizard.

**2** Complete the wizard, specifying

- The slide-show name.
- That you want to use the Pictures Library.
- The group and individual photos you want to use.
- The order in which the photos will be shown.

**3** Click Create.

**4** To adjust the way the slide show is displayed, right-click the completed slide show, and choose Settings from the shortcut menu. In the Settings window, select Pictures, and, in the Pictures Settings window, choose Slide Shows to display the Slide Shows Settings window.

**5** Make any changes to the settings.

**6** Click Save.

**7** To play the slide show, in the Pictures Library, select Slide Shows if it isn't already selected, click the slide-show name, and then click Play Slide Show.

**Tip**

To play music with your slide show, right-click the slide show, and choose Play Music from the drop-down menu.

**See Also**

"Arranging Your Media with Playlists" on pages 178–179 for information about managing your music and creating playlists.

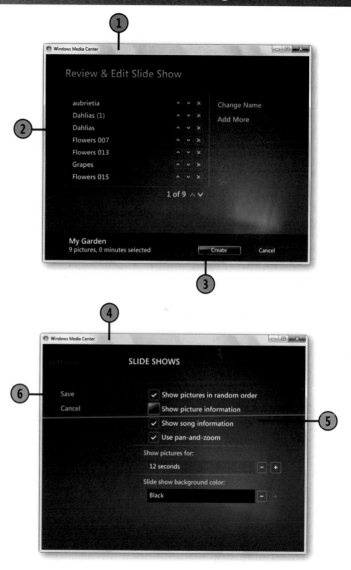

# Viewing Photos with Windows Live Photo Gallery

It's easy to become overwhelmed by the proliferation of photos on your computer, especially when they're stored in a variety of locations. Although the Pictures Library is a powerful tool for managing your photos, we've found that a really great way to access and sort all those photos, and to organize them so that you can easily locate them, is to use Windows Live Photo Gallery, an add-on program that you can download for free. It automatically includes all the pictures and photographs that are stored in your Pictures Library, as well as any that are contained in subfolders.

## Browse Your Photos

1. Click the Start button, type **photo** in the Search box of the Start menu, and click Windows Live Photo Gallery to start the Photo Gallery.

2. Scroll through the photos.

3. Point to a photo to see an enlarged version of it, as well as other details.

4. To rotate a photo, click to select it, and then click the Rotate Clockwise or the Rotate Counterclockwise button.

5. To view a photo in detail, double-click it.

6. Use the controls to see additional photos, and to rotate, delete, or change the magnification (zoom) of the photo.

7. Click the Back To Gallery button when you've finished.

> **See Also**
>
> "Setting up Windows Live Essentials Programs" on page 285 for information about installing Windows Live programs if Windows Live Photo Gallery isn't already installed.

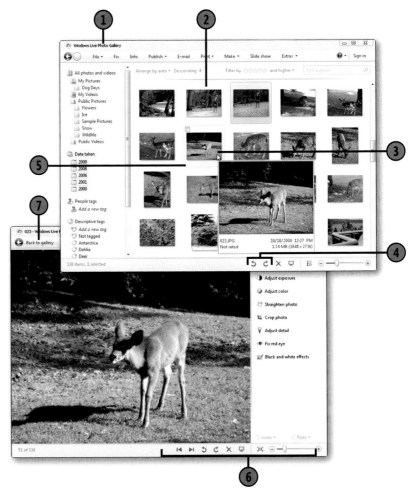

## Classify and Find Your Photos

**1** Click the type of category you want to use to classify the photos, if the list isn't already expanded.

**2** Click the category you want to use. If necessary, click any subcategories to expand them, and then select the category you want.

**3** View the photos in that category.

**4** If you want to find a specific photo within the selected category, click in the Search box, and start typing a name, file type, or tag (classification) for the photo.

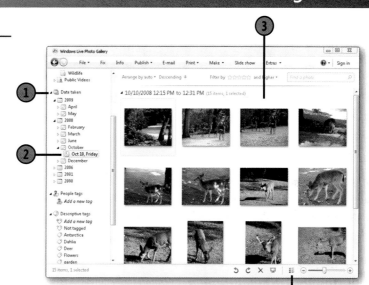

**Tip**

To search all the items in Windows Live Photo Gallery, either click the All Pictures And Videos category, or click the down arrow at the right of the Search box and choose Search All Items In Photo Gallery from the list. Then conduct your search.

Click to display details about all the photos.

**Try This!**

Click the Info button to display the Info pane. Click to open a photo, and note the detailed information that's shown. Add information to the Info page, including tags, a caption, a rating, and the author's name. Click a photo that shows your friends or family. In the Info pane, under People Tags, click People Found. Point to one of the People Found listings, note whose face is selected in the photo, and then click Identify. Enter a name, or select one from the list. Repeat to identify the other faces. Repeat the procedure for your other photos. After you've identified everyone, try using a People tag to find someone in the various photos he or she is in.

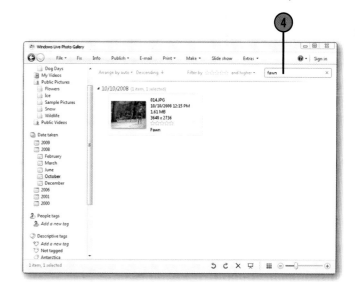

# Editing Your Photos

Often, on closer inspection, the photo that looked so perfect in the camera seems to have a few flaws. The lighting or the color is slightly off, the subject is tilted a bit or has those disconcerting red eyes, or the photo is under- or overexposed.

You can adjust these problems using the tools in Windows Live Photo Gallery, and, if you don't like the result, you can easily revert to a copy of the original photo.

## Adjust the Picture

**(1)** In the Pictures Library, click to select the photo you want to edit; then click the down arrow at the right of the Preview button, and choose Windows Live Photo Gallery. If Windows Live Photo Gallery is already running in Photo Gallery view, double-click the photo.

**(2)** If the editing tools aren't visible, click Fix to display them.

**(3)** Click Auto Adjust to allow the computer to adjust the exposure and color, and to straighten the photo.

**(4)** Use the sliders to make further changes if you're not satisfied with the adjustments made by Auto Adjust.

**(5)** Click Adjust Detail, and use the slider to sharpen the photo.

**(6)** Click Analyze to reduce the visual "noise" in the photo. Use the slider to modify the suggested changes if you want.

**(7)** If you don't like one of your changes, click the Undo button. To undo a series of changes, click the down arrow next to the Undo button, and choose from the series of items that you can undo.

**(8)** To edit another photo, use the Next or the Previous button to display additional photos.

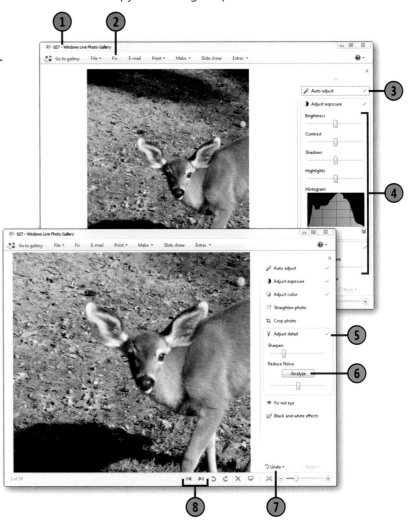

## Crop a Photo

(1) Click Crop Photo to specify which part of the photo you want to keep while the remaining parts are discarded.

(2) Click Proportion, and specify the finished size you want for the photo.

(3) Use the mouse to drag the frame to include the parts of the photo you want to keep. If the frame is oriented incorrectly, click Rotate Frame.

(4) When the photo is cropped exactly the way you want, click Apply.

## Remove "Red Eye"

(1) In a photo in which a person or a creature has red eyes caused by the camera flash, use the Zoom Control to enlarge and pinpoint the red eyes, and click Fix Red Eye.

(2) Drag a rectangle over the red part of the eye. Repeat for other red eyes.

(3) Click Close to return to your library, or choose Back To Gallery to return to the Photo Gallery. Note that your changes are saved automatically as you work, but Photo Gallery keeps a copy of the original file. To undo all your editing, click the File button in the editing window, and choose Revert To Original from the drop-down menu.

# Viewing a Custom Photo Slide Show

Instead of clicking through a static view of your photos, or using the standard slide show available from your Pictures Library, you can use Windows Live Photo Gallery to view your pictures in a dynamic slide show that can include zooming, panning, and transitions.

## View the Show

1. Start Windows Live Photo Gallery, and select a category, tag, rating, or folder to display only the photos you want in your slide show.

2. Click Slide Show.

3. Move your mouse to display the slide-show controls.

4. Click Themes, and select the slide-show style you want. If the controls don't appear, Photo Gallery is running in Basic mode due to the limitations of your computer's graphics display, and so you can't use the advanced controls. If this is the case, right-click the slide show, and control it using the commands on the shortcut menu that appears.

5. Click the Settings button to set the speed at which the pictures advance, to specify whether you want the photos to be shown in order or at random, and to specify whether the show is to be played in a continuous loop or as a single show.

6. When you've finished viewing the show, move the mouse if the controls aren't visible, and click Exit or press the Esc key.

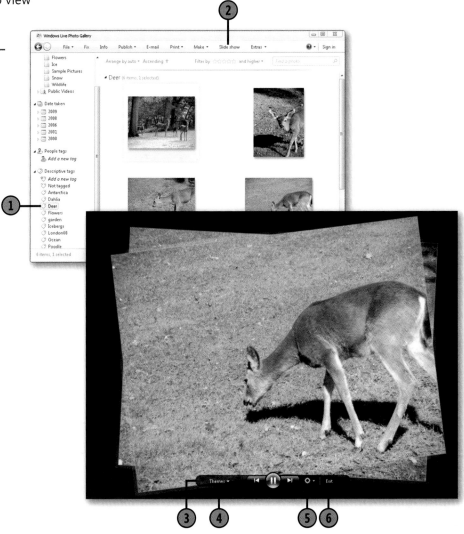

# Creating a Panoramic Photo

Photos are great for capturing scenery, but what if the view is too wide to capture in a single photo? The answer is to "stitch" several photos together to create a single panoramic view. Although the preparation for this can be a bit tricky, Windows

Live Photo Gallery analyzes your photos, figures out where they overlap and where they align, and then merges them into a single panoramic photo.

## Merge Your Photos

(1) Click the Start button, type **photo** in the Search box of the Start menu, and choose Windows Live Photo Gallery from the menu to start Photo Gallery.

(2) Select the photos that will be part of the final panoramic photo, and clear the check boxes for the photos you don't want to include.

(3) Click the Make button, and choose Create A Panoramic Photo from the drop-down menu. Wait for the photos to be analyzed and stitched together. Save the panoramic photo when you're prompted to do so.

(4) If necessary, click the Fix button, and use the tools to modify or crop your panoramic photo.

**Tip**

To download additional tools, including a more powerful program for creating panoramic photos, choose Download More Photo Tools from the Extras menu.

**Tip**

Use a tripod when you're shooting the series of photos for the panorama so that all the photos are on the same plane. Doing this also minimizes the amount of blank space in the final panoramic photo. Also, make sure that some content in each photo overlaps the content of the previous photo.

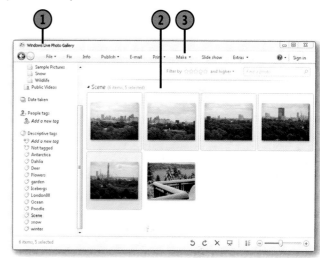

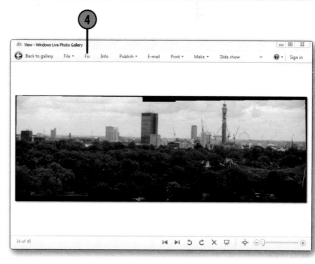

# Creating an Online Photo Album

With Windows Live Photo Gallery and a Windows Live ID, you can create and post an online photo album that can be viewed by other people. You select which photos you want to be included and who can view the album. The online album is then posted to your Windows Live account, which is a free account that includes all the Windows Live services.

## Create the Album

①  Click the Start button, type **photo** in the Search box of the Start menu, and choose Windows Live Photo Gallery from the menu to start Photo Gallery.

②  Click Sign In to sign in to your Windows Live account. (MSN, Hotmail, and Live IDs are all acceptable as Windows Live identification.)

③  Select the photos you want to use.

④  Click Publish, and choose Online Album from the drop-down menu.

⑤  Type a name for the album.

⑥  Specify who can view the album.

⑦  Select the photo quality you want for the album.

⑧  Click Publish, and wait for the photos to be uploaded. When they've been uploaded, click View Album to see the album. Use the Windows Live tools to send out invitations to the people you want to view your album.

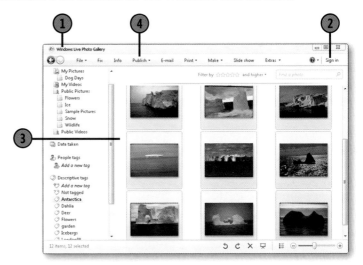

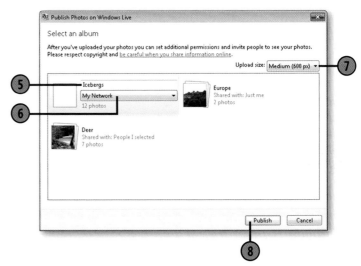

> **Tip** ✓
>
> You can create a group online album, which is an album you share with a group you defined in Windows Live. You can also create an event album that's shared among the members of an event you defined in Windows Live. You can post photos to other online services by pointing to More Services on the Publish drop-down menu and selecting the service from the submenu.

# Importing Photos from Your Camera or Removable Media

Many digital cameras come with their own software for downloading your photos and managing them on your computer. However, Windows 7 makes it so simple to download and organize the photos from your camera that you might want to try both systems to see which one you like better. Windows also uses the same method to transfer photos from a CD, a DVD, a memory card, or a USB storage device. However, how Windows handles this task depends on the way you have your AutoPlay settings configured for the device or the type of media you're using.

## Import Your Photos

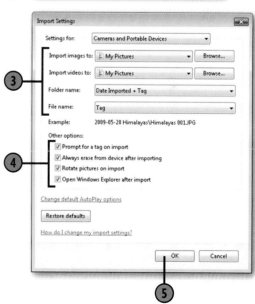

1. Connect or insert the device you're using, and, if necessary, turn it on. If the AutoPlay dialog box appears, click Import Pictures And Videos. If the Device And Printers window for your device appears, click Import Pictures And Videos to display the Import Pictures And Videos dialog box.

2. Click Import Settings.

3. In the Import Settings dialog box, select the location, the folder, and the file-naming method you want for your photos.

4. Make any other changes you want to the way your photos are imported.

5. Click OK.

6. Type a tag for the pictures if you want.

7. Click Import.

8. For future imports using the same settings, skip steps 2 through 5.

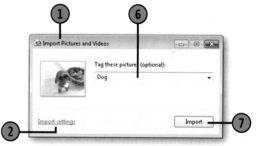

**See Also**

"Set the AutoPlay" on page 103 for information about adjusting the AutoPlay settings.

"Scanning a Picture into Paint" on page 223 and "Scanning Anything" on page 224 for information about scanning photos and other pictures.

# Drawing Pictures

If you're feeling artistic, you can create a picture in the Paint program, which comes with Windows 7. Paint was designed so that you can create and edit *bitmap* pictures in a variety of formats. (A bitmap is just that: a map created from small dots, or *bits*.) Although you can print your pictures if you want to, Paint pictures are usually inserted into other documents. You can also create a Paint picture and use it as the wallpaper for your Desktop.

## Create a Picture

1. Click the Start button, type **pain** in the Search box of the Start menu, and click Paint to start the Paint program.

2. On the Home tab, do any of the following:
   - Click the Pencil drawing tool to draw a freehand line.
   - Click Brushes, and select the type of brush you want.
   - Click a shape to drag out that shape. Click Outline to choose the type of outline you want, and then click Fill to choose the type of fill.

3. Click Size, and select a size to use with your selected item.

4. Click Color 1, and click the primary color you want. Click Color 2, and then click a secondary color.

5. Drag out the line or the shape you want.

6. Click the Text tool, and draw out the area where you want the text. Use the tools on the Text Tools tab that appears on the Ribbon to specify the text format. Type your text, and then click outside the text area.

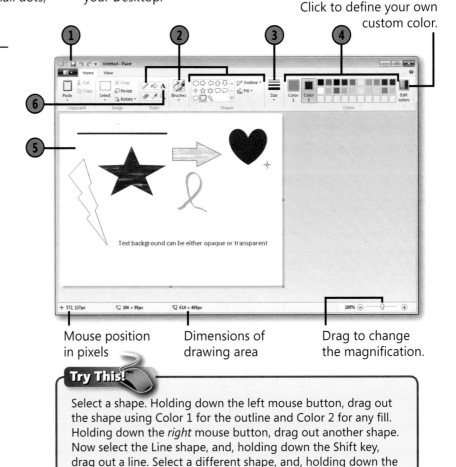

Click to define your own custom color.

Mouse position in pixels

Dimensions of drawing area

Drag to change the magnification.

**Try This!**

Select a shape. Holding down the left mouse button, drag out the shape using Color 1 for the outline and Color 2 for any fill. Holding down the *right* mouse button, drag out another shape. Now select the Line shape, and, holding down the Shift key, drag out a line. Select a different shape, and, holding down the Shift key, drag out the shape.

## Edit a Picture

**1** Click the View tab, and select the Rulers, Gridlines, and Status Bar check boxes if they aren't already selected. Change the magnification if you want to see the picture in more or in less detail.

**2** Click the Fill With Color tool, point to the interior of an item, and click the left mouse button to fill the area with Color 1, or click the right mouse button to fill the area with Color 2.

**3** Click the Eraser button, and drag over the area to replace everything with Color 2. To replace Color 1 with Color 2, drag while holding down the right mouse button.

**4** Click Select, drag a selection rectangle around the item, and do any of the following:

- Drag the selected item to a new location. Hold down the Ctrl key to copy instead of move the item, or hold down the Shift key to create a series of overlapping images of the selection.

- Click Rotate, Resize, or Crop to change the orientation or the size of the selection. Clicking Crop keeps only the selected portion of the picture.

- Click either Copy or Cut to copy or cut the item to the Clipboard, or click Paste to paste an item from the Clipboard.

**5** Click the Paint button to save, print, or use the picture as your Desktop background.

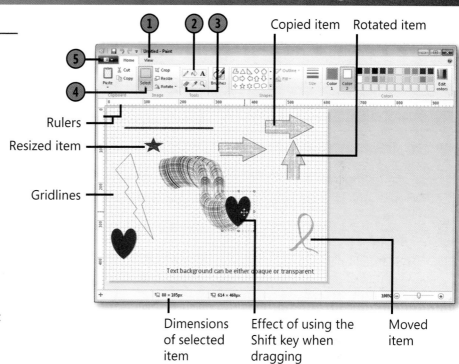

Copied item   Rotated item

Rulers

Resized item

Gridlines

Text background can be either opaque or transparent

Dimensions of selected item

Effect of using the Shift key when dragging

Moved item

**Tip**

To substantially reduce the file size of pictures stored in *png*, *bmp*, *dib*, or *tif* format, store them in a compressed folder; *jpeg* and *gif* files have their own compression.

**Tip**

To change the size of the drawing area, either drag a sizing handle at a corner of the drawing area or, with no item selected, click Resize. In the Resize And Skew dialog box, select Pixels, specify the size of the area, and click OK.

# Changing a Picture's Resolution

A problem with digital photos and drawings is that their file sizes can be immense. If you don't need to have a picture at its highest-possible resolution, you can resize it. Its true size will be a bit smaller and it will have a bit less detail, but it will also have a much smaller file size.

## Resize with Paint

1. In the Pictures Library, click the photo whose resolution you want to change, click the arrow at the right of the Preview button, and choose Paint from the drop-down menu to display the photo in Paint.

2. On the Home tab, click Resize.

3. In the Resize And Skew dialog box, specify whether you want to change the photo by a set percentage, or specify the size you want in pixels.

4. Make sure the Maintain Aspect Ratio check box is selected to prevent the photo from being distorted.

5. Enter the percentage or the pixel size.

6. Click OK.

7. Click the Paint button, choose Save As from the drop-down menu, and save the file with a different name and/or file format to create a smaller copy of the original photo.

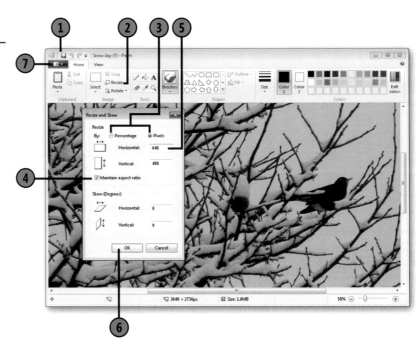

### See Also

"E-Mailing Your Photos" on page 228 for information about resizing photos when you e-mail them, and "Sending Photos with Windows Live Mail" on pages 244–245 for information about editing and formatting your photos.

### Try This!

If you have Windows Live Photo Gallery installed and running, right-click a photo you want to resize, and choose Resize from the shortcut menu. Select a size, and then click Resize And Save. Many other photo-editing programs also have commands that let you easily resize a photo.

# Working with Multimedia

In Windows 7, the term "multimedia" covers a lot of ground: music, videos, television, movies, and more. The tools you use to work with your multimedia depend on the way you want to configure your system and how you intend to use the multimedia. Do you want an all-encompassing system hooked up to your television or to a large monitor so that you can listen to music, play movies, watch and record TV, catch Internet shows, and so on? If so, you'll probably want to spend the time hooking everything up and using Windows Media Center. However, if you want a straightforward program that helps you organize, share, and use your media, Windows Media Player is probably the right choice for you.

If your computer is part of a homegroup, you can easily share your media with others on your network; and if you have devices that are capable of receiving media from your network, such as a network-enabled picture frame or a video extender, you can send music or videos to those devices.

If you use a video camera and you've downloaded Windows Live Photo Gallery and Windows Live Movie Maker, you can easily download all or parts of your recordings. You can then turn them into flashy video DVDs and send them to friends via e-mail or load them onto a Web site.

# Playing Multimedia with Media Player

Media Player makes it easy to play your music or videos. There are two main views in Media Player: Now Playing and Library. You use Now Playing view to watch your videos or to display album art or visualizations for the music. You use Library view to access the media in all your libraries and, if you want, to set up a series of items to be played by creating a playlist. In Library view you can also access your music based on categories such as artist, album title, or genre.

## Start Playing

**1** Insert a music CD or a video DVD, or, in a music or video library, double-click the media file you want to play.

**2** In Now Playing view, use the controls to stop, fast-rewind, pause, or fast-forward the file, or to set the volume.

**3** Click the View Full Screen button if you want to enlarge the viewer to full-screen size. In Full-Screen mode, move the mouse to make the controls visible. Click the Exit Full-Screen Mode button to return the viewer to its previous size.

**4** Right-click the viewer to

- Add visualizations to music.
- Change the video size.
- Display video enhancements.
- Turn on or off the options for displaying lyrics, captions, and subtitles.
- Select features for playing a DVD.

**5** To play the playlist in a continuous loop, click the Turn Repeat On button. Click it again to turn off Repeat mode.

**6** When you've finished, select the action you want, or close Media Player.

Switch To Library button

**See Also**

"Create an Auto Playlist" on page 179 for information about setting AutoPlay options so that Media Player will start when you insert a music CD or a video DVD.

## Play Anything

**(1)** If Media Player isn't already running, click the Start button, type **media** in the Search box of the Start menu, and choose Windows Media Player from the menu to start Media Player with Library view displayed. If Now Playing view is displayed, click the Switch To Library button.

**(2)** Click a library, playlist, or device. For the music library, select a category if you want to sort the contents by that category. Double-click Artist, Album, or Genre to display the songs if they aren't already displayed.

**(3)** To play a series of files, click the Play tab if it isn't already displayed. Click the Clear List button if there are items in the list that you don't want, and then drag the files you want onto the list. Drag the files up or down to set the play order.

**(4)** If you want to save the list as a playlist for future play, click the Save List button, type a name for the list, and press Enter.

**(5)** Click Play to play the media. To temporarily stop play without losing your place in the media file, click Pause. To stop playing the media, click Stop.

**(6)** To play the files in the playlist in random order, click the Turn Shuffle On button. Click the button again to turn off Shuffle mode.

**(7)** To play an existing playlist, double-click it.

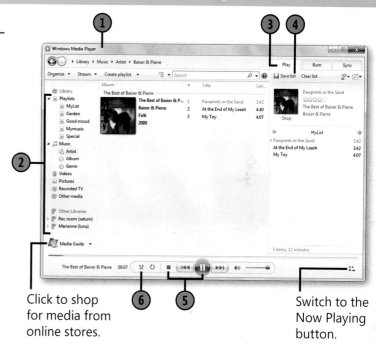

Click to shop for media from online stores.

Switch to the Now Playing button.

**See Also**

"Arranging Your Media with Playlists" on pages 178–179 for information about creating a personal playlist that programs the items to be played.

**Tip** ✓

When you play music from the Media Player library, Media Player usually displays Library view. When you play other media, Media Player switches to Now Playing view. You can switch between views using the Switch To Now Playing button and the Switch To Library button.

# Arranging Your Media with Playlists

When you've amassed a large number of media files, it can be difficult to keep track of them and even more difficult to figure out how to organize them. Media Player comes to your rescue with two tools that can relieve your frustration: Playlists to help you go through your files and decide which items you want to group together; and Auto Playlists, with which Media Player assembles various playlists depending on the criteria you've specified.

## Create a Playlist

① With Media Player running in Library view, click Create Playlist.

② Type a descriptive name for the playlist, and press Enter. Double-click the new playlist to make it the active list.

③ Drag an item you want in the playlist from the library onto the list. Continue adding files from the library to your list. Drag a file up or down in the list to change the order of play.

④ Click Save List to create the playlist.

⑤ If you want to modify the list at any time, double-click it to make it the active playlist, make your changes to the list, and then click Save List.

**See Also**

"Sharing Media Libraries on Your Network" on pages 186–187 for information about accessing media libraries on other computers.

**Tip**

To quickly add any media file in the library to an existing playlist without opening the playlist, drag the media file onto the playlist in the Navigation pane.

**Tip**

You can include in your playlist music or other media files that reside on another computer on your home network, provided the library on the other computer has been shared over the network. Of course, that computer must be turned on and available over the network for you to be able to play the media.

## Create an Auto Playlist

1. In Library view, click the down arrow at the right of the Create Playlist button, and choose Create Auto Playlist from the drop-down menu to display the New Auto Playlist dialog box.

2. Type a name for the playlist.

3. Click to specify the criteria you want to use to assemble the playlist.

4. Click each underlined item to specify conditions for that criterion.

5. Click to add other criteria.

6. Click to add limitations to the criteria you've added to the list.

7. Click OK to create your list.

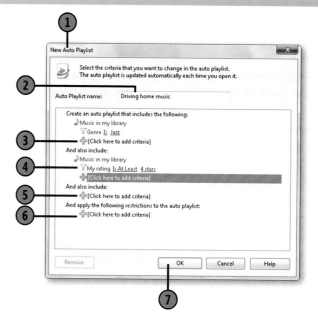

**Tip**

If you no longer want a playlist, right-click it in the Navigation pane, and choose Delete from the shortcut menu.

**Tip**

After you've created an auto playlist, it's included in the list of all your playlists, so make sure that you use a descriptive name to remind yourself what parameters you used to create the auto playlist.

# Copying CD Music

Instead of inserting a CD into your computer every time you want to hear a particular song or piece of music, you can *rip*—that is, copy—individual tunes or entire CDs onto your computer's hard disk, after which you can play the saved music in any order you like. When you copy the music, you can set the file type for compatibility and the bit rate for balancing file size and quality, or you can just set the defaults and forget about the individual settings.

## Rip from a CD

①  Place the music CD in its drive. If the AutoPlay dialog box appears, choose to play the CD using Media Player.

②  Clear the check boxes for any tracks you don't want to copy.

③  Click Rip Settings to display the Rip drop-down menu, and make any file-format or bit-rate settings you want. If the Rip Settings button isn't visible, click the Display Additional Commands button to display it.

④  Click Rip CD, and wait for the selected tracks to be copied.

Additional Commands button

**See Also**

"Create an Auto Playlist" on page 179 for information about setting what action is automatically taken when you insert a music CD.

**Tip**

Before you rip any music, check the file-type requirements of any portable or external device you want to use to be sure that you'll save the music in a compatible format.

**Tip**

To create your own default settings, such as the file location and file type, click Rip, choose More Options from the drop-down menu, and make your changes on the Rip tab of the Options dialog box.

## Create a Music CD

1. Make sure you have a blank CD in your CD drive. Click Burn to display the Burn tab.

2. Use the Navigation pane to locate what you want to copy, and then select the music genre, the album, the playlist, or the track that contains the music you want to copy.

3. Drag the track or tracks onto the Burn List. Move through additional categories to locate any other tracks you want to copy, and drag them onto the Burn List. Drag items up or down in the Burn List to specify the order in which you want the tracks to be placed on the CD.

4. Click the Burn Options button, and make any changes you want from the drop-down menu. For additional settings, choose More Burn Options from the menu, and make your changes on the Burn tab of the Options dialog box.

5. Click Start Burn, and wait for the tracks to be copied onto your CD.

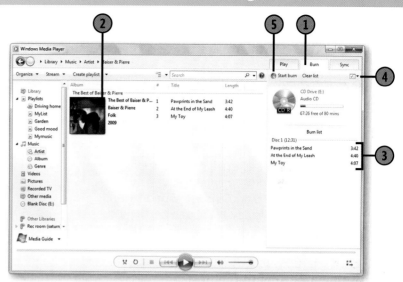

**See Also**

"Synchronizing Media with a Portable Device" on pages 184–185 for information about copying music automatically or manually to a portable device.

**Tip**

Many media files have restrictions regarding how often you can copy each file and to how many devices you can copy it. This restriction, called Digital Rights Management, often restricts copying a file to only one or two devices and might allow the file to be copied only a couple of times. To find out whether a file you want to copy has these restrictions, right-click the file, choose Properties from the shortcut menu, and view the license terms on the Media Usage Rights tab of the Properties dialog box.

# Controlling Video Playback

Watching video with Windows Media Player is fairly straight-forward, whether it's streaming video from the Web or video files on your computer. All you need to do is click the link on the Web page for the streaming video or choose the video from your Media Library, and then watch it on the Now Playing tab of Windows Media Player. However, you can also control the speed of the video playback and can even examine it frame by frame.

## Adjust the Playback

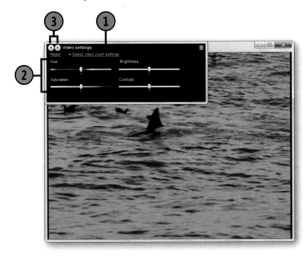

① With your video playing in Now Playing view, right-click the player, point to Enhancements on the shortcut menu that appears, and choose Video Settings from the submenu to display the Video Settings panel.

② Use the sliders to adjust the hue, brightness, saturation, and contrast of the video.

③ Keep clicking the Next Enhancement or the Previous Enhancement button until the Play Speed Settings controls are displayed.

④ Drag the slider to set the speed of the playback. The blue area shows the range of available speeds.

⑤ Click the Next Frame button to pause the video. Then click the Previous Frame or the Next Frame button to move the image backward or forward by single frames.

⑥ Click the Next Enhancement or the Previous Enhance-ment button, and then use the other enhancements to adjust the sound and video size.

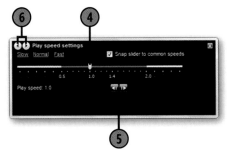

**Tip**

The Enhancement window isn't attached to Media Player, so if Media Player is in a window and isn't maximized or at full-screen size, you can move the Enhancement window to the side or above or below the player and make your adjustments without obscuring any of the video.

# Changing Media Player's Appearance

Although Windows Media Player has only two basic views—Library view and Now Playing view—it can assume many different shapes and appearances. You can make this happen by switching to Skin mode. In Skin mode, you can apply one of many different "skins" to personalize your player. After you've applied a new skin, it might take you some time to figure out where your controls are, but that's the cost of individuality! Of course, some shapes aren't appropriate for all types of media, but you can play around with the shapes to see which is best for you.

## Apply a Skin

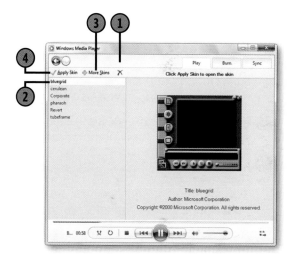

① In Library view, choose Skin Chooser from the View menu to display Skin Chooser view. If the menus aren't displayed, press the Alt button to temporarily display them.

② Select a skin to preview it.

③ If you don't see any skins you like, click More Skins, and download additional skins from the Windows Media Web site.

④ When you've selected the skin you want, click Apply Skin.

⑤ Use Media Player with its new skin to see whether you like its appearance and to determine whether it fits your needs.

⑥ Use Media Player's controls to switch views, or press Ctrl+1 to switch to the standard Media Player in Library view.

**Try This!**

In Library view, start playing a music playlist. Press Ctrl+2 and use Skin mode. Press Ctrl+3 to switch to Now Playing view. Click the Minimize button. Point to the Media Player icon on the taskbar, and use the controls in the thumbnail window to go to the previous or the next track, or to pause the player. Click in the thumbnail window to restore the player. Press Ctrl+1 to return to Library view.

# Synchronizing Media with a Portable Device

If you want to take your media files with you on a compatible portable device, you can have Media Player synchronize the content in your media library with the content on your portable device. The content can be synchronized either manually or automatically. Media Player will initially select which method to use, depending on the capacity of your device and the size of your media library.

## Synchronize

1. In Windows Media Player, attach your portable device, and click the Sync tab if it isn't already selected. Click Sync Options, and choose Set Up Sync from the drop-down menu to display the Device Setup dialog box.

2. If this is the first time you're synchronizing the device with your media library, enter a name for the device.

3. Click Finish. If the device has more storage capacity than the size of your media library and has more than 4 gigabytes of storage, wait for the contents of your media library to be copied to your portable device.

4. If the device didn't sync automatically, drag the playlist or the file that you want to add onto the Sync List. Continue adding playlists and/or files until all the items you want have been placed on your device.

5. Click Start Sync, and wait for the items to be copied.

6. After the files have been synchronized, click the device's name to expand the list, and then click Sync Status to verify that the files you want on the device have been synchronized.

## Control the Synchronization Settings

1. With your device set up, attached, and synchronized, click Sync Options, and then click Set Up Sync to display the Device Setup dialog box.

2. Clear this check box, if it's selected, to stop the device from automatically synchronizing when connected, or select the check box to automatically synchronize the device with your libraries.

3. If the device is set to sync automatically, choose Sync Playlists or Personal Playlists to see the available playlists you want to sync that aren't already included in the playlists. Choose to add playlists you want to sync, or remove playlists you no longer want to sync.

4. Adjust the way the playlists are to be synchronized:

   • Click the Shuffle What Syncs check box if the quantity of media in your library is too large to fit on your device and you want access to different materials each time you synchronize.

   • With the Shuffle What Syncs check box cleared, click a playlist to select it, and then use the Priority arrows to move the playlist up or down in priority.

5. Click Finish when you've finished.

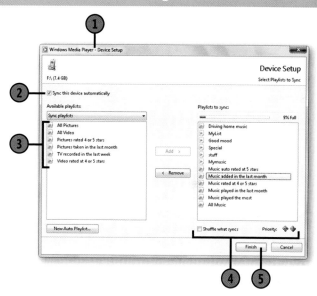

**See Also**

"Create an Auto Playlist" on page 179 for information about creating an auto playlist to specify the type of media you want to be included.

**Tip**

To see the contents of a playlist in the Device Setup dialog box, double-click the playlist.

**Tip**

In addition to dedicated portable music or video players, you can synchronize with a removable memory device such as a USB flash-memory device that you can then use with a different computer or device.

# Sharing Media Libraries on Your Network

With so many households having more than one computer or more than one user on a computer, media libraries can become scattered and inaccessible. By sharing your media libraries among users and across your home network, you can play your music, your videos, or whatever other media you want on one computer, regardless of where the media are stored.

## Share with Specific Computers and Devices

(1) With Windows Media Player running and in Library view, click Stream, and choose More Streaming Options from the drop-down menu to display the Media Sharing Options window.

(2) Type a descriptive name for the media library.

(3) Click Choose Default Settings to display the Default Media Streaming Settings dialog box.

(4) Specify what you want to share, and then click OK.

(5) Click one of the devices to select it.

(6) Click Customize if you don't want to use the default sharing settings with this device.

(7) Click this button, and choose Allowed to permit the device to access your media library, or choose Blocked to prohibit access to your library.

(8) Click the other devices, change any settings you want, and choose to either allow or block access.

(9) Click OK.

**See Also**

"Sharing with Your Homegroup" on pages 250–251 for information about sharing libraries with other members of your home network.

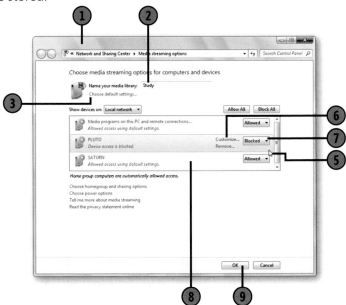

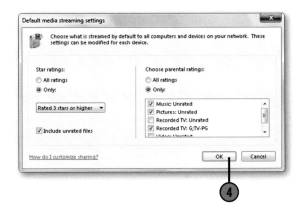

## Share with Everyone

 Click Stream, and choose Automatically Allow Devices To Play My Media from the drop-down menu.

Ⓐ In the Allow All Media Devices dialog box that appears, click Automatically Allow All Computers And Media Devices to confirm your choice.

Ⓑ If you decide that you no longer want to share your media, click Stream, choose Automatically Allow Devices To Play My Media, and, in the Allow All Media Devices dialog box, click Do Not Automatically Allow Computers And Media Devices.

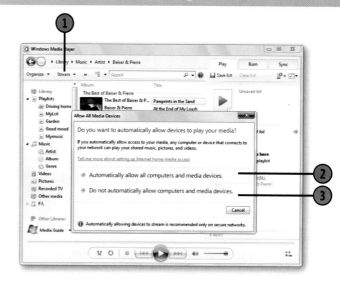

**Tip**

Shared Libraries are listed in Media Player's Library view under Other Libraries; they list both the descriptive name of the library and the computer it resides on.

**Caution**

If you share all your media with everyone, any media file added to any file in any folder that's included in any of your media libraries will be accessible by every computer or every device attached to the network. Be sure that your network is secure and that there are no media files in your libraries that might be embarrassing or vulnerable if they were accessed by anyone who gains access to the network.

**Tip**

Be aware of the differences between sharing media libraries using Media Player and sharing files over a homegroup. Media Player can share your library with other computers on your network that are using different operating systems, provided the other computers are using Media Player. When you're sharing with a homegroup, only computers that are running Windows 7, and that have joined the homegroup, can access the media libraries. However, the homegroup provides a higher level of security when you're sharing over a network. Note also that when you share a library with Media Player, the contents can be accessed only by using Media Player, whereas libraries shared over the homegroup can be accessed by any program you want to use.

# Accessing Your Media over the Internet

If you have computers both at home and away that run Windows 7, you might be able to access your home Windows Media Player library over the Internet. You do this by enabling both your home computer and your computer-away-from-home network to connect to each other. Then you use an online ID that's linked to your Windows user account to verify that you're authorized to make the connection. Your home computer must be turned on and not asleep in order for your other computer to access it. If you can't establish the connection, Media Player can help you figure out the problem.

## Set Up the Connection

1. With your home computer configured with a linked online ID signed in to the online ID service, and with Windows Media Player running, click Stream.

2. Click Allow Internet Access To Home Media in the drop-down menu, if there's no check mark next to it, to display the Internet Home Media Access dialog box. If there is a check mark, then the computer is already configured to share the media.

3. Click Allow Internet Access To Home Media, provide Administrator credentials if necessary, and then, in the dialog box that appears, click OK to confirm the setting.

4. With the computer that isn't part of your home network configured with the same linked online ID as your home computer, in Media Player, click Stream, and repeat steps 2 and 3 on the computer.

5. The media available from your home computer's media library should appear under Other Libraries.

6. When you no longer want the connection, click Stream, and then click Allow Internet Access To Home Media to display the Internet Home Media Access dialog box. Click Do Not Allow Internet Access To Home Media.

**See Also**

"Creating a Linked Online ID" on page 326 for information about linking an online ID with your Windows user name.

## Troubleshoot the Connection

1. Go through the steps to make the connection. If the connection can't be established, click Stream, and then click Allow Internet Access To Home Media to display the Internet Home Media Access dialog box.

2. Click Diagnose Connections.

3. In the Internet Streaming Diagnostic Tool, note the results of each test.

4. Click Port Forwarding Information to show the Port Forwarding Information dialog box. Note the information, and then click Close.

5. Click Close.

6. Click Stream, click Allow Internet Access To Home Media again, and, in the Internet Home Media Access dialog box, click Change Online ID. In the Link Online IDs window, verify that the online ID is the one you want to use, and then click OK.

7. Repeat steps 1 through 6 for your other computer.

8. Use your router documentation to determine how to change the port-forwarding settings for your router, if necessary. Apply any changes, and then try again to establish the connection.

### Caution

This connection can be very tricky to create for reasons unrelated to Windows. Corporate networks use security protocols that often block this type of connection. Also, the firewall settings for your home network's router might need to be manually changed, and any anti-virus and firewall settings on the home computer might need to be modified.

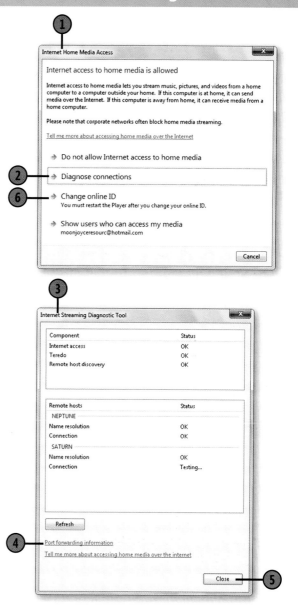

# Playing Your Media on Another Computer or Device

You can use Windows Media Player to play your media files on devices throughout your home network, on another computer, and on network-enabled electronic picture frames, audio systems, and extenders such as Xbox 360. You use your computer to select what you want to send to which device.

## Set Up a Computer or a Device to Receive Media

**1** Start Media Player, if it isn't already running, on the computer that is to receive and play the media, and, in Library view, click Stream. Choose Allow Remote Control Of My Player from the drop-down menu, if there isn't already a check mark next to the command, to display the Allow Remote Control dialog box.

**2** Click Allow Remote Control On This Network.

**3** If you're using a device, follow the device's instructions for connecting to your network.

---

**Tip**

To play to an Xbox 360, you first need to set up the extender. On the Xbox, choose Media Center, and follow the instructions for setting up the Xbox as an extender on your network. You'll also need Media Player running on your computer each time you want to reestablish the connection to the Xbox.

---

**Tip**

A device should be a DLNA-certified Digital Media Renderer to ensure that it will work with the Play To feature of Media Player. Devices designed specifically to work with Windows carry a "Compatible With Windows" logo. (In case you're wondering, DLNA stands for Digital Living Network Alliance.)

---

**Tip**

To confirm that a device is properly connected to your network, choose View Devices And Printers from the Control Panel, and review the devices listed.

---

## Play Media to a Device

**1** Start Media Player, if it isn't already running, on the computer that's sending the media. Click Stream, and verify that media streaming is turned on.

**2** In Library view, add the media you want to play to your playlist.

**3** Click the Play To button.

**4** Select the device you want to send the media to.

**5** Use the Play To window to control your play.

**Tip**

Multimedia files can require a lot of bandwidth when you're streaming them over a network. For music and most pictures, this should work fine. However, when you're streaming high-resolution pictures and video, you might encounter unacceptable slowdowns or poor image quality, especially if you're using a wireless connection on one or both of the devices. In that case, consider using removable media such as a USB memory device or a DVD to transfer the media to a computer or to a device.

**See Also**

"Sharing Media Libraries on Your Network" on pages 186–187 for information about enabling and controlling media streaming on your computer.

# Using Windows Media Center

Windows Media Center is a powerful program that produces a user-friendly environment for watching TV and movies, showing off your pictures, listening to your music, accessing and playing media from the Internet, and much, much more. What you can do with Media Center depends very much on the equipment you have, such as a TV tuner or a cable card, lots of disk space, and access to high-definition video. You can even link up an Xbox 360 or another type of extender accessory over your network to extend Media Center throughout your house. For information about setting up a computer or a device to receive media, see "Playing Your Media on Another Computer or Device" on pages 190–191.

You access your resources through Media Center's main menu. After you've selected a feature, you'll often find many more options. Most of these options are self-explanatory; you can find what you need by exploring the menus. Note, however, that some features won't be available if you don't have the proper equipment installed, and that some features are available only in certain countries or regions. For example, you need a device that supports radio reception if you want to listen to over-the-air radio. If you want to watch one show while simultaneously recording another one, you'll need to have two TV-tuner or cable cards (or one of each) installed on your computer. Following is a brief description of the main menu items and their features.

**Extras** for accessing online features, including online games, news and entertainment sites, and, in some locations, even Internet TV.

**Pictures+Videos** for viewing the contents of your pictures and video libraries. You can also create slide shows to display your photos.

**Music** for playing music from your music library and, if equipped with a radio tuner, to listen to radio stations. You can also create playlists to organize what you play and can search your library for specific music files.

**Movies** for viewing and playing your movie files, playing DVDs, and, if equipped with a TV tuner or a cable card, for viewing a guide to movies on TV.

**TV** for accessing and playing recorded TV files, viewing a guide for Internet TV, and, if equipped with a TV tuner or a cable card, for viewing a guide to available TV shows and for viewing live TV.

**Sports** for viewing sports scores, tracking players and teams, and, if equipped with a TV tuner or a cable card, for viewing a listing of sports on TV.

**Tasks** for customizing settings, setting up a screen saver, burning a CD or DVD, synchronizing media with a portable device, adding an extender, locking the Media Center display in Full-Screen mode, and shutting down the computer.

# Watching Windows Media Center

Windows Media Center is a specialized tool that's designed to run primarily on a computer that's customized with TV and radio cards or connectors, and that has a very large amount of disk storage space, a large high-resolution display, and a remote control. However, with some—or even none—of these features on your computer, you can still use parts of Media Center.

## Control Media Center

① If Media Center isn't running, start it from the Start menu. If a Setup wizard starts, complete it to configure your system.

② Scroll through the menus using either the mouse or the arrow keys on your keyboard or remote control. Click an item, or press Enter when the item you want is selected.

③ Move the mouse to display the controls, and then use the controls with the mouse to change channels, fast-forward, and so on; or use the arrow keys and the numeric keypad on your keyboard or remote control to control the play.

④ To return to the previous page, click the Back button, or press the Back key on your remote control or the Backspace key on your keyboard.

⑤ To return directly to the main menu, click the Main Menu button.

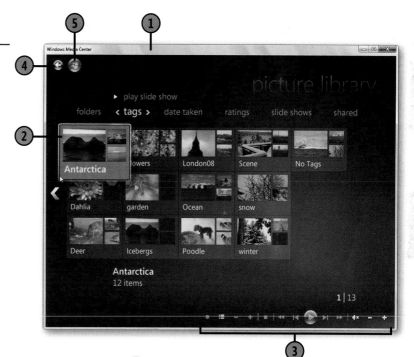

**See Also**

"Create and Play a Slide Show" on page 163 for information about creating a slide show for viewing your photos using Media Center.

**Tip**

If you're using a fully equipped Media Center computer, follow the directions for using the remote control and any specialized keyboard that came with the system. You can also control all the functions of Media Center from the keyboard. To find the extensive list of keyboard shortcuts, search Windows Help for Media Center keys.

# Creating a Video DVD

If there's a video that you want to share with others, and you don't need to edit it or add titles, transitions, or a soundtrack—or if you've already done so in another program—you can create a video DVD, complete with an opening menu and a visual layout scheme.

## Create the DVD

1. With a recordable DVD disc in your DVD burner, click the Start button, type **dvd** in the Search box of the Start menu, and choose Windows DVD Maker from the menu.

2. In the Windows DVD Maker window, click Add Items, locate and select the videos, and click Add. Drag the videos up or down to set the order of play.

3. Click Options to customize the video playback, the video aspect ratio, the video format, the DVD writing speed, and the location of the temporary files.

4. Type a name for the video DVD.

5. Click Next.

6. Click the menu style you want.

7. Click Menu Text to modify the font and the menu text and to add any notes; then click Change Text.

8. Click Preview to make sure the video appears as you want it. Click OK.

9. Click Burn to create the DVD.

> **See Also**
>
> "Making a Movie" on page 198 for information about editing your video.

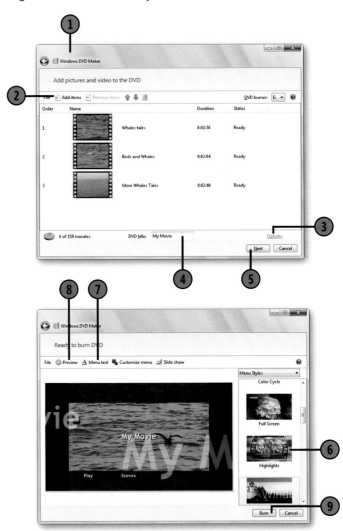

# Recording Video from a Camera

Although Windows 7 doesn't provide tools for viewing and recording live feeds from your digital video camera, you can use Windows Live Photo Gallery to do so if you choose to download and install this free program. With the proper connection, you can record a live feed from your video camera directly onto your computer, creating a video file (or files) in the format of your choice.

## Record Live Video

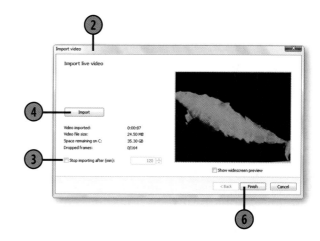

1. Attach your camera to your computer, turn on the camera, and, if necessary, set it to Record Video mode, but don't start recording yet.

2. Start Photo Gallery if it isn't already running, click File, and choose Import From A Camera Or Scanner from the drop-down list. In the Import Photos And Videos dialog box, select your camera if it isn't already selected, and click Import to start the Import Video wizard. Type a name for the video, and click Next to display the Import Live Video page of the wizard.

3. Select this option if you want to specify a maximum length of recording.

4. Click Import to start recording the feed; click Stop if you want to pause the recording.

5. Repeat steps 3 and 4 until you've completed the recording.

6. Click Finish.

**See Also**

"Setting Up Windows Live Essentials Programs" on page 285 for information about downloading and installing Windows Live programs, including Windows Live Photo Gallery.

**Tip**

Different cameras have different methods of connecting, but you usually get the best results by using a Firewire (IEEE 1394) connection. If you have any difficulties connecting, try using the software that came with your camera to download both live and recorded video.

# Downloading Recorded Video from a Camera

With the digital video camera attached to your computer and Windows Live Photo Gallery installed, you can transfer all the recorded video to your computer or directly to a DVD, or you can download only selected portions of the video.

## Download the Entire Video

(1) With your camera attached to the computer, turn on the camera, and set it to play the recorded video.

(2) Start Photo Gallery if it isn't already running, click File, and choose Import From A Camera Or Scanner from the drop-down list. In the Import Photos And Videos dialog box, select your camera if it isn't already selected, and click Import to start the Import Video wizard.

(3) Choose either to import the entire video or to burn it to a DVD. If you want to burn it to a DVD, type a name for the DVD, and make sure that you have a blank, recordable DVD in your DVD burner.

(4) Click Next, and wait while the videotape is being rewound and then played and recorded.

(5) If you want to stop the recording before the entire tape has been transferred, click Stop.

(6) Click Finish when the video has been transferred. If you're transferring it to a DVD, wait for Windows DVD Maker to burn it onto the disc.

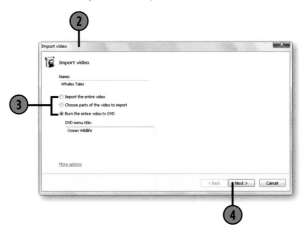

## Download Video Clips

**(1)** With the camera turned on, attached to your computer, and set to play the recorded video, click File in Photo Gallery, and choose Import From A Camera Or Scanner. In the Import Photos And Videos dialog box, select your camera if it isn't already selected, and click Import to start the Import Video wizard.

**(2)** Type a name for the video.

**(3)** Select this option to import parts of the videotape.

**(4)** Click Next.

**(5)** Use the controls to move through the video until you locate the part you want to record. Use the Next Frame and the Previous Frame controls to find the exact location where you want to start the recording.

**(6)** Click Import, and watch your clip.

**(7)** Click Stop when you reach the spot where you want to stop the importing.

**(8)** Repeat steps 5 and 6 until you've imported all the clips you want, and then click Finish.

**See Also**

"Making a Movie" on page 198 for information about editing your video clips.

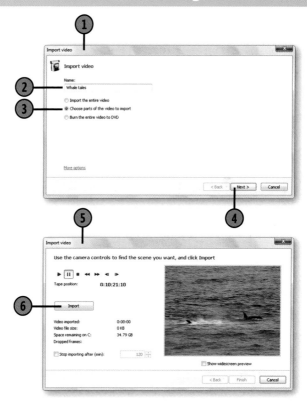

# Making a Movie

Why not transform your multimedia files into a movie with titles, transitions between scenes, special effects, and even a soundtrack? Windows 7 doesn't provide video-editing tools, but you can download Windows Live Movie Maker and add a lot of pizzazz to your videos.

## Create a Movie

1. With Movie Maker running, click Add on the Home tab, and select the video and/or photo files you want to include in the movie.

2. Move the files around so that they're in the order you want.

3. To add a soundtrack, click Add, and choose the music file you want. To balance the soundtrack with the audio, start playing the video, click Mix, and drag the slider to achieve the balance you want. If you're creating a slide show, click Fit so that the length of the slide show matches the length of the soundtrack.

4. On the Visual Effects tab, with a file or a group of files selected, choose the transition you want to use at the beginning of each selected file, and then apply any special effect you want to all the selected files.

5. On the Edit tab, select a file, and click Text Box to add a text box. Select a font you like, and type your text. Move the text box into the location you want, and then click outside it.

6. Use the other editing tools to trim the video clip, mute the audio of the video, or set the duration for which each slide is displayed.

7. Click Publish to send your movie to a Web site, or click Output to save the video as a file.

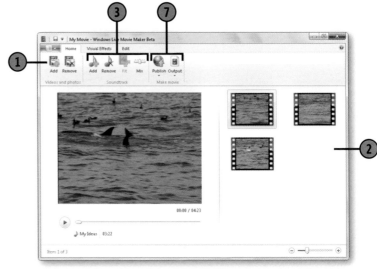

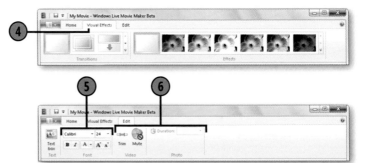

**See Also**

"Setting Up Windows Live Essentials Programs" on page 285 for information about downloading and installing Windows Live Movie Maker.

# 10 Using Voice and Sounds

If the sound your computer emits to signal an event—the logon or logoff sound, for example—is an earsplitting assault, relief in the form of adjusting the volume is just a click or two away with Windows 7's volume control. And, if you can't stand the startup sound, you can simply turn it off! You can also use the volume control to keep your music and other sounds muted so that you don't disturb the people around you.

If you'd like to command your computer verbally instead of typing and using the mouse, try Windows 7's powerful speech-recognition program. We must stress how important it is to go through the tutorial so that you learn the correct commands, and so that the program can recognize your voice and the way you pronounce words. Be patient! It can take a bit of trial and error, but you'll know it was time well spent when you can dictate letters or long documents without touching the keyboard!

Instead of saving your fingers, perhaps you want to save your eyes by using the Narrator program, which actually reads aloud to you. Using your sound system, Narrator can describe items on your screen and can read blocks of text to you. But what if you can't—or don't want to—hear any sounds from your computer? You can set it to give you visual cues, including flashes and captions, instead.

# Controlling the Volume

Although a computer blaring loud music can be fun when you're relaxing or having a party, it's not a good idea when you're around other people in a crowded room or office or using a notebook computer at a meeting.

## Set the Master Volume Level

① Click the Volume icon in the notification area of the taskbar.

② Do either of the following:

- Drag the slider to adjust the volume.

- Click the Mute button to mute the sound or to turn off muting.

③ If you want to fine-tune the settings for your speakers or another output device, including the balance between speakers, click the icon for the device, and make the changes in the device's Properties dialog box.

④ Click outside the Volume Control to close it.

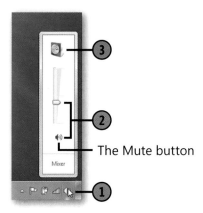

The Mute button

**See Also**

"Controlling the Sound System" on pages 200–203 for information about selecting your default output device and adjusting speaker balance.

**Tip**

Many, but not all, computers have volume controls on their keyboards so that you can easily change the volume or mute the entire system. These buttons accomplish the same thing as using the Volume Control on the taskbar.

**Try This!**

Right-click the Volume icon on the taskbar, and choose Volume Control Options from the shortcut menu. If there's more than one sound device listed in the Volume Control Options dialog box, select the check boxes for all the devices, and then click OK. Click the Volume icon, and note that each sound device has its own volume control.

## Set the Volume for Events and Programs

① Click the Volume icon in the notification area of the taskbar, and click Mixer to display the Volume Mixer dialog box.

② Adjust the volume for the device.

③ Adjust the volume for the event sounds used with Windows.

④ Adjust the sound level for each running program.

⑤ If you want to turn off the sound for one of the events or programs but retain the sound for the others, click the event's or the program's Mute button. Click the button again to restore the sound to the item.

⑥ Close the Volume Mixer dialog box when you've finished.

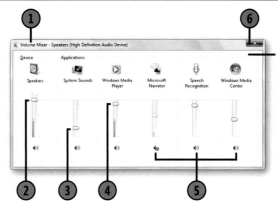

Some items appear in the Mixer only if they're currently running.

**See Also**

"Customizing the Taskbar" on pages 96–97 for information about displaying the Volume icon if it isn't already displayed on the taskbar.

"Creating a Sound Theme" on pages 204–205 for information about modifying which Windows sounds are used for specific events.

**Tip**

If the Volume icon isn't displayed on the taskbar, open the Start menu, type **vol** in the Search box of the Start menu, and choose Adjust System Volume to display the Volume Mixer.

# Controlling the Sound System

Just like your house or your car, your computer might have a really terrific sound system—or perhaps one that isn't so great. You can tweak the sound system to get the most out of it, including customizing it for different types of speakers and for the various types of activities for which you use your computer.

## Set the Speaker Defaults

1. Click the Start button, type **sound** in the Search box of the Start menu, and choose Sound from the menu to display the Sound dialog box.

2. On the Playback tab, select your speaker system.

3. Click Configure, and, in the Speaker Setup wizard that appears, step through the wizard to specify the appropriate configuration for your speakers. Click Finish when you've finished.

4. Click Properties to display the Properties dialog box for your speakers. Make any device-specific settings that you want as the default settings for that device, including volume levels and enhancements, and click OK.

5. If there's more than one device listed, select another device, and make any changes you want to it by repeating steps 3 and 4.

6. Select the device you want as the default device, and click Set Default.

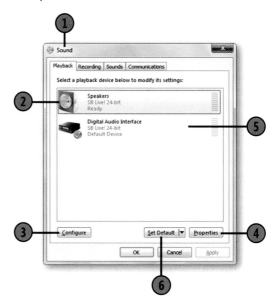

Tip

Many computer sound systems are available, each with different features, so what you see on your computer might list different items from the ones shown here. Additionally, some sound systems come with their own mixers and sound controls that give you additional control of the system. Check with your computer documentation to make sure that you're getting the most from your sound system.

## Set the Input Defaults

① On the Recording tab of the Sound dialog box, select an input device, and click Properties to display the device's Properties dialog box.

② Click the tabs to configure the input:

- Listen to configure the connection for an external device such as a portable music player

- Custom for any special features of the device

- Levels to set the input levels for the device

- Advanced to specify the default format to be used in shared mode, and whether to allow programs to take exclusive control of the device

③ Click OK.

## Set the Background Level

① Click the Communications tab of the Sound dialog box.

② Select the sound levels you want when you're using the computer for phone calls.

③ Click OK.

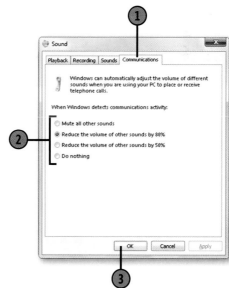

# Creating a Sound Theme

When you personalize your computer by changing themes, you're also often switching the sound scheme used by Windows and other programs that alert you to an event—the closing of a program or the arrival of new e-mail, for example. You can change which sound scheme is associated with your custom theme, and you can even create your own scheme.

## Change the Sounds in a Theme

1. Right-click a blank spot on the Desktop, and choose Personalize to open the Personalization window. In the Personalization window, select the theme you want to modify, and click Sound to display the Sound dialog box, with the Sounds tab selected.

2. Click the Sound Scheme list, and select a scheme.

3. Click any event that's marked with a sound icon.

4. Click the Test button to preview the sound scheme.

5. If you never again want to hear the Windows startup sound when you turn on your computer, clear this check box.

6. If you like the sound scheme, click OK.

7. In the Personalization window, click Save Theme, enter a name for the modified theme, and click Save.

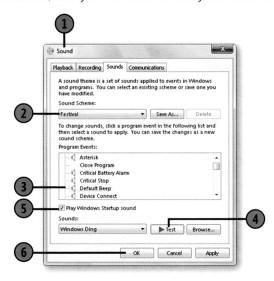

**See Also**

"Changing the Overall Look" on pages 84–85 for information about changing themes.

**Tip**

If you find the use of the terms *sound scheme* and *sound theme* confusing, you're not alone! You create, modify, and save as many *sound schemes* as you want in the Sound dialog box. When you apply a specific *sound scheme* by selecting it and clicking OK, it becomes the *sound theme* for your computer.

## Create a Sound Scheme

**1** Right-click a blank spot on the Desktop, and choose Personalize to open the Personalization window. In the Personalization window, select the theme you want to modify, and click Sound to display the Sound dialog box, with the Sounds tab selected.

**2** On the Sounds tab, click an event to which you want to assign a sound.

**3** Click a sound in the Sounds list, or use the Browse button to find a sound in another folder. Click None in the Sounds list to remove a sound from an event.

**4** Click the Test button to preview the sound. Continue to select events and assign the sounds you want to them.

**5** If you want to assign a unique name to a sound scheme, click Save As, enter a name for the sound scheme you've created, and click OK.

**6** Click OK.

**7** In the Personalization window, click Save Theme, enter a name for the modified theme, and click Save.

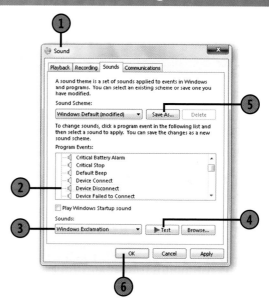

### Tip

If you want to use a different sound scheme without saving it with a theme, click the Start button, type **sound** in the Search box of the Start menu, and click Sound to display the Sound dialog box.

### Tip

The sound files used in a sound scheme are .*wav* (Waveform Audio Format) files. These are uncompressed files, so any long series of notes creates a large file. Therefore, sounds in the sound schemes should preferably be very short. You can obtain additional .*wav* files from many sources or can create your own using third-party software.

### Caution

Don't try to use the Windows Sound Recorder to create sounds for your sound scheme. Sound Recorder creates sound files in the Windows Media Audio File format, not the .*wav* format used in sound schemes.

# Directing Your Computer with Voice Commands

Windows 7 includes a powerful speech-recognition program that lets you use your voice to direct the computer. Although the speech-recognition program is designed primarily for people who have difficulty using the keyboard and/or the mouse, the ability to direct Windows and your other programs with your voice has a certain authoritative appeal. And, as with using the mouse or the keyboard, there are numerous ways to accomplish any specific task.

## Start Speech Recognition

① Click the Start button, type **speech** in the Search box of the Start menu, and choose Windows Speech Recognition from the menu. If this is the first time you've started Speech Recognition, the Set Up Speech Recognition wizard will appear. Work your way through the wizard to set up your system, select your settings, and then go through the tutorial.

② With Speech Recognition running, use the commands that you learned in the tutorial or from Help, or from those listed in the table on the facing page.

③ If you want to access something in a window but can't figure out how, say "Show numbers." Say the number for the item, and then say "OK."

Microphone button

Visual feedback for the spoken command

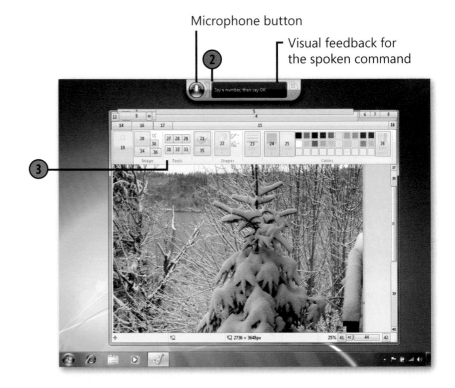

**See Also**

"Dictating Text" on pages 208–209 for information about using the Alternates Panel if a command isn't clearly understood.

**Tip**

If you can't remember a command, say "What can I say?" to display Windows Help And Support, which lists all the commands you can use.

## Use the Commands

| To do this | Say this |
| --- | --- |
| Start a program | "Start," and then the name of the program |
| Open the Start menu | "Start" |
| Open a menu in a program or window | The name of the menu |
| Activate a toolbar button | The name of the button |
| Activate a link | The name of the link |
| Click an item | "Click," and then the name of the item |
| Double-click an item | "Double-click," and then the name of the item |
| Use the equivalent of keystrokes | "Press," and then the name of the key or the name of the keyboard shortcut |
| Switch to a program | "Switch to," and then the name of the program |
| Scroll in a window | "Scroll down," "scroll up," "scroll left," "scroll right" |
| Scroll a specific number of lines | "Scroll," and then the number of lines |
| Move the speech-recognition program out of the way | "Move speech recognition" |
| Work without using speech recognition | "Stop listening" |

**Tip**

Depending on your settings, if the speech-recognition program is running but is sleeping, say "Start listening" or click the Microphone button, or press Ctrl+Windows key to activate it.

**Caution**

Don't skip the tutorial! As you work your way through it, the speech-recognition program is learning to understand your voice and the way you pronounce words. If you skip the tutorial, the speech-recognition program won't be very effective.

# Dictating Text

The speech-recognition program lets you issue commands to your computer and dictate text in a document. Of course, while you're dictating, you'll also be issuing some commands—for example, telling the computer to correct or change some words, to start paragraphs, and to scroll through the document. Fortunately, the speech-recognition program is usually smart enough to know when you're dictating text and when you're issuing commands. Even if the speech-recognition program gets something wrong, however, you can easily correct it.

## Dictate Your Text

1. In a document that accepts text, start dictating your text. If the speech-recognition program is sleeping, say "Start listening" or click the microphone button before you start dictating.

2. Speak as you did in the tutorial, pausing only after completing a phrase or sentence. The text will be inserted after a brief pause. As necessary, use any of the commands in the table at the right.

### See Also

"Directing Your Computer with Voice Commands" on pages 206–207 for information about moving around windows, choosing menu commands, and improving the program's recognition of your voice.

## Use the Commands

| To do this | Say this |
| --- | --- |
| Insert a punctuation mark | The name of the mark—"period," "comma," "question mark," and so on. |
| Insert a number | The name of the number. |
| Insert special characters | The name of the character—"double quote," "open parenthesis," "close parenthesis," "hyphen," "ampersand," and so on. |
| Insert an unusual name or word | Spell the word one letter at a time. |
| Start a new paragraph | "Enter." |
| Undo your last entry | "Undo." |
| Move the insertion point around in a document | The type of move—"end," "backspace," "move down two lines," and so on. |
| Select text | "Select," and then the word or range—"sentence" or "paragraph." |
| Apply formatting or other items on a toolbar | The name of the item—"bold," italic," and so on. If you don't know the name of the item, say "show numbers," say the number of the item, and then say "OK." |
| Figure out how to enter or edit something if you can't remember the command | "What can I say?" and then review the Help file. |

## Correct Errors

**①** Say "Correct," and then say the word or phrase that needs to be corrected to display the Alternates Panel.

**②** Say the number of the correct item, and then say "OK." If the correct word or phrase doesn't appear in the Alternates Panel, say the word or phrase again, say the number of the correct item, and then say "OK."

**③** If you're trying to correct a word that the program never recognizes, say "Spell it" to display the Spelling Panel.

**④** In the Spelling Panel, spell the word slowly, one letter at a time. If you make a mistake, say the number of the wrong letter, and then say the correct letter. If a letter is routinely misunderstood, say it with an example, such as "H, as in hotel." When the spelling is correct, say "OK."

**Tip**

To directly add, delete, or correct words in the dictionary, say "Show speech options," and, on the shortcut menu that appears, say "Open the speech dictionary."

**Tip**

Dictating text can be quite frustrating at first, but as you use the program, both you and the program get better at it. Also, for better recognition, you can take advantage of the additional training the speech program offers.

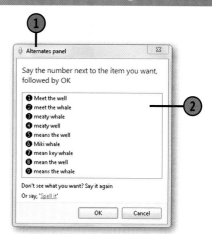

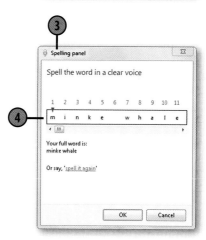

# Customizing Speech Recognition

You can customize the way the speech-recognition program works so that it adjusts to your preferences, including the language you want to use, the way the program spaces sentences, and its ability to recognize a *profile*—that is, to recognize someone else's voice and/or adjust to different background sounds.

## Customize

1. If you want to change the way the speech-recognition program works, say "Show speech options." On the shortcut menu that appears, say "Configuration" to open the submenu, and then say "Open speech-recognition control panel." In the Speech Recognition Options Control Panel that appears, say "Advanced speech options" to display the Speech Properties dialog box.

2. On the Speech Recognition tab of the Speech Properties dialog box, make the modifications you want:

   - Select the language for the speech recognition.

   - Create a new profile or select a different profile.

   - Do additional training to improve speech recognition.

   - Specify the way you want speech recognition to start, learn, and space sentences.

   - Adjust the microphone.

3. Say "OK" to close the dialog box.

4. Make any other changes in the Speech Recognition Options Control Panel, and then say "Close."

**Tip** ✓

Use the Speech Recognition window that you opened to access additional training, to adjust your microphone, or to read more about the way you can use the speech-recognition program.

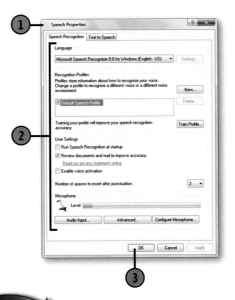

**See Also**

"Letting Your Computer Do the Talking" on page 212 for information about using Narrator.

**Tip** ✓

The Text To Speech tab of the Speech Properties dialog box is used in association with any text-to-speech programs you've installed on your computer. By default, the Text To Speech settings are set to work with Narrator, the text-to-speech program that comes with Windows 7.

# Talking to the Mouse

If you want to work with the mouse when you're using voice commands, you use a large grid that encompasses the entire screen to specify where you want the mouse to go. Using the grid is especially useful if you have any problems with navigating around the screen and making windows or other areas active.

## Use the Grid

**1** With speech recognition running and listening, say "Mouse grid" to display the large grid.

**2** Say the number that identifies the region in which you want to work to display a small grid for that region.

**3** In the small grid, do any of the following:

- Say "Click" to click in the middle of the grid.

- Say a number on the grid to show a detailed grid of that region.

- Say a number, and then say "Click" to click in the center of that region.

- Say a number, and then say "Right-click" to right-click in that region.

- Say "Back" to move back to the large grid.

- Say "Cancel" to remove the mouse grid.

**Tip** ✔

Most voice commands, except those used with the mouse grid, aren't recognized while the mouse grid is displayed. The mouse grid will remain on the screen if you type any information, but it will go away if you click the mouse, press the Windows key, or say an appropriate voice command.

# Letting Your Computer Do the Talking

Windows 7 provides a program called Narrator that speaks to you! Narrator can describe aloud the items that are currently displayed on your screen, and it can even read long blocks of text. Narrator has some limitations, but it can be very useful in the right circumstances. Of course, for Narrator to work, your computer must have a sound system.

## Listen to Narrator

1. Start Narrator from the Start menu to display the Microsoft Narrator dialog box.

2. Select this check box if you want Narrator to describe aloud each keystroke you make so that you can verify that you're pressing the keys you want.

3. Select or clear any of the check boxes to make Narrator work the way you want.

4. Click the Voice Settings button to display the Voice Settings dialog box.

5. Adjust the reading speed, volume, and pitch of Narrator's voice. Click OK when you've finished.

6. Press Alt+Spacebar, and choose Minimize from the Control menu to minimize Narrator when you've adjusted all the settings to your satisfaction.

7. To close Narrator, keep pressing Alt+Tab until Narrator is selected, and then click the Exit button in the Microsoft Narrator dialog box.

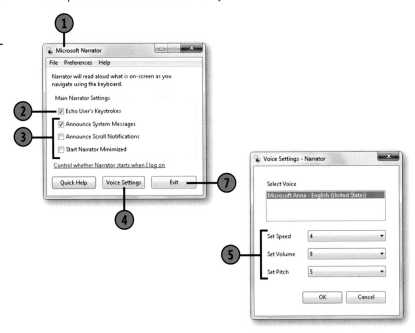

**See Also**

"Directing Your Computer with Voice Commands" on pages 206–207 and "Dictating Text" on pages 208–209 for information about talking to your computer.

**Tip**

Narrator works very well with the speech-recognition program, but it's designed primarily to work with the keyboard, so you'll need to use the Tab key to move around in a dialog box, or use keyboard shortcuts to activate commands. To temporarily stop Narrator while it's reading or describing something, press the Ctrl key. To have Narrator describe the contents of a window at any time, press Ctrl+Shift+Spacebar. To hear a description of the layout, press Ctrl+Alt+Spacebar.

# Creating a Sound File

You can record your own Windows Media Audio (*.wma*) file from a variety of sources, depending on your computer's equipment. These sources can include live or recorded music, narrations, or notes. After you've recorded a *.wma* file, you can play it back using Windows Media Player or Windows Media Center.

## Record Sounds

① Start Sound Recorder from the Start menu.

② Click the Start Recording button, and record the sounds you want.

③ Click the Stop Recording button when you've finished. If you've completed the recording, use the Save As dialog box to save the sound file with the name you want in the location you want. To continue recording to the same sound file, click Cancel in the Save As dialog box.

④ Click the Resume Recording button, record what you want, and then click the Stop Recording button when you've finished. Use the Save As dialog box to save the file with the name you want in the location you want.

⑤ Close Sound Recorder when you've finished.

**Tip**

To adjust the recording volume of your microphone, click the Start button, type **sound** in the Search box of the Start menu, and choose Sound from the menu to display the Sound dialog box. On the Recording tab, double-click your microphone, and adjust the settings on the Levels tab.

**Caution**

Sound Recorder is a fine application for recording voice notes or a sample of music, but the recording quality isn't adequate for quality music recordings.

**Tip**

To add a sound recording to the Windows Media Player library, right-click the sound recording file, and choose Add To Windows Media Player List from the shortcut menu.

# Using Alternatives to Sound

If you're unable to hear the sounds your computer makes (or if you simply don't want to) you can set up a visual cue—for example, a flash when a sound would normally be played. You can also set captions to be displayed by programs that normally signal an event with a sound. However, not all programs support the caption alternative, so you won't always have the option of seeing the captions displayed.

## Turn on Visual Cues

**1** Open the Ease Of Access Center from either the Start menu or the Control Panel. In the Ease Of Access Center, choose Use Text Or Visual Alternatives For Sounds to display the Use Text Or Visual Alternatives For Sounds window.

**2** Select this check box to see visual cues for sounds.

**3** Specify the visual cue you want:

- None to show no visual warnings

- Flash Active Caption Bar to flash the title bar and surrounding border for the active window or dialog box

- Flash Active Window to flash the entire active window or dialog box

- Flash Desktop to flash everything

**4** Select this check box if you want programs to display captions for sound events.

**5** Click OK.

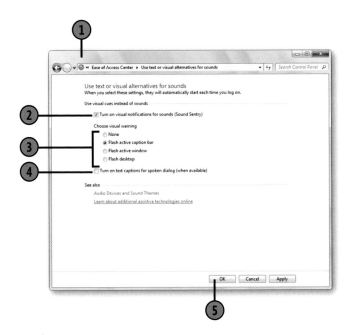

### See Also

"Using Alternative Ways of Working" on page 104 for information about other methods of customizing the way Windows 7 works.

# Printing and Scanning

Unless you've been unusually lucky, we're willing to bet that you've had a frustrating experience with a surly printer at least once! This section of the book will guide you painlessly through the printing process. If you have multiple printers installed on your computer, on your homegroup, or on your network, we'll show you how to designate one of them as your default printer—that is, the one you set up to automatically print all your documents—and how to target another printer when you can't or don't want to use the default printer.

Printing your photographs is a snap too, with a great wizard to help you arrange your photos on the page. With just a few clicks, you can choose the size and orientation of each picture, the required number of copies, and the way you want the pictures to be laid out on the page.

Also, if you've ever printed a Web page and been unhappily surprised by the chaotic result, you'll appreciate the ability Internet Explorer gives you to print readable Web pages. We also discuss creating and printing a document in the universal XPS format, which makes it possible for your document to look exactly the same as it did originally, even if you open or print it on a different computer.

# Printing a File

In most programs, you can print a document on any printer that's installed on your computer or shared by your homegroup or over a standard network. By using the Print dialog box, you can specify which printer to use and can customize the way your document is printed.

## Print a Document

**1** With the document open in its program, choose Print from the File menu or the program menu to display the Print dialog box.

**2** Specify the printer you want to use.

**3** Click Preferences if you need to change the printer settings—the size of the paper being used, whether the document is to be printed in color or in black and white, and so on. (Note, however, that sometimes the program's settings will override your own settings.)

**4** Click Find Printer to find and use a printer on a network that isn't listed in the Select Printer section.

**5** Specify which pages you want to print.

**6** Specify how many copies of each page you want.

**7** Specify whether you want multiple copies to be printed with the pages in order (collated) or whether you want each page to be printed multiple times before the next page is printed. (Collated printing is usually slower than uncollated printing.)

**8** Click Print.

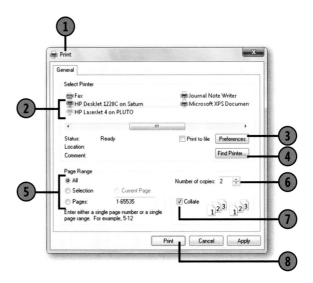

### See Also

"Specifying a Default Printer" on the facing page for information about setting a printer as your default printer.

### Try This!

Select a document in a library or folder and right-click it. Choose Print from the shortcut menu to print the document on your default printer. Now select several files of the same type, right-click one of them, and choose Print to print all the selected files on your default printer.

# Specifying a Default Printer

Some programs are set up to print only on the system's default printer. Other programs are set up to print on the system's default printer but allow you to *target*, or change

to, a different printer. If several printers are available, you can designate any one of them as your default printer.

## Change the Default Printer

① Choose Devices And Printers from the Start menu to display the Devices And Printers window.

② Right-click the printer you want to use.

③ Choose Set As Default Printer from the shortcut menu that appears.

④ Close the Devices And Printers window when you've finished.

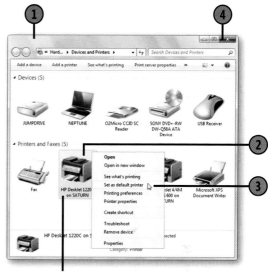

The current default printer

> **Tip**
>
> If there's a check mark next to the printer icon, the printer you've chosen is already designated as the default printer.

> **Tip**
>
> In Windows 7 Professional, Enterprise, and Ultimate editions, you can select a different default printer for each network you connect to. That way, when you connect to a work network, you'll have one of the printers at your workplace as your default printer, and when you connect to your home network, a printer at home will be the default printer. To specify the default printers, click Manage Default Printers in the Devices And Printers window.

> **See Also**
>
> "Printing a File" on the facing page and "Controlling Your Printing" on pages 218–219 for information about printing on different printers.

# Controlling Your Printing

When you send your documents to be printed, each print job is *queued,* or lined up, in the order in which it's received by the print server. You can see the progress of your print job in the print queue and can temporarily suspend the printing of your document or remove it from the queue if you decide that you don't want to print it. You can also suspend or cancel all printing, and you can make changes to your printing preferences.

## Control the Print Queue

1 Choose Devices And Printers from the Start menu to display the Devices And Printers window.

2 Click the printer you're using to select it.

3 Click See What's Printing to open the print queue for that printer.

4 Note the names and details of the documents in the print queue.

5 To manage the printing of a document, right-click the document's name, and choose the action you want from the shortcut menu:

- Pause to temporarily stop your document from printing.

- Resume to resume printing after the document printing has been paused. Note that Resume appears on the menu only after you've chosen Pause.

- Restart to restart printing the document from the beginning after the document printing has been paused.

- Cancel to delete the document from the print queue.

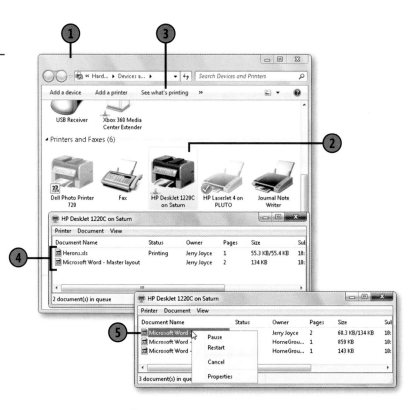

**Tip**

Don't be surprised if, after you've paused or canceled a print job, the printer continues to print another page or two. This is because those pages have already been stored in the printer.

# Control the Printer

1. On the computer to which the printer is connected (or on the computer to which the Administrator for the printer is signed on), open the Devices And Printers window if it isn't already open, click the printer, and click See What's Printing to open the print queue for that printer.

2. In the print queue window, click Printer, and choose either of the following:

   - Pause Printing to temporarily stop all printing. Click Pause Printing a second time to resume printing.

   - Cancel All Documents to remove all documents from the queue.

3. Close the print queue window.

4. Double-click the printer in the Devices And Printers window to display the window for the printer.

5. In the printer's window, review the information about that printer.

6. Use the commands to check the status of the printer, to customize the settings, and to change the print options. Use any additional links or information to get support and/or supplies from the manufacturer, if these are available.

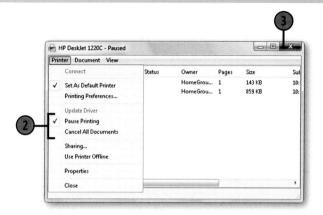

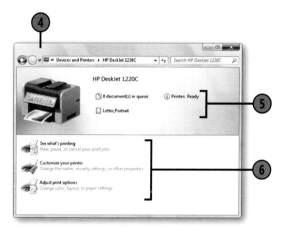

> **Tip**
>
> The information displayed in the printer's window depends on items supplied by the manufacturer, so the information for each printer will be different. Some printers that don't support supplying this information display the print queue window instead. In this case, right-click the printer, and choose Printer Preferences or Printer Properties from the shortcut menu.

# Printing Your Photographs

In the past, printing your photographs used to be quite a challenge; depending on their format and resolution, your pictures might have been printed in different sizes or in different orientations on the page. Windows 7 now makes your life a lot easier by providing a wizard that lets you lay out the pictures just as you want them, so you get exactly the desired results every time.

## Print the Photos

1. In the Pictures Library, select all the photos you want to print, and click Print.

2. In the Print Pictures window, select your printer and the printer settings you want. The printer settings will differ depending on which printer you chose.

3. Select the layout you want.

4. Click Options to display the Print Settings dialog box if you want to make additional printer settings.

5. Select this check box to enlarge or crop each photo to a specified size.

6. Specify the number of copies you want of each photo.

7. Look at the preview to verify that the pictures will be printed the way you want. Use the arrows to view all your pages.

8. Click Print to print the photos.

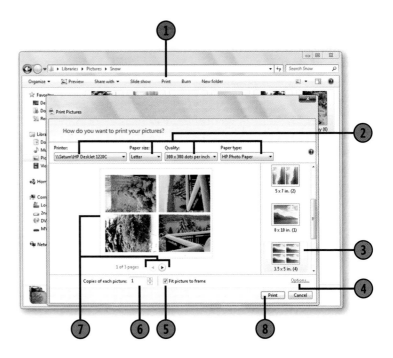

**Tip**

To send your pictures over the Internet to a photo-printing service, in the Pictures Library, select the photos you want, and click Preview. In the Windows Photo Viewer, click Print, and choose Order Prints from the drop-down menu.

# Printing Web Pages

Perhaps you've visited a Web page or site whose content you found interesting or informative enough that you wanted to print it out for yourself or for someone else to read, only to find that the printed result was less than satisfactory. You ended up with odd-looking pages filled with cut-off text, for example, and an indecipherable hodgepodge of disconnected graphics, tables, frames, and text. Now, however, using Internet Explorer, you can convert Web pages into a printable form. All you need to do is specify how you want the pages to be set up, take a quick look at the layout to make sure it includes the items you want to print, and then print the pages.

## Fix the Layout

1️⃣ With the Web page you want to print displayed in Internet Explorer, click the down arrow at the right of the Print button, and choose Print Preview from the drop-down menu to display the Print Preview window so that you can preview the page.

2️⃣ Select the orientation you want for the printed page.

3️⃣ Click the Page Setup button to display the Page Setup dialog box, in which you can change the paper size, the margins, the header and footer information, and the font; include the background colors and images; or disable the shrink-to-fit feature. Click OK when you've finished.

4️⃣ Click this button to specify whether you want to show or hide the header and footer.

5️⃣ Click these options to adjust your view of the page or pages.

6️⃣ Select the *scaling* to fit the material onto the printed page. Select Shrink To Fit to automatically scale the page so that the entire width of the Web page is included, or select a scaling value for a custom fit.

7️⃣ Examine the layout based on your changes, and then click Print to print the Web page, or click Close to return to the normal view without printing the page.

Page Setup button

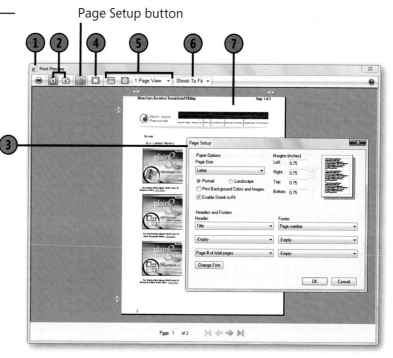

# Creating an XPS Document

The XPS file format is a universal format that produces a document that looks exactly the same as it looked originally, regardless of which computer you use to open or print the document. To create an XPS document, you print it to the Microsoft XPS Document Writer from whichever program you used to create the content.

## Create a Document

**1** Create or open a document or another item—a photo, for example—in the program you normally use, and choose to print it to display the Print dialog box. If the program doesn't display the Print dialog box or doesn't let you choose a printer before printing, set the Microsoft XPS Document Writer as your default printer.

**2** In the Print dialog box, select Microsoft XPS Document Writer if it isn't already selected, make any other settings you want, and then click Print.

**3** In the Save The File As dialog box that appears, specify where you want the file to be stored.

**4** Enter a name for the file.

**5** Click Save to create the file.

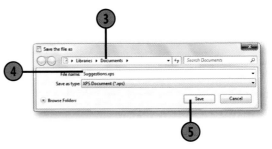

---

**Tip**

XPS stands for XML Paper Specification, and XPS documents are usually viewed either with a dedicated XPS viewer or with Internet Explorer that has an XPS viewer add-on. Windows 7 comes with an XPS viewer. If you're using a different operating system, you can download an XPS viewer from Microsoft.

# Scanning a Picture into Paint

You can scan any item—a drawing, a newspaper article, a piece of patterned fabric—directly into Windows Paint, using the settings you want, provided the scanner uses a WIA (Windows Image Acquisition) driver rather than a TWAIN (yes, this *really* stands for Technology Without An Interesting Name) driver. Then you can save the scan of the item in the format and location you want.

## Scan a Picture

1. In Windows Paint, choose From Scanner Or Camera from the Paint menu to display the Scan dialog box.

2. Select the type of scan result you want.

3. If you want to modify the settings, click Adjust The Quality Of The Scanned Picture to display the Advanced Properties dialog box.

4. Make any changes you want, and click OK.

5. Click Preview to make a quick scan of the picture and then preview the scan.

6. If the selected area doesn't match your item or the part of it you want, drag the handles in the preview to adjust the selected area.

7. Click Scan.

8. Preview the scan in Paint, and make any modifications you want. When you've finished, click the Paint button, choose Save from the drop-down menu, and save the scan in the file format and location you want.

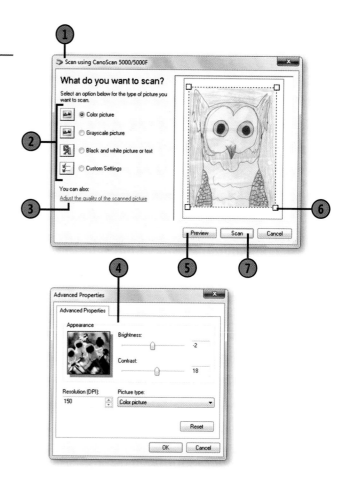

**Tip**

If your scanner doesn't use a WIA driver, the From Scanner Or Camera command won't be available. In that case, check with the scanner manufacturer to see whether there's a WIA driver available; otherwise, use the software that came with your scanner to make your scans.

# Scanning Anything

A scanner is an excellent tool for creating digitized images of printed documents, photos, drawings, fabrics, and so on, and making them available on your computer. The Windows Fax And Scan program provides tools to scan and manage the scanned files.

## Scan an Item

1. Click the Start button, type **scan** in the Search box of the Start menu, and choose Windows Fax And Scan from the menu to start the Windows Fax And Scan program.

2. If it isn't already selected, click Scan to switch to Scan view.

3. Click New Scan.

4. Make any changes to your settings in the New Scan dialog box.

5. Click Preview to make a quick scan of the item, and then preview the scan. Make any settings changes you want—brightness, for example—and click Preview again.

6. Drag the handles of the selection rectangle, if necessary, to include the entire item or only the part of it that you want.

7. Click Scan, and wait for the item to be scanned.

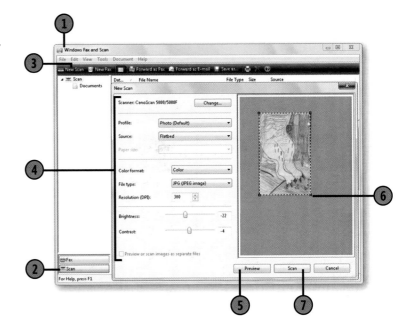

> **See Also**
>
> "Understanding E-Mail Clients and Webmail" on page 239 for information about e-mail clients and other mail programs.

> **Caution**
>
> To use the Windows scanning program, the scanner must use a Windows Image Acquisition driver (WIA) rather than a TWAIN driver. To e-mail the scan from the program, you must have an e-mail client installed. To fax the scan from the program, you need to have a fax modem or a fax server available.

## Manage Your Scans

Toggle Preview Pane button

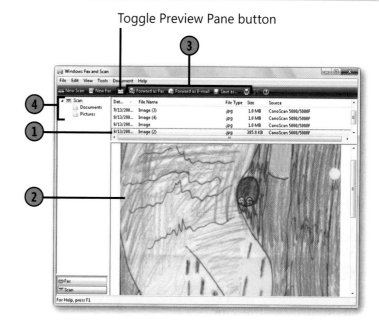

1. Click a scan to select it.

2. Use the Preview pane to preview your scan. If the Preview pane isn't visible, click the Toggle Preview Pane button to display it.

3. Click any of the following:

   - Forward As Fax to send the image as a fax

   - Forward As E-Mail to enclose the image in an e-mail message

   - Save As to save the image in a different location, with a different name and/or in a different format

   - Print to display the Print Pictures dialog box and to print the scan in the size and orientation you want

4. To organize your scans by type, right-click Scan, choose New Folder from the shortcut menu, and name the new folder. Select the scans you want to move into that folder, right-click one of them, and choose Move To from the shortcut menu. In the Move To dialog box, select the new folder you just created and named, and then click OK.

**See Also**

"Sending a Fax" on pages 230–231 for information about using the Windows Fax And Scan program to send faxes.

**Try This!**

If you have Windows Live Photo Gallery installed and open, choose Import From A Camera Or Scanner from the File menu. In the New Scan dialog box that appears, make any changes you want, and then click Scan. In the Importing Pictures And Videos dialog box that appears, type a tag for the scan, and click Import. Note that the scan goes directly into your Pictures Library.

# Quickly Scanning an Item

You can quickly scan an item by pressing the Scan button on your scanner, and the item will be scanned using your default scan profile. All you need to do is select the appropriate profile, make any modifications to it that you want, and—provided no other program has been programmed to respond to the scanner's Scan button—you're all set.

## Choose Your Scanning Settings

**1** Click the Start button, type **scan** in the Search box of the Start menu, and choose Windows Fax And Scan from the menu to start the Windows Fax And Scan program. From the Tools menu, choose Scan Settings to display the Scan Profiles dialog box.

**2** If you want to modify a profile, select it, and click Edit. To create a new profile from scratch, click Add.

**3** In either the Edit Profile or the Add New Profile dialog box, type a name for the profile.

**4** With an item typical of what you'll be scanning placed in the scanner, click Preview, and wait for the item to be scanned. Modify the settings, and preview the scan again until you're satisfied with the settings.

**5** Click Save Profile.

**6** Select the profile you want to use.

**7** Click Set As Default.

**8** Click Close, and then close the Windows Fax And Scan program.

**9** When you want to scan a document, press the Scan button on the scanner. The Windows Fax And Scan program will open, and the item will be scanned using your default profile.

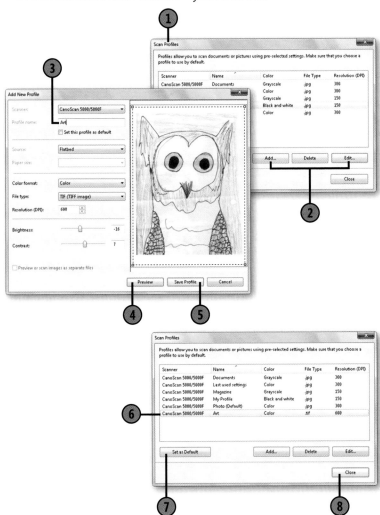

# 12 Communicating

The ability to communicate electronically is one of a computer's most used and most valued features. However, although Windows 7 provides support for the necessary communication tools, it doesn't provide many of those tools. So, first we'll talk about the features that are built into Windows 7, and then we'll discuss some add-on programs that you might find helpful.

Microsoft Fax And Scan, one of the built-in programs, lets you send a fax without needing a printed copy of what you're faxing and makes it possible for you to receive a fax as an electronic file. You can then forward the received fax as a fax or as an e-mail, or you can print it out for your records. Internet Explorer 8 is another powerful gateway to various types of communication, giving you—among other options—access to Web-based e-mail accounts. Another program, Windows Explorer, works with your e-mail program so that you can easily send photos and other files in an e-mail. And your Contacts folder is a great way to organize and access information about all your contacts.

If you want more tools, you can download some of the Windows Live programs. Live Mail is a powerful mail client you can install on your computer; it adds even more power from the Web when you sign in. Other useful Windows Live programs are Live Messenger, Live Call, and Live Writer.

# E-Mailing Your Photos

We all want to share those wonderful pictures we've taken of our families, our friends, our pets, our gardens. If you have an e-mail client installed on your computer, Windows 7 makes it oh, so easy—just select the pictures and send them on their way. What's really useful is that Windows 7 gives you the ability to set the size of your pictures, so you can send several at a time without incurring the wrath of your e-mail service provider for overloading the system—or the eye-rolling of the recipient when the pictures take an hour to download! Also, if you size the pictures, they'll fit nicely on a screen when viewed.

## Send Your Photos

1. In your Pictures Library, click a picture you want to send. If you want to send several pictures, hold down the Ctrl key and click each picture.

2. Click the E-Mail button. If there is no E-Mail button, you don't have a compatible e-mail client installed and set up as your default program for e-mail.

3. In the Attach Files dialog box, select the size (in pixels) at which you want the pictures to be sent.

4. Click Attach.

5. In the mail message that appears, address your message, modify the subject and text if necessary, and then click Send.

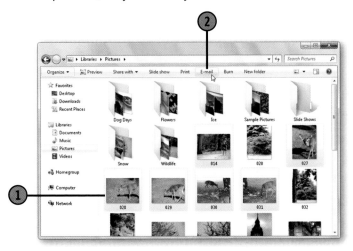

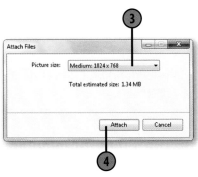

> **See Also**
>
> "Understanding E-Mail Clients and Webmail" on page 239 for information about the differences between using an e-mail client and using Webmail.
>
> "Sending Photos with Windows Live Mail" on page 244 for information about using Windows Live Mail features to share your photos.

# E-Mailing Your Files

If you have an e-mail program installed on your computer, you can easily e-mail files to friends and colleagues. Windows helps you by taking the file or files you select and starting a new message in your default e-mail program; it then attaches the file or files to the message. All you have to do is complete the message and send it to the people who need it.

## E-Mail Your Files

① In Windows Explorer, open the folder or the library that contains the file or files you want to send.

② Select the file or files.

③ Right-click a file. If you've selected multiple files, right-click any selected file.

④ In the shortcut menu that appears, point to Send To, and click Mail Recipient.

⑤ In the e-mail message that appears, address the message, add any content you want, and send the message.

⑥ Switch to your e-mail program, and verify that the message was sent.

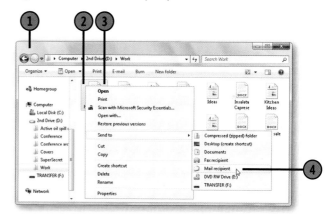

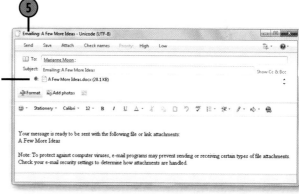

The file is attached to the message.

**Tip**

If Windows recognizes the type of file you're sending as being a document or a picture, the E-Mail button will appear on the toolbar of Windows Explorer, and you can then click the button to e-mail the selected file or files. However, if you choose the Mail Recipient command from the Send To submenu of the shortcut menu, you can send any type of file, and you can even send an entire folder.

# Sending a Fax

With the Windows Fax And Scan program, you can send a fax directly from your computer, whether it's a single document or a collection of items. You can also decide whether or not to include a cover page.

## Fax a Document

**1** Open or create the document in its program, and then choose Print from either the File menu or the program menu.

**2** In the Print dialog box that appears, choose Fax as your printer, and make any other changes you want to the settings. Click Print.

**3** In the New Fax window that appears, select a cover page if you want to use one. If this is the first time you're using a cover page, complete the user and fax information.

**4** Enter the fax recipients in any of the following ways, separating each entry with a semicolon:

- Type the contact's name, and then click the Confirm Recipient button.

- Click the To button, select the recipient or recipients, click To, and then click OK.

- Click the Fax Number Properties button, enter the recipient's name, fax number, and long-distance calling details, and then click OK.

- Type the entire fax number.

**5** Type a subject for the fax, and add any notes you want to appear on the cover page.

**6** Select a dialing rule if you want to use specific calling rules.

**7** Enter any text that you want to include on a page that comes after a cover page and before the first page of your document.

**8** Click Send.

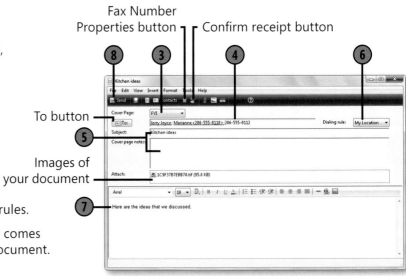

Fax Number Properties button — Confirm receipt button

To button

Images of your document

# Fax Anything

① Click the Start button, type **fax** in the Search box of the Start menu, and choose Windows Fax And Scan from the menu to open the Windows Fax And Scan program.

② Click New Fax to display the New Fax window.

③ Select a cover page if you want one, and complete the information you want to appear on the cover page. Enter the fax number or the contact's name; then enter the subject, and select a dialing rule.

④ Type the text you want, and format it using the formatting tools.

⑤ Click to insert the contents of a file.

⑥ Click to insert a picture from a file.

⑦ Click to scan an item and insert it into the fax.

⑧ Click to preview the fax. Click again to close the preview.

⑨ When you've finished, click Send.

**See Also**

"Setting Up Your Modem" on page 282 for information about setting up dialing rules for long-distance calling.

"Set Up the Fax" on page 288 for information about configuring your fax settings, and "Personalize the Fax" on page 289 for information about entering the Sender Information and creating a custom cover page.

**Tip**

The cover page is a separate page sent with your fax. It usually contains information about the sender, such as the sender's name and contact information, the company name, and the name of the recipient of the fax. The cover page is usually a document you can use repeatedly, with the contact information filled in from the Sender Information you've completed, and the address of the recipient, the subject, and any notes you want to add in the New Fax window.

# Receiving a Fax

If you have a computer equipped with a fax modem and connected to a phone line, you can receive faxes directly on the computer. If the line is a dedicated line, you can have the computer receive incoming faxes automatically. However, if the line is used for both voice and faxes, you can set it to answer the call as a fax call only when you tell it to.

## Manually Receive a Fax

①  When you receive a phone call and a notification that the line is ringing, click to receive the call.

②  In the Windows Fax And Scan Fax Monitor that appears, click the View Details button to see the details of the call, if they're not displayed already. (Note that after you've used the View Details button, it changes into the Hide Details button.)

③  Close the Windows Fax And Scan window if you don't want it on your Desktop, or leave it open to answer and track future faxes.

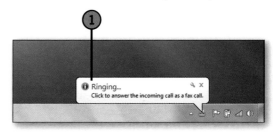

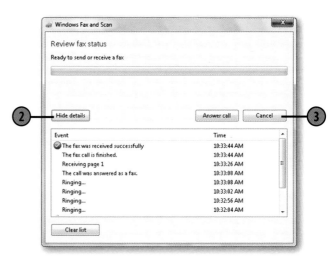

**See Also**

"Setting Up for Faxing" on pages 288–289 for information about permitting faxes to be received, setting automatic or manual answering, displaying notifications, and setting your fax identification name.

**Tip**

You can also manually answer calls by clicking the Answer Call button in the Windows Fax And Scan Fax Monitor or by clicking the Receive A Fax Now button in the Windows Fax And Scan program.

## View a Fax

Preview button

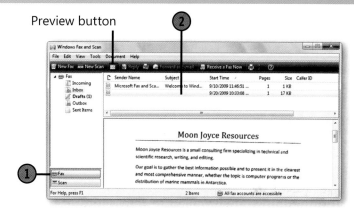

1. Open the Windows Fax And Scan program if it isn't already running. If Fax view isn't showing, click Fax.

2. Click the new fax. If a preview of the fax isn't shown, click the Preview button.

3. Double-click the fax name to open the Fax Message window.

4. Review the fax.

5. Use any of the commands to print, to reply with a fax, or to forward the fax as a fax or as e-mail.

6. Use the Next or the Previous button if you want to view another fax.

7. Close the Fax Message window when you've finished.

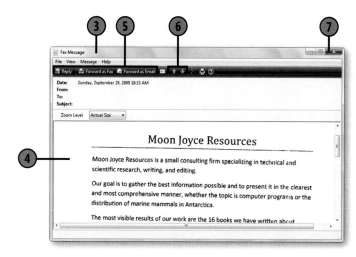

**Tip**

Many commercial faxes are sent with little additional information, so these types of faxes might not show the sender's name and/or the subject. However, the banner at the top of the fax should include some sender information.

# Connecting with Your Contacts

You can use your Windows Contacts folder to keep all sorts of information about your contacts in addition to their e-mail addresses. You can include their home and workplace addresses and phone numbers, their birthdays and anniversaries, their family members, and so on. You can access this information from numerous programs or directly from your Contacts folder.

## Enter Your Contacts

1. Click the Start button, type **contacts** in the Search box of the Start menu, and choose Contacts from the menu to open the Contacts window.

2. Click New Contact.

3. On the various tabs of the Properties dialog box that appears, enter the information you want to record. You can include as much or little as you like, but you'll need a valid e-mail address if you intend to send e-mail to that contact.

4. To include an identifying picture, click here, and choose Change Picture from the menu that appears. In the Select A Picture For Contact window, locate and select the picture you want, and click Set.

5. Click OK.

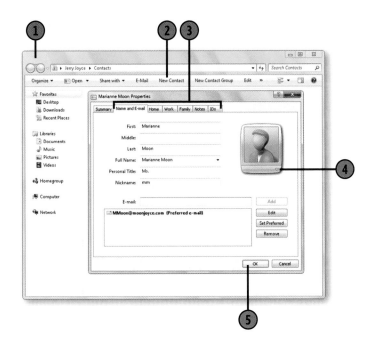

**Caution**

Don't confuse the contacts in your Contacts folder with the contacts list created in your e-mail program. Although they might contain similar information, that information isn't automatically shared between the Contacts folder and your e-mail program. You can, however, use import and export tools to make sure that you have the same information in both locations.

**See Also**

"Sharing Your Contacts" on pages 236–237 for information about exchanging contacts information.

## Use Your Contacts

1. In the Contacts window, double-click a contact to open the Properties dialog box. Review the information, and close the Properties dialog box when you've finished.

2. To send e-mail, click the contact's name to select it, and then click E-Mail to start an e-mail message to the contact, using your default e-mail client.

3. To make a phone call to a contact using the modem on your computer, right-click the contact's name, point to Action on the shortcut menu, and choose Call This Contact from the submenu. In the New Call dialog box that appears, select the correct phone number, and place the call.

4. To create a printed copy of the contact information, select the contact or contacts you want, and click Print.

5. In the Print dialog box, select your printer to print information for the selected contacts or for all your contacts, specifying the print style and the number of copies you want. Click Print.

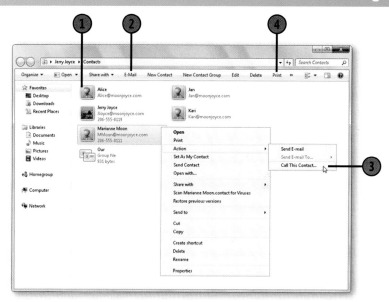

**See Also**

"Setting Up a Modem" on page 282 for information about configuring your dialing rules before you make your first phone call.

"Understanding E-Mail Clients and Webmail" on page 239 for information about mail clients.

# Sharing Your Contacts

Contact information can contain as little as a name and an e-mail address, or it can be rich with information: home and workplace mailing addresses and phone numbers, notes about the family, birthdays and other significant dates, and even digital certificates for keeping your messages secure. You can share a single contact or even all your contacts with others using *vCards*, a popular electronic business-card format used by many programs. You can also include contact information from others in your Contacts folder.

## Send Contact Information by E-Mail

**1** Click the Start button, type **contacts** in the Search box of the Start menu, and choose Contacts from the menu to open the Contacts window.

**2** If you have an e-mail client on your computer, right-click the contact you want to send, and choose Send Contact from the shortcut menu.

**3** Complete the e-mail message that appears, and send the message with the business card.

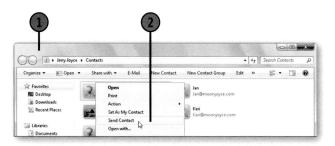

The contact information is attached as a business card.

> **Tip** ✓
>
> You can share an individual contact with other people on your network by selecting the contact, clicking Share With, and specifying with whom you want to share the contact information. You can share the entire Contacts folder by selecting the folder and clicking Share With.

> **Caution** !
>
> If you transfer contact information from your Contacts folder without using either the Send Contact or the Export command, the contact files will be in the Contacts file format instead of the in the vCard format. The Contacts file format isn't compatible with as many e-mail programs as is the vCard format.

> **Tip** ✓
>
> If you want to export contacts from, or import them into, an e-mail or other contacts program that doesn't support the vCard format, use the CSV (Comma-Separated Values) format. This format can also be used to import or export contact information to or from a database or a spreadsheet.

## Share Multiple Contacts

**1** In the Contacts window, click Export to display the Export Windows Contacts dialog box.

**2** Select vCards from the list, and click Export. In the Browse For Folder dialog box that appears, specify where you want all the contact files to be stored, and click OK.

**3** Share the vCards you exported with other people as attachments in e-mails, on your network, or by using a portable storage device.

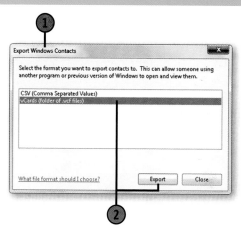

## Receive Contacts

**1** In your Contacts window, click Import to display the Import To Windows Contacts dialog box.

**2** Select vCard, and click Import.

**3** In the Select A vCard File For Import dialog box that appears, locate and select the vCard or vCards you want to import, and click OK.

# Creating a Contacts Group

If you frequently send one message to the same group of people, you can gather all their addresses into a *group*, and then all you need to do is enter the group name to send the message to all the individuals. It's a real time-saver.

## Create a Group

**1** Click the Start button, type **contacts** in the Search box of the Start menu, and choose Contacts from the menu to open the Contacts window. In the Contacts folder, click New Contact Group.

**2** On the Contact Group tab of the Properties dialog box, type a descriptive name, or *alias*, for the group.

**3** Click Add To Contact Group.

**4** In the Add Members To Contact Group dialog box, click to select the name of a person you want to include in the group. Hold down the Ctrl key and continue clicking names until the contact-group list is complete.

**5** Click Add.

**6** Type the name and e-mail address of a person you want to add to the list but don't want to save as a contact, and then click Create For Group Only.

**7** Add any further information to the Contact Group Details tab.

**8** Click OK.

**Tip**

When you use a group, the names of all the individual members are still listed in the e-mail. If you want to send an e-mail without showing the names of all the recipients, add their names or their group only to the Bcc line in the e-mail.

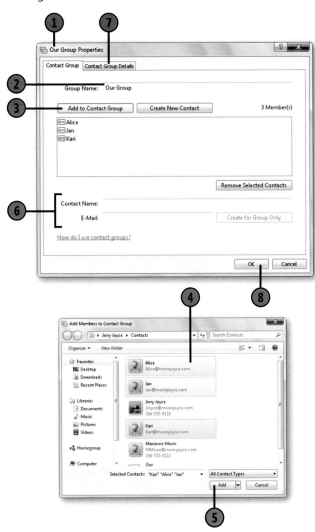

# Understanding E-Mail Clients and Webmail

Windows Live Mail is a popular, easy-to-use e-mail program, but it's just one of many options you can use to read and send e-mail. The ways you can handle your e-mail fall into two main categories. You can use a program that's installed on your computer—an *e-mail client*—or you can use your Web browser to use Webmail. Whichever e-mail program you use, however, it has the same function: connecting you to an e-mail server that stores your received e-mail and sends your outgoing e-mail along its way on the Internet. Although the function is the same, the functionality is different, and each category has advantages and disadvantages. Understanding these differences will help you have the best experience with your e-mail.

**An e-mail client** is a program that exists on your computer. It downloads messages from the e-mail server to your computer, and it sends the messages you write from your computer to the e-mail server. You can also use a single e-mail client to access more than one e-mail account. Your e-mail client provides tools to help you compose and read your messages, read and save attachments, and organize your e-mail. Your e-mail client also helps you customize the way you manage your messages, including letting you automatically delete a message from the e-mail server once the message has been downloaded. Other than its ease of use, another advantage of your e-mail client is that the downloaded messages are available on the computer even when you're not connected to the Internet or another network. Also, with an e-mail client on your computer, you can take advantage of the Windows 7 commands to e-mail items such as pictures or other files. Some examples of e-mail clients are Windows Live Mail, Microsoft Outlook, Eudora, and Opera Mail.

**Webmails** are Web programs that allow you to access your e-mail using your Web browser. This means that you can access your e-mail and your Contacts list from any computer that connects to the Internet. However, the working interface is often less helpful in managing and composing messages than the e-mail clients are. Webmail often offers connections to additional features, including online and shared calendars. Some examples of Webmail are Hotmail, Gmail, and Yahoo. Many e-mail servers also support e-mail clients and Webmail.

Whichever type of e-mail interface you're using, many of its features are determined by the functionality of the e-mail server. For example, some e-mail servers allow you to create an automated out-of-office message; other servers don't. In order to get the best service from your e-mail, find out what features are available to you from the e-mail server so that you'll get the most from your e-mail client or your Webmail. Unfortunately, because there are so many different choices, we're unable to cover every option in detail. For information about setting up your e-mail accounts, see "Setting Up Windows Live Essentials Programs" on page 285 and "Setting Up Windows Live Mail" on pages 286–287.

# Using Windows Live Mail

Windows Live Mail is a downloadable multipurpose tool with many options. You can use it for sending and retrieving e-mail with most types of e-mail accounts, for keeping track of your appointments using the Calendar, for reading RSS feeds, and for reading and posting messages to Internet newsgroups. If you sign in to a Windows Live account, you can also synchronize your Live Mail information with the content of your online Live account, including mail messages, calendar entries, and contacts. Signing in with a Live account also provides additional features, such as online storage of high-resolution copies of your photos when you're using Photo E-Mail.

## Use Windows Live Mail

1. If Windows Live Mail isn't already running, click the Start button, type **mail** in the Search box of the Start menu, and choose Windows Live Mail from the menu to start Windows Live Mail.

2. If you haven't yet signed in to a Windows Live account, and if you want to, click the Sign In button.

3. Click one of the shortcuts to access the feature you want.

4. Use the appropriate buttons to take the actions you want.

5. To modify the color scheme of your window, click the Colorizer button, and choose the color you want.

6. Click to see the most common menu commands. Choose Show Menu Bar from the drop-down menu if you want to see all the menus with all the available commands.

**Tip**

A Windows Live ID is associated with one of several types of accounts provided by Microsoft. For more information about these accounts, click the Sign In button.

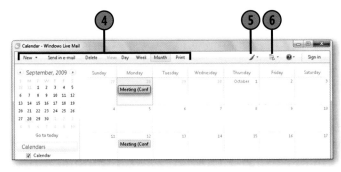

# Sending E-Mail with Windows Live Mail

Most of us can't imagine life without e-mail! You don't have to address an envelope or trek to the mailbox on a cold, rainy day. With Windows Live Mail, all you do is type a name, create a message, and click a Send button. The Windows Live Mail client and your e-mail server do the rest. What could be quicker or more convenient?

## Create a Message

**①** With Windows Live Mail running, click Mail if it isn't already selected.

**②** Click New.

**③** In the New Message window that appears, start typing the recipient's name. If the name you want is selected in the drop-down list, press Enter. If you want a different recipient from the list, either continue typing the name until it becomes selected, or click the name in the list. To add more names, type a semicolon (;), and then type all or part of another recipient's name.

**④** Press Tab to move to the Subject line, type a subject, and press Tab again to move into the message area.

**⑤** Type your message. Use any of the formatting tools to format your message.

**⑥** Click Send to send the message.

**⑦** Click Sync to send the messages in the Outbox to your e-mail server.

**Tip**

To send an e-mail to someone who isn't in your Contacts list without adding that person to the list, simply type his or her e-mail address in the To line.

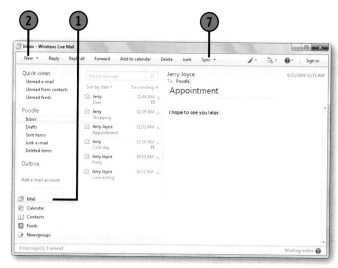

Click if you want to send a copy of the message to others.

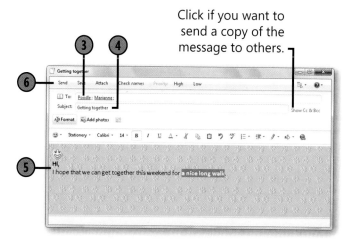

# E-Mailing a File with Windows Live Mail

A great way to share a file, or several files—a Microsoft Word document, a picture, or even an entire Web page—is to include it as part of an e-mail message. The file is included as a separate part of the message—an *attachment*—that the recipient can save and open at any time. Although the procedure we show here is specific to Windows Live Mail, most e-mail clients and Webmail programs use very similar procedures.

## Send a File by E-Mail

① Use Windows Live Mail to create a message to your intended recipient, including the e-mail address, subject, and any accompanying text.

② Click the Attach button.

③ Locate and select the file in the Open dialog box. If you want to send multiple files, hold down the Ctrl key as you select each file.

④ Click Open.

⑤ Click Send to send the message just as you'd send any other message.

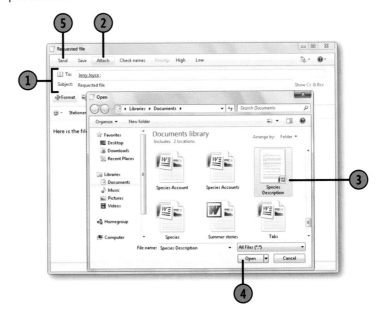

---

**See Also**

"Sharing Files with Other Users" on page 44, "Sharing with Selected Users" on page 45, and "Copying Files to a CD or DVD" on pages 46–47 for information about other ways to transfer files.

"Sending Photos with Windows Live Mail" on page 244 for information about creating a specialized photo e-mail.

"Setting Up Windows Live Mail" on pages 286–287 for information about setting up e-mail accounts in Windows Live Mail.

---

**Tip**

If you include photos as attachments, Windows Live Mail might ask you whether you want to turn the message into a photo e-mail. Click No if you simply want to transfer the photo files to the recipient; click Yes if you want to create a specialized e-mail to display your photos.

## Receive an Attachment

**(1)** Select a message you've received that contains an attachment.

**(2)** Right-click the attachment's name.

**(3)** Choose the action you want from the shortcut menu:

- Open to open the selected file using the default program for that type of file.

- Print to print the selected file using your default printer. (You must have a program on your computer that's capable of opening this type of file to be able to print it.)

- Save As to save the attachment in its original format in a location you select.

- Save All to save all the attachments in the message (or those that you select in the Save Attachments dialog box that appears) in their original file formats to a single location that you select.

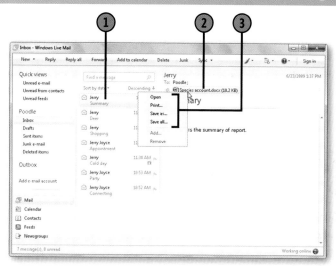

**See Also**

"Compressing Files" on pages 48–49 for information about using compressed folders.

"E-Mailing Your Files" on page 229 for information about quickly attaching a file to an e-mail message using any e-mail client program.

"Transferring Files" on page 259 for information about various methods of transferring files.

**Caution**

Viruses are often distributed in attached files, so *don't* open an attachment from an unknown sender, and *do* make sure that you have a good anti-virus program installed on your computer.

**Tip**

Different e-mail systems can send or receive different sizes of attachments—some as small as or smaller than 1 MB and others as large as 10 MB or more. If you need to transfer a large file or numerous files, try compressing the file or files, or use a different transferral method.

# Sending Photos with Windows Live Mail

Windows Live Mail has a special functionality called Photo E-Mail that you can use when you're sending photos. When you add photos to your message, Live Mail provides some photo-editing and layout tools. When you send the e-mail message, smaller, lower-resolution versions of the photos are included in the message, and the original photo files are stored on a Web server. The recipient then has the opportunity to view the photos as a slide show on a Web page, to select individual files to download and view, or to download and save all the photo files.

## Add Your Photos

**1** If Live Mail isn't already running, click the Start button, type **mail** in the Search box of the Start menu, and choose Windows Live Mail from the menu to start Live Mail. If you haven't yet signed in to a Windows Live account, sign in now. Click New to display a New Message window. Address the message as you normally would. Add any introductory text you want.

**2** Click Add Photos.

**3** In the Add Photos dialog box, select the photos you want to include.

**4** Click Add. Continue selecting photos until you have all the items you want, and then click Done.

**5** Click Layout.

**6** Choose the layout you want.

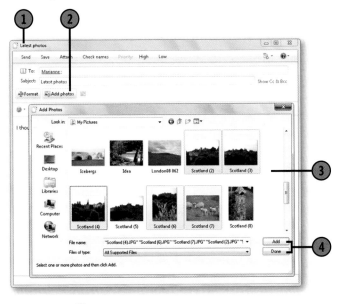

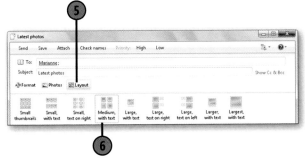

> **Tip**
>
> You can start a new message and automatically display the Add Photos dialog box by clicking the down arrow at the right of the New button and choosing Photo E-Mail from the drop-down menu.

## Format the Photos

1. Click Photos.

2. Choose the borders you want for all the photos. Click Border Color if you want to change the color of the borders.

3. Click each photo, and make whatever changes you want to individualize the photo:

   • Click one of the editing tools to modify the photo.

   • Add a label or other text. Click Format to format the text.

   • Click a different border and/or choose a different border color.

4. Select the resolution you want to use. Note the upload time and total size of all the files.

5. Click Send.

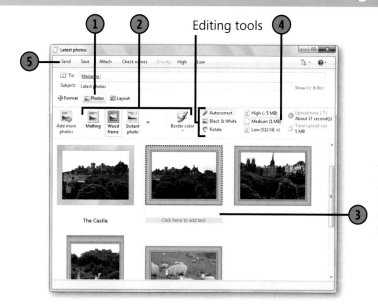

Editing tools

**Tip**

If you haven't signed in to a Windows Live account, the Upload Time and the Total Upload Size information won't be available. Additionally, the photos included in the e-mail won't have any links to the higher-resolution photos.

**See Also**

"E-Mailing Your Photos" on page 228 for information about sending your photos by e-mail without signing in using a Windows Live ID.

# Communicating with Windows Live

You can install many, many programs on your computer that provide you with all sorts of ways to communicate. Which programs you choose depend on your needs, your budget, and perhaps the need to be compatible with what someone else is using on his or her computer. Microsoft provides a set of Windows Live programs that are designed to work seamlessly with Windows 7 and that you can download for free. Depending on your needs, you can download a group of the programs and install all of them at once, or you can select only those that fit your needs. Microsoft continues to develop the Windows Live programs, and will make additional ones available when they're ready for release. Following are descriptions of the communications programs that were available at the time this book was written.

**Windows Live Messenger** is a multifunctional communications program. Unlike the way most of the other Windows Live programs work, you can use the program only after you've signed in with a Windows Live ID. What you can do with Windows Live Messenger depends on the hardware you have in your computer system and on the way you connect to the Internet. Communications can be as simple as sending an instant message to a contact or as complex as having a voice and video meeting. However, Live Messenger is designed primarily for social networking, and for sending and responding to instant text messages with your friends. You can also use it to share or transfer files, including photos. With a good sound card, you can have voice conversations, and, with a Webcam, you can let a contact view your Webcam, hold a video call, or watch a contact's Webcam. When you're using video, you can connect with only a single contact, and you need a fast Internet connection. To explore what you can do, with Messenger running and with yourself signed in, move the mouse over various contacts and see some actions you can perform. To see everything you can do, press the Alt key to display and explore each menu.

**Windows Live Call** is a subscription-based service you can use to make calls from your computer to someone's telephone. Live Call is integrated into Live Messenger, but, after you've signed in to Live Messenger, you can also start Live Call from the Start menu. The calls are routed over the Internet for most of their way, so long-distance and international calls are inexpensive, but this service is available only in some locations.

**Windows Live Mail** handles your e-mail, of course, but you can do a lot more with it because it incorporates Calendar, Feeds, and Newsgroups. **Calendar** lets you keep track of your schedule, and you can view other people's shared calendars and see their schedules. If you share your calendar, friends and colleagues can also see your schedule. When you enter a new event in your calendar, you can send the information to others via e-mail. **Feeds** lets you view the RSS feeds that you've subscribed to. You can forward an entry via e-mail, print an entry, and add or remove the feeds that you're subscribed to. **Newsgroups** provides access to Internet newsgroups so that you can subscribe to those that are of interest to you. When you've subscribed, you can read postings, reply to existing postings, and create your own postings.

**Windows Live Writer** is a special word processor that's designed to help you write blog entries and publish them to your blog. Live Writer is designed for working with several types of blogs, and it lets you add various features, including pictures, a photo album, a table, a map, or a video. It also prevents you from adding certain elements, such as formatting that isn't compatible with a particular blog. When you start Live Writer, you connect it to your blog. With Live Writer configured, you can create a draft entry, save it, check your spelling and word count, and preview the entire entry. When the draft is completed, you can classify the entry by category, set the publication date and time, and then publish the item to your blog.

# 13 Networking

Networking, once a requirement only in large corporations, is now almost a necessity in a multi-computer household, home office, or small business. If your home network has computers running Windows 7, sharing libraries and printers is as simple as joining your homegroup. Even with a mix of operating systems on your network, you can access files and folders on other computers that have been set up for sharing without being part of your homegroup, and you can share the files and folders on your computer with friends and colleagues.

If you want to limit other people's access to certain items—your private files, for example—you can do so. If you're working from home, you can connect to your office network by creating a secure VPN (Virtual Private Network) connection over the Internet, or simply call up the network over your phone line.

If your computer has a wireless network adapter, Windows recognizes the wireless networks that are within range, some of which might be open and free and others that require a security key before you can connect wirelessly. If you don't have a network, you can still connect using an *ad hoc,* or improvised, wireless network.

# Joining a Homegroup

A *homegroup* is an easy and powerful way to share libraries on a home network. When you connect to a homegroup, you can access items on other computers on the network, as well as items stored by different users on the same computer.

However, the Homegroup feature is available only on computers running Windows 7 and only when those computers are connected to a home network.

## Join a Homegroup

1. Start Windows Explorer if it isn't already running, and click Homegroup in the Navigation pane to display the Homegroup window.

2. Click Join Now.

3. In the Join A Homegroup wizard, select the items to be shared.

4. Click Next.

5. Type the password that was supplied by any other member of the homegroup.

6. Click Next, and then click Finish.

**See Also**

"Setting Up a Homegroup" on page 278 for information about creating and managing a homegroup and getting the homegroup password.

**Tip**

You can change the password to set up a homegroup, but you can't customize the homegroup's name. Note that the password is case sensitive, so make sure you type it exactly as it was given to you.

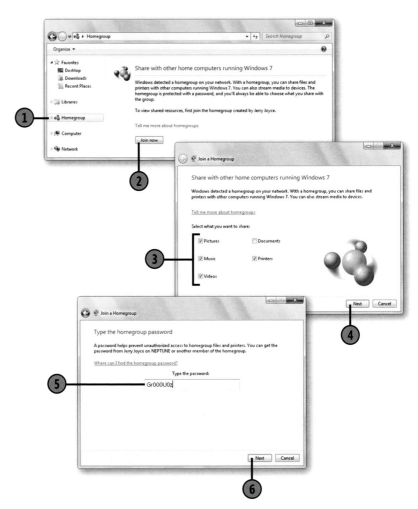

# Accessing Your Homegroup

After you've joined a homegroup, you have access to all the libraries shared in the homegroup by other users. In most cases, you can open, use, or play the files in the libraries, but you can't rename, delete, or change any of them.

## Access Shared Libraries

① Make sure that the computer or computers you want to access are turned on and awake, are connected to the home network, and are members of your homegroup.

② Start Windows Explorer if it isn't already running.

③ In the Navigation pane, click Homegroup.

④ Double-click the member of the homegroup you want to access.

⑤ Double-click a library to access it.

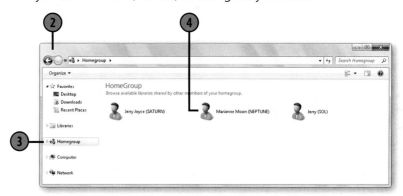

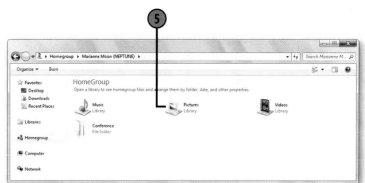

**Tip**

By default, libraries are shared with other members of the homegroup with Read permission. This means that although members of the group can use the file, they can't delete or rename it. They can, however, usually copy the file to their own computers, where they can then do anything they want with it. To allow more control by other people of the files in a library, you can change the sharing permission to Read/Write.

**See Also**

"Sharing Media Libraries on Your Network" on pages 186–187 for information about sharing media libraries.

"Sharing with Your Homegroup" on pages 250–251 for information about changing access permission so that you can modify files.

# Sharing with Your Homegroup

As a member of a homegroup on your home network, you can control which libraries you want to share with other members of the homegroup. You can also decide whether you want to share any printers attached to your computer. If you've created your own custom library, you can also share it with the homegroup.

## Share Your Libraries

**1** Click the Start button, type **home** in the Search box of the Start menu and choose HomeGroup from the menu to open the HomeGroup window.

**2** Select the check boxes for the libraries you want to share, and clear them for libraries you don't want to share.

**3** Select the Printers check box if you want to share the printer or printers attached to your computer, or clear the check box if you don't want to share them.

**4** Select this check box if you want to share your media files with all the devices on your network, including computers that aren't part of the homegroup as well as other devices attached to the network.

**5** Click Save Changes.

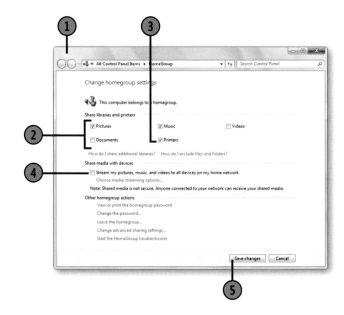

### See Also

"Organizing Library Folders" on pages 50–51 for information about adding folders to, or removing folders from, a library, and for information about creating a new library.

### Tip

If several people use your computer, if even just one person joins his or her computer to the homegroup, all users of the computer (except a Guest User) are then joined to the homegroup. However, none of your own libraries are shared until you allow them to be shared.

## Share a Custom Library

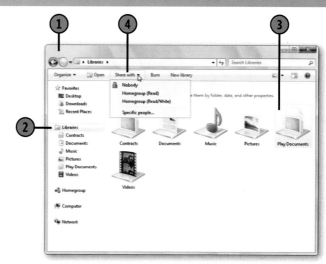

1. Start Windows Explorer if it isn't already running.

2. In the Navigation pane, click Libraries.

3. Select the library you want to share.

4. Click Share With, and choose the option you want from the drop-down menu:

   - Homegroup (Read) to allow access to the files but not to allow any changes to them

   - Homegroup (Read/Write) to allow access and to allow changes to the files

5. If at some point you decide that you no longer want to share this library, repeat steps 1 through 4, but this time, in step 4, choose Nobody from the Share With drop-down menu.

### See Also

"Controlling Homegroup Sharing" on page 252 for information about changing access settings for all your libraries and shared files.

### Try This!

Click Libraries in the Navigation pane of Windows Explorer, and then click the New Library button. Name the new library, and then double-click it. Add any folders you want to the library. Click the Share With button on the toolbar, and specify how you want to share the library with your homegroup.

# Controlling Homegroup Sharing

By default, all the files in the shared libraries are shared, but only with Read permission. This means that other members of the homegroup can view or play the files, but they can't change, delete, or rename them. However, you can allow files in your libraries to be changed, and you can prevent individual files from being shared.

## Allow Changes to a File

1. In Windows Explorer, click Libraries in the Navigation pane.

2. Select the library you want to change.

3. Click Share With, and choose Homegroup (Read/Write).

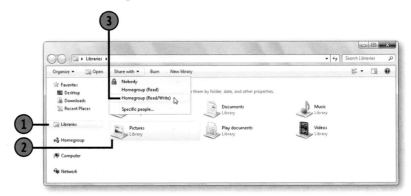

## Prevent Access to a File

1. Select the file.

2. Click Share With, and choose Nobody. The file will be marked with a padlock in your library and won't be visible to other members of the homegroup.

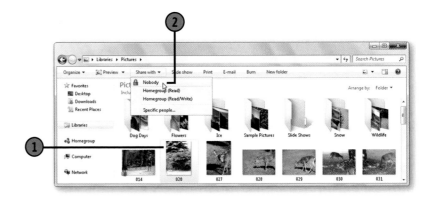

# Understanding Networks in Windows 7

Windows 7 classifies networks into four main categories: Home, Work, Public, and Domain. The Domain network configuration (which isn't available in Windows 7 Home Premium), is used in corporate networks. Each network type has its own default configuration and security settings. However, you can modify many of these settings, creating a custom configuration that's exactly right for the way you work and share information.

A **Home** network is designed...well, to be used at home. It assumes that every computer and device on your network is secure and can be trusted. Computers on the network can be detected by each other, and sharing files, media libraries, and printers is fairly easy. One very useful feature of a home network is its ability to use a homegroup on computers that are running Windows 7. A **Homegroup** provides an easy way to share libraries and printers among users on the same computer and on different computers on the network.

A **Work** network is similar to a home network and is intended to be used in a small-business setting. All the computers on the network are detectable, and the files can be shared. Like a home network, a work network assumes that all the computers and devices on the network are safe and can be trusted. However, you can't create a homegroup on a work network.

A **Public** network is one whose users you don't always know. Because you don't know who's connected to the network, it follows that you can't trust everyone. With the default settings for this configuration, you can't see or access the other computers and devices on the network, and they, likewise, can't see or access your computer. You also can't share files over this type of network. A public network is a useful configuration that helps to protect you from malicious software when you connect to the Internet using wired or wireless access from public places: coffee shops, hotels, airports, and anywhere the network might not be secure. The increased security settings

used in this configuration are also useful on any network when you don't need to access or share anything with any other computers on your network.

A **Domain** network, available in Windows 7 Professional, Enterprise, and Ultimate editions, is designed for a computer that's part of a corporate-type client-server domain. If you're running one of these versions of Windows 7, your computer will be aware of the type of network you're attached to. If, for example, you bring your computer home, it will recognize the home network and switch its settings from the domain network to the home network. The Enterprise and Ultimate versions also provide an easy way to automatically connect to the corporate network over the Internet, called **DirectAccess**.

Even without having the Professional, Enterprise, or Ultimate edition, you might still be able to connect to a corporate network using a specialized connection. Depending on the configuration hosted by the network, you can use a **Virtual Private Network (VPN)** connection over the Internet, or you can use **Remote Access Service (RAS)** using a telephone connection. In these connections, the corporate network uses specialized servers to receive your connection, to verify your identity and access privileges, and then to connect you to the network. Many corporate network administrators now issue a smart card that's necessary for making and verifying a connection. For you to use a smart card, your computer needs to be equipped with a smart-card reader.

An **Ad Hoc** network is another specialized connection among computers that are in close proximity to each other. This temporary network uses the wireless network adapters on the computers to connect directly to each other without using a network router. This type of connection is made by mutual agreement and creates a secure connection, useful for transferring files between computers or playing some multiplayer games.

# Allowing Your Files to Be Shared

You can share your files and folders in your public folders with anyone who uses your computer, or you can share the public folders with anyone who can access your home or work network. You can also share the files or folders on your computer with only specific people or with anyone whose computer is on your network.

## Set Up Sharing Permission

**1** In Windows Explorer, click Network in the Navigation pane, and, in the Network window, click Network And Sharing Center. In the Network And Sharing Center window, click Change Advanced Sharing Settings to display the Advanced Sharing Settings window.

**2** Click Turn On Network Discovery to make your computer visible on the network and to be able to see other computers on the network.

**3** Click this option to allow the files and printers that you've shared to be accessed.

**4** Click the first option to allow people anywhere on your network to access and modify files in your public folders. Select the second option to deny access to these folders over the network but to allow any other users on your computer to access them.

**5** Click the first option for the highest security, or select the second option for greater compatibility with computers that aren't running Windows 7.

**6** Click Turn On Password Protected Sharing to allow sharing only to those with user accounts on your computer, or select the second option to allow access to anyone who can access your network.

**7** Click Save Changes.

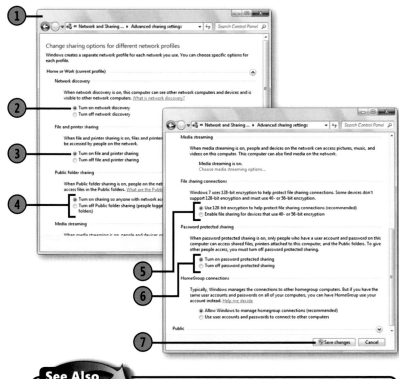

**See Also**

"Sharing Files with Other Users" on page 44 and "Sharing with Selected Users" on page 45 for information about using public folders and setting permissions to share your files over the network.

"Sharing Media Libraries on Your Network" on pages 186–187 for information about using media streaming over your network.

# Viewing Your Network

Windows 7 will automatically explore your home or work network and will look for various computers, devices, and connections, provided you have Network Discovery enabled on your computer. You can then see the structure and status of your connections and what's currently connected and available on the network.

## View the Network

(1) In Windows Explorer, click Network in the Navigation pane, and, in the Network window, click Network And Sharing Center to display the Network And Sharing Center window.

(2) Review the information about your network structure, network type, and type of access.

(3) Click See Full Map.

(4) Examine the computers and devices that are available on the network.

**See Also**

"Allowing Your Files to Be Shared" on the facing page for information about enabling Network Discovery.

**Tip**

Several items in the Network And Sharing Center provide useful shortcuts. Move the mouse pointer over an item and, if the mouse pointer turns into the Link Select pointer (usually a pointing hand), you can click it to make settings or to access locations. In the Network Map, point to a computer or a device to see details about the computer or the device, or right-click it for more options.

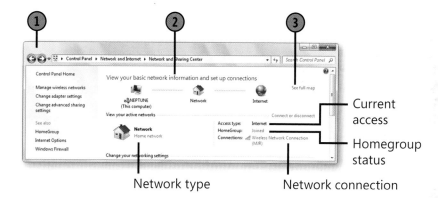

Current access

Homegroup status

Network type

Network connection

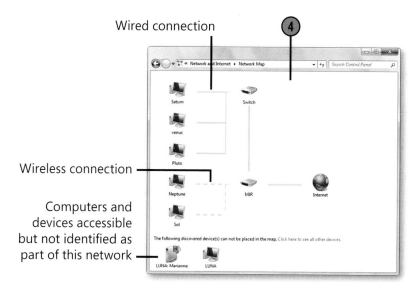

Wired connection

Wireless connection

Computers and devices accessible but not identified as part of this network

# Connecting to a Network Computer

When your computer is connected to a home or work network, and when other computers on the network are set up to share items, you can connect to a computer on the network and access items on that computer. The type of access you have to the contents of another computer depends, as it should, on the sharing settings on that computer to ensure that private files are kept private and public files are made available. Although networking is easiest between computers that are running Windows 7, you can still connect to computers running other types of operating systems, provided those computers are properly configured.

## Connect to a Computer

1. In Windows Explorer, click Network in the Navigation pane.

2. Double-click the computer whose files or folders you want to access. If the Windows Security dialog box appears, enter a user name and password for that computer, and then click OK. The user name and password must be those that have been set up on that network computer.

3. Double-click a folder to access its contents. To access the public folders, double-click Users, double-click Public, and then double-click the public folder you want. Use the folder and its contents as you would any other folder, depending on the permission you've been granted.

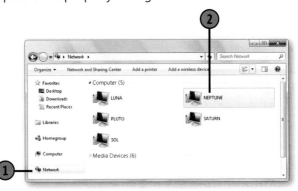

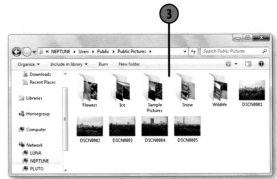

**See Also**

"Sharing Files with Other Users" on page 44 and "Sharing with Selected Users" on page 45 for information about using public folders and setting permissions to share your files over the network.

"Allowing Your Files to Be Shared" on page 254 for information about setting password-protected sharing.

**Tip**

The Windows Security dialog box appears when the network computer has Password Protected Sharing turned on and you're not listed as one of the users on that computer.

## Connect to a Computer That's Not Listed

**1** Click Network in the Navigation pane of Windows Explorer.

**2** If the computer you want to connect to isn't listed, click the Network icon in the Address bar.

**3** Type the address of the computer in the form **\\computername**, with *computername* being the name of the computer on the network. If you were given the full path to a shared folder, type the entire address in the form **\\computername\sharedfolder**, with *sharedfolder* being the name of the folder that's shared on that computer. Then press Enter to locate the computer or the shared folder on the computer.

**4** Use the shared folders as you would any other network folders.

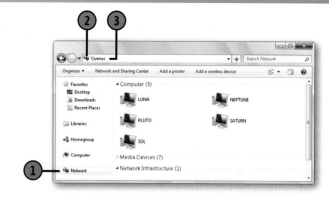

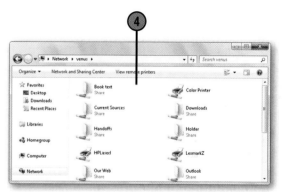

### Try This!

Click Network in the Navigation pane, and then click one of the listed computers. Open a shared folder. Now click the Network folder icon in the Address bar. Note how the address changes to show the traditional path address to that shared folder. You can use this type of path address in the Address bar whenever you want to go directly to a folder, regardless of where it's located.

### See Also

"Adding Direct Access to a Folder or Library" on pages 38–39 for information about adding a folder to a jump list or to the Favorites list in the Navigation pane of Windows Explorer.

"Creating a Connection to a Network Folder" on page 258 for information about creating quick access to a folder using a drive letter for compatibility with certain programs.

### Tip

A computer is usually not listed if it uses an operating system other than Windows or if it uses a version of Windows earlier than Windows XP. A computer running Windows XP might not be visible if it hasn't been updated with the most recent service pack. Computers that have Network Discovery turned off or that haven't been set to share files might not be visible or accessible.

# Creating a Connection to a Network Folder

If you frequently use one particular shared folder on the network, you can access that folder quickly by assigning a drive letter to it. By doing so, you'll not only gain quick access to the folder from Windows Explorer, but you'll also be able to access the folder in programs that don't allow you to browse the network to find a file.

## Assign a Drive

1. Start Windows Explorer if it isn't already running, and click Computer in the Navigation pane.

2. Click Map Network Drive.

3. Select a letter for the drive. Only unused drive letters are shown.

4. Click Browse. In the Browse For Folder dialog box that appears, locate and select the folder you want, and click OK.

5. Select this check box if you always want to connect to this folder. Clear the check box if you want to connect only during this session.

6. Select this check box if you'll be using a different user name and password to log on to the shared folder. In the Windows Security dialog box that appears, enter the user name and password that have been assigned to you, and click OK.

7. Click here to start the Add Network Location wizard if you want to connect to a Web site or to a File Transfer Protocol (FTP) location that you want to use for file storage.

8. Click Finish.

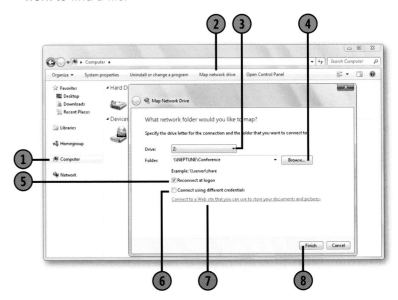

**Tip**

If you know the name and location of the folder you want to connect to, type it in the Folder text box, using the form **\\computer\folder**.

# Transferring Files

In most cases, transferring files is a simple task. For example, if you want to transfer a few small files, you can easily send them by e-mail. You can copy larger or more numerous files to a removable disc or to a removable USB (Universal Serial Bus) memory device. On a home network, you can add the folder containing the files to a library shared with your homegroup, or you can share items with individuals. On a business network, you can simply move the files to a public or shared location or post them to a SharePoint site. There are also more and more Internet sites that provide free storage of files and the ability for other people to access the files and collaborate on the work. However, if you need to transfer a number of large files electronically but none of the foregoing options works for you, there are several possible solutions. Listed below are additional methods for directly transferring files; you should find at least one among them that's appropriate for your situation. To find more information about any of these methods, look in the index of this book and/or search the Windows 7 Help And Support Center.

**Ad Hoc Wireless Connection:** You can create a temporary ad hoc connection between two or more computers in the same vicinity by using each computer's wireless network adapter. You can transfer files from public and shared folders.

**Compressed (Zipped) Folders:** Windows 7 provides the Compressed Folders feature, which reduces the size of the files it contains and keeps all the compressed files in one location. When you transfer a compressed folder, the receiving computer sees either a compressed folder on most Windows computers, or a ZIP-type file that can be opened using one of several third-party programs.

**FTP Transfer:** You can use FTP (File Transfer Protocol) to transfer files to an FTP server over the Internet. In most cases, you'll be able to use Internet Explorer to connect and manage the files. In addition, if you connect to an FTP site with Internet Explorer, you can choose Open FTP Site In Windows Explorer from the Page menu to use the familiar interface of Windows Explorer to manage the transfer of files. You can also use the Add Network Location wizard to create a direct connection from Windows Explorer to the FTP site.

**RAS:** A RAS (Remote Access Service) connection is a telephone connection between your computer and a RAS server on a network. You'll need to have credentials supplied to you by the System Administrator of the server.

**VPN:** A VPN (Virtual Private Network) connection creates a secure connection over the Internet between your computer and another network or computer. You'll need to have credentials supplied to you by the System Administrator of the VPN server.

**Windows Live Messenger:** With Windows Live Messenger, you can send a file to or receive a file from any online contact. However, the recipient must agree to receive the file before you can send it. Although it isn't a part of Windows 7, Windows Live Messenger is available for download as part of Windows Live Essentials.

# Connecting to a Network over the Internet

To connect to a company network over the Internet, you can use a VPN (Virtual Private Network), which provides a secure connection between your computer and the network. The computer you connect to must be configured as a VPN server and must be connected to the Internet. Before you connect, verify that you have the correct name of the host computer, the correct user name and password that have been assigned to you, and instructions on the proper security and protocol settings.

## Create a VPN Connection

1. In Windows Explorer, click Network in the Navigation pane, and then click Network And Sharing Center. In the Network And Sharing window, click Set Up A New Connection Or Network.

2. In the Set Up A Connection Or Network wizard, select the Connect To A Workplace option, and then click Next. Click Use My Internet Connection (VPN) to select a VPN connection.

3. Type either the domain name or the IP address that was assigned to you.

4. Enter a name for the connection, and select any options you want.

5. Click Next, and enter the user name and password that were assigned to you for this connection. Then click Connect and wait to be authorized and connected.

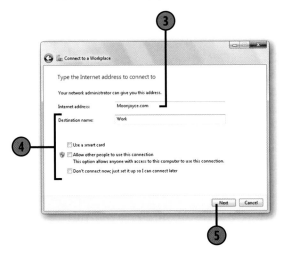

## Configure the Connection

**①** Click the Network icon in the notification area of the taskbar, and click Open Network And Sharing Center to display the Network And Sharing Center window.

**②** Verify that you're connected to a network using the VPN connection.

**③** If you want to change the network location, click the current location and, in the Set Network Location dialog box that appears, click the location you want. Click Close.

**④** Click the VPN connection.

**⑤** In the VPN Connection Status dialog box, click Diagnose if you're having problems with the connection.

**⑥** If you need technical details about the connection, click the Details button to view information about connectivity protocols, or click the Details tab to view information about the connection.

**⑦** If you need to change settings, click Properties.

**⑧** When you've finished using the connection, click Disconnect.

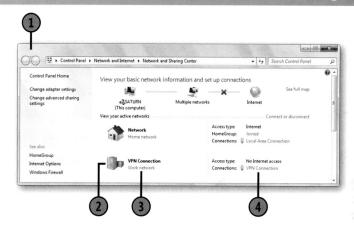

# Connecting to a Network over the Telephone

Although technology has provided us with numerous fast ways to connect remotely to a network, sometimes there's no choice but to use a standard telephone land line to make the connection. The computer you connect to must be configured as a RAS (Remote Access Service) server.

## Call In

(1) In Windows Explorer, click Network in the Navigation pane, and then click Network And Sharing Center. In the Network And Sharing window, click Set Up A New Connection Or Network.

(2) In the Set Up A Connection Or Network wizard, select the Connect To A Workplace option, and then click Next. Click Dial Directly to select the dial-up connection.

(3) Type the phone number, enter a name for the connection, and select any options you want.

(4) Click Next, enter the user name and password that were assigned to you for this connection, and click Connect.

(5) When you're verified and connected, use the connection in any way you want. When you've finished, click the Network icon in the notification area of the taskbar, click the connection, and click Disconnect.

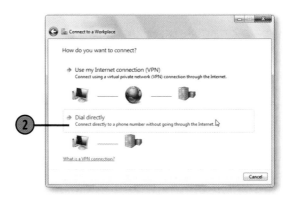

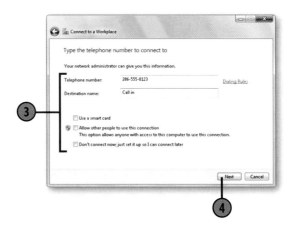

### See Also

"Reconnecting to a Network" on the facing page for information about quickly reconnecting to a network after the connection has been created.

"Setting Up a Modem" on page 282 for information about setting up your dialing rules.

# Reconnecting to a Network

After a VPN or dial-up connection to a network has been created, you can quickly and easily connect to it and manage it.

## Use Your Connections

① Click the Network icon in the notification area of the taskbar to display the Available Network Connections window.

② If you don't see any connections listed that you've already created, click Dial-Up And VPN to expand the list.

③ Click the connection you want.

④ Click Connect and wait to be connected.

⑤ When you've finished with the connection, click the Network icon in the notification area of the taskbar again. Click the connection, and then click Disconnect.

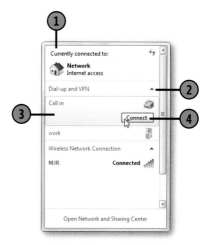

> **See Also**
>
> "Connecting to a Network over the Internet" on page 260 for information about creating a VPN connection and "Connecting to a Network over the Telephone" on page 262 for information about creating a dial-up connection.
>
> "Managing Your Network Connections" on pages 266–267 for information about modifying the settings for your existing connections.

A computer with a wireless network adapter also lists all the available wireless network connections.

# Connecting to a Public Wireless Network

The world is bristling with wireless networks, some of which are free with open access, and others that require a security key for access. Windows 7 recognizes the wireless networks that are within range and broadcasts their identity, making it easy for you to connect to them. For privacy reasons, a wireless network may not broadcast its identity, but if you know its name and security settings, you can still connect to it.

## Connect to a Network

1. Click the Network icon in the notification area of the taskbar to display the Available Network Connections window.

2. Click the network you want.

3. Click Connect.

4. If you're asked to provide the security key, type the one that was assigned to you, and then click OK.

5. Use the network. When you've finished your work, click the Network icon in the notification area of the taskbar again, select the network, and click Disconnect.

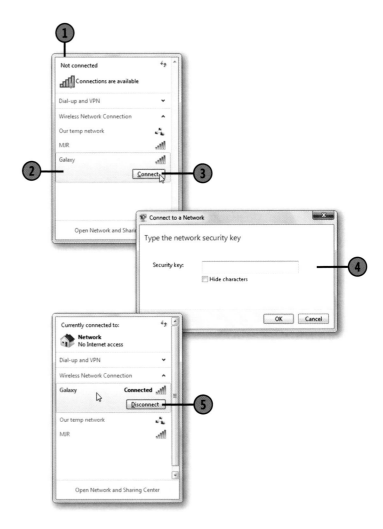

**See Also**

"Connecting Without a Network" on pages 268–269 for information about creating an ad hoc (improvised) wireless network between two computers.

## Connect to a Hidden Network

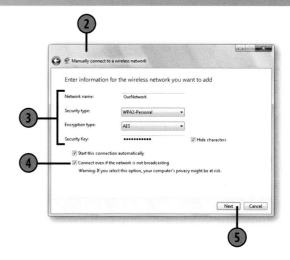

**1** Click the Network icon in the notification area of the taskbar, and click Open Network And Sharing Center. In the Network And Sharing Center window, click Set Up A New Connection Or Network.

**2** In the Set Up A Connection Or Network wizard, click Manually Connect To A Wireless Network, and then click Next to start the Manually Connect To A Wireless Network wizard.

**3** Enter the name and security information that was supplied to you.

**4** Select this check box to make the connection visible.

**5** Click Next, and then click Close.

**6** Click the Network icon in the notification area of the taskbar, click the network you want, and then click Connect.

---

**Caution**

Do *not* connect to any network, especially a hidden wireless network, unless you're certain that it is a legitimate network and that you're allowed to have access to it. Also, always be cautious about sending any confidential information, including passwords and account names, to a network you're not sure about.

**See Also**

"Reconnecting to a Network" on page 263 for information about using the Available Network Connections window to connect to or disconnect from a network.

# Managing Your Network Connections

As you create multiple connections—wireless networks, VPN connections, or RAS connections—you'll probably want to delete some network connections you no longer use and modify other connections for which the settings have changed.

## Manage Wireless Network Connections

**1** Click the Network icon in the notification area of the taskbar, and click Open Network And Sharing Center. In the Network And Sharing Center window, click Manage Wireless Networks to display the Manage Wireless Networks window.

**2** Click an old connection that you no longer want, click Remove, and then, in the dialog box that appears, click Yes to confirm your choice.

**3** To modify the settings for a network, right-click it, and choose Properties from the shortcut menu to display the Wireless Network Properties dialog box.

**4** On the Connection tab, select this check box if you want to connect automatically.

**5** Select this check box if you have more than one network connection set to connect automatically and you want the connections to try to connect in a specific order.

**6** On the Security tab, make any changes you want to your security settings and your security key. Click OK when you've finished.

**7** To change the order in which Windows tries to connect to the networks, click a network to select it, and use the Move Up or Move Down button to re-order the networks.

**8** Close the Manage Wireless Networks window when you've finished.

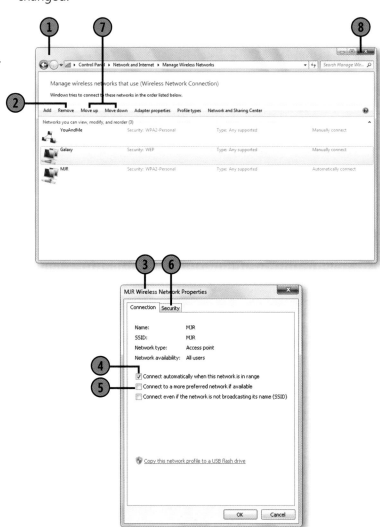

## Manage Other Network Connections

① Click the Network icon in the notification area of the taskbar. In the Available Network Connections window, right-click the connection you want to modify, and choose Properties from the shortcut menu to display the Properties dialog box.

② Make the changes you want:

- On the General tab, make any changes to the connection's Internet address (for a VPN) or to the phone number (for a RAS).

- On the Options tab, make any changes to your connection options.

- On the Security tab, make any changes to data encryption and authentication settings. For a VPN connection, select a different type of VPN connection, if necessary.

- On the Networking tab, add or remove any network protocols necessary for the connection.

③ Click OK when you've finished.

**See Also**

"Reconnecting to a Network" on page 263 for information about using the Available Network Connections window to connect to or disconnect from a network.

**Tip**

To manage all your network connections and to delete or rename connections, open the Control Panel, type **network connections** in the Search box, and choose View Network Connections from the Search Results to open the Network Connections window.

# Connecting Without a Network

How can you network when you don't have a network? As illogical as it sounds, you can do it using two or more computers that have wireless adapters and are within range of each other. You connect them using an ad hoc network. This temporary network can work just like any wireless network and, provided you use proper security procedures, is as secure as a standard wireless connection. When it's established, you can access files, play shared games, and do whatever you normally do over any network.

## Create a Network

(1) In Windows Explorer, click Network in the Navigation pane, and then click Network And Sharing Center. In the Network And Sharing Center window, click Set Up A Connection Or Network to open the Set Up A Connection Or Network window.

(2) Click Set Up A Connection Or Network to start the Set Up A Connection Or Network wizard.

(3) Click Set Up A Wireless Ad Hoc (Computer-To-Computer) Network to set up a wireless ad hoc network.

(4) Click Next, and then type a name for the network, select the type of security you want, and enter your security key.

(5) Select this check box if you want to use the same network connection in the future.

(6) Click Next, and then click Close. Provide others with the name of the network and the security key you used.

> **Caution**
>
> Always use some level of security encryption; otherwise, anyone within 30 feet (and probably more) of any computer on your ad hoc network can access your computer.

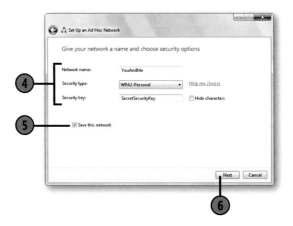

## Connect to the Network

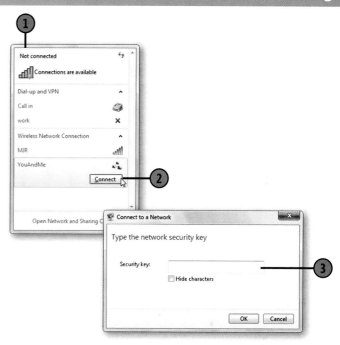

1. With the computers you want to connect situated closely enough to receive each other's signals, on the computer that created the network, click the Network icon in the notification area of the taskbar to display the Available Network Connections window.

2. Click the network name, and then click Connect.

3. On the other computer that's connecting to this network, click the Network icon, click the connection, and then click Connect. In the Connect To A Network dialog box that appears, type the security key that you were assigned, and then click OK.

4. When the network connection is established, click Network in the Navigation pane of Windows Explorer, and connect to the other computer or computers. If you don't see the other computers or you're unable to connect, click Open Network And Sharing Center, and change your sharing options. When you've finished with the connection, click it in the Available Network Connections window, and then click Disconnect.

**Tip**

Ad hoc connections are sometimes blocked by the computer's firewall. If you use a firewall other than Windows Firewall, check with the manufacturer about modifying the firewall settings to allow the ad hoc connection.

**Tip**

You can connect to only one network at a time unless you have multiple network adapters.

**See Also**

"Allowing Your Files to Be Shared" on page 254 for information about changing your network-sharing settings.

"Configuring the Windows Firewall" on pages 302–303 for information about allowing programs access through the firewall.

# 14 Setting Up

Something that can take all the fun and excitement out of buying a new computer is having to set up all over again the files and settings that took such a long time to get exactly right on your old computer. Well, we have good news for you! You can transfer your files and settings easily and quickly with the help of a wizard that walks you through the process.

You'll also find information in this section about setting up dial-up Internet access, if a broadband connection isn't available, so that you can explore the Web's vastness. We also talk about getting and installing Windows Live programs, setting up Windows Live Mail for sending and receiving e-mail messages and subscribing to newsgroups, and setting up a printer that's attached to your computer or that's available on your network.

In addition, we discuss turning on or off Windows 7 features or parts thereof, and setting up your fax and backup programs.

If these all sound like daunting tasks, rest assured that they're not. With the instructions on the pages that follow, and with help from the wonderful wizards of Microsoft, you'll sail right through them.

# Transferring Files and Settings

When you need to transfer your accounts—personal files, computer settings, and the contents of shared folders—from your old Windows computer to a new super-duper computer loaded with Windows 7, Windows provides a wizard that helps you transfer the files—automatically, using a network or a transfer cable, or manually, using removable media. Each method has its own procedures, and the wizard guides you through the specific steps. When your computers are connected by a network or a cable, the wizard transfers the information directly from one computer to the other when you enter the key code that's generated by the wizard. If you're using a USB (Universal Serial Bus) flash memory device or an external hard drive, you record the information on one computer, remove the device, connect the device to the other computer, and then have the wizard copy the information to the second computer. You can use this method to transfer files and settings from a computer that's running Windows 7, Windows Vista, Windows XP, and, to a limited extent, to a computer running Windows 2000.

## Set Up the Computers

① On the new computer, log on as an Administrator, click the Start button, type **easy** in the Search box of the Start menu, and choose Windows Easy Transfer from the menu to start the Windows Easy Transfer wizard. Step through the wizard, completing the following information and actions:

- Specify which device you're going to use for the transfer: an Easy Transfer cable, a network, or an external hard drive or a USB flash drive.

- Specify that this is the new computer.

- Specify that you haven't already saved the files from the old computer.

- Specify the way you're going to install Easy Transfer on your old computer.

- Copy the Easy Transfer setup files to a USB device or to a network folder, if necessary.

**Tip**

An Easy Transfer Cable is a specialized cable designed to work with the Windows Easy Transfer wizard. You can't use a standard USB or serial cable for this purpose. The Windows Easy Transfer cable is available from numerous retailers and computer manufacturers.

## Transfer the Information

**1** If it isn't already running, start the Easy Transfer wizard on the new computer.

**2** On the old computer, close all your running programs; then connect any cable or device you'll be using in the transfer, or connect to the network folder that contains the Easy Transfer installation files. If the Easy Transfer wizard doesn't start automatically, double-click the Windows Easy Transfer shortcut. Step through the wizard, specifying the way you want to transfer the information, that this is the old computer, and what you want to transfer.

**3** If you're transferring the information over a network or a cable, write down the Easy Transfer Key that's displayed in the wizard, and then enter it on the other computer when it's requested. The transfer will take place automatically. If you're using removable media or copying the material to a shared network folder, enter a password to protect the material, and then click Save to copy it.

**4** Take the completed transfer file created by the Easy Transfer wizard to the new computer; or access the shared network folder, double-click the transfer file on the removable media or in the shared folder to open it, enter the password when requested, and step through the Easy Transfer wizard to copy the information you want.

**5** Examine the results of the transfer to verify that the files you want have been transferred from the old computer to the new one.

Click to modify the items to be transferred.

# Setting Your Default Programs

When you set up Windows 7, certain programs are designated as the default programs for specific tasks: Windows Photo Viewer to view photos, Windows Media Player for playing videos and digital music, and Windows Media Center for recording TV programs. However, if there are other programs you'd prefer to use, you can set them as your default programs. You can also modify which file types are associated with which programs.

## Set the System Defaults

**1** Click the Start button, choose Default Programs from the Start menu, and, in the Default Programs window, click Set Program Access And Computer Defaults.

**2** In the Set Program Access And Computer Defaults window, click the down arrows for any configurations you might want to use.

**3** Select the type of configuration you want to use. If you choose the Custom configuration, make whatever changes you want to it.

**4** If you don't want the Microsoft program to be available on your computer, clear this check box.

**5** Click OK.

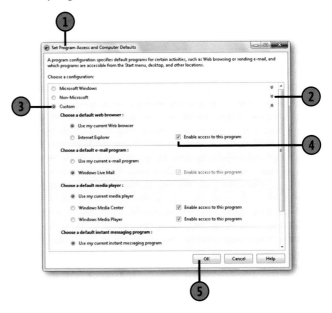

**Tip**

Because of the need to customize Windows in certain locales, what you see in the Set Program Access And Computer Defaults window might be different from what you see here, and might offer different options.

**See Also**

"Associating a File Type with a Program" on page 277 for information about quickly setting the default program for a specific file type.

## Customize the Settings

1. In the Default Programs window, click Set Your Default Programs to display the Set Default Programs window.

2. Click a program.

3. Click Choose Defaults For This Program.

4. In the Set Program Associations window that appears, specify which file types (extensions) and protocols you want this program to use. Items that are currently checked are already defaults for this program.

5. Click Save.

6. Continue going through the list of programs until you've customized all of them.

7. Click OK when you've finished.

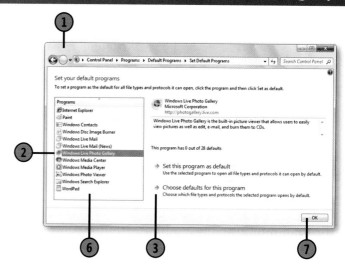

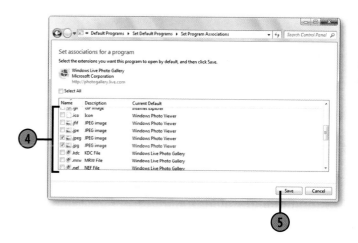

**Tip**

In case you're curious, a protocol is a set of defined rules used to enable communications. For example, you might want to set Windows Media Player as the default to handle the MMS (Microsoft Media Server) protocol so that you can receive streaming media over the Internet.

**Tip**

You can't clear a check box for a default setting in the Set Program Associations window. You switch the association by assigning that extension or protocol to a different program.

# Turning Windows Features On or Off

When Windows 7 is installed on your computer, some—but not all—of its features are available. If any features you need aren't active, you can turn them on, and, by the same token, if there are active features that you never use, you can turn them off.

## Turn a Feature On or Off

1. Save any documents you're working on, and close all your running programs.

2. Click the Start button, and choose Control Panel from the Start menu. In the Control Panel, choose Programs, and, in the Programs window that appears, click Turn Windows Features On Or Off to display the Windows Features dialog box.

3. If a plus sign (+) appears next to a feature, click it to see the items listed under that features group.

4. To turn a feature on, select its check box, or to turn a feature off, clear its check box.

5. Click OK.

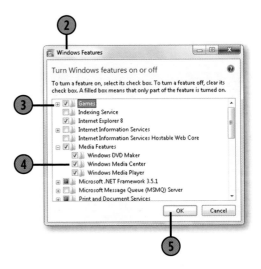

**See Also**

"Installing Critical Fixes" on page 316 and "Downloading Free Software" on page 355 for information about updating existing Windows features or adding recently released features.

**Tip**

Because the Control Panel has different views, you can access items in different ways. If the view is set to Category, you can click a main category (in this case *Programs*) to access the Programs window, where you'll see additional items under the Programs And Features subcategory. If the view is set to either Large Icons or Small Icons, you can bypass the main category and go directly to the subcategory of Programs And Features. Either way, you'll still be able to access the Turn Windows Features On Or Off command to adjust the features you want.

# Associating a File Type with a Program

Most of us seem to end up with different programs installed that handle the same file types, although not always in the same way; for example, you might have one program for viewing and organizing your photos and another program for editing them. You can tell Windows 7 which program you want to open which file type.

## Set a Program to Always Open a File

① Right-click the file that you want to be associated with a specific program, point to Open With on the shortcut menu, and choose Choose Default Program from the submenu.

② In the Open With dialog box that appears, click the program you want to use.

③ Select this check box to make the program the default program for all the files of this type.

④ Click OK.

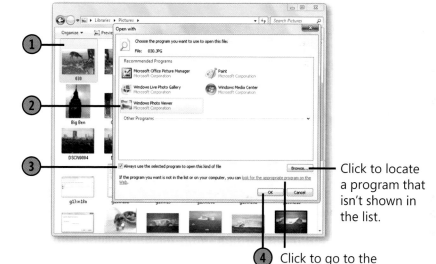

Click to locate a program that isn't shown in the list.

④ Click to go to the Windows File Associations Web page, where you'll see links to makers of software that's designed to work with the type of file you're trying to open.

---

**Tip**

To set the association for any of the file types or protocols on your computer, choose Default Programs from the Start menu, and choose Associate File Types Or Protocols With A Program.

**Tip**

If you choose a program listed on the shortcut menu, the file will open in that program this one time, but the program won't become the default for future use.

# Setting Up a Homegroup

A homegroup provides a powerful way to share libraries and printers among computers that are running Windows 7 on a home network. To set up a homegroup, one person creates it and provides a password to other people, who can then join the homegroup. To make it simple for the people who'll be joining the homegroup, you—or whoever is creating the homegroup—can change the randomly generated password to an easily remembered one.

## Create the Homegroup

① In Windows Explorer, click Homegroup in the Navigation pane, and then click Create A Homegroup to display the Create A Homegroup wizard.

② Select the items you want to share with the homegroup.

③ Click Next.

④ Write down the randomly generated password, or click to print the password along with instructions on how other people can join the homegroup.

⑤ Click Finish to create the homegroup.

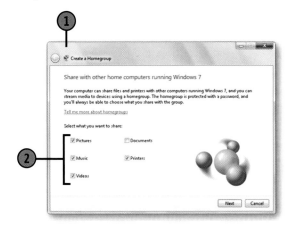

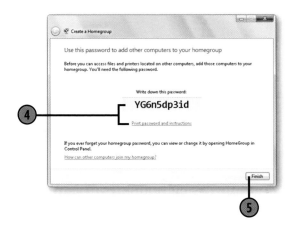

### Tip ✔

If you see the Join Now button instead of the Create A Homegroup button when you select Homegroup in the Navigation pane, it means that a homegroup already exists on your home network and that you can join that homegroup.

### See Also

"Joining a Homegroup" on page 248 for information about joining an existing homegroup.

## Change the Password

Click to generate another random password.

1. Click the Start button, type **home** in the Search box of the Start menu, and choose HomeGroup from the menu to display the HomeGroup window. Click Change The Password to display the Change Your Homegroup Password wizard.

2. Type the new password. The password can contain up to 16 characters and is case sensitive.

3. Click Next.

4. Verify the new password, write it down or print it, and then click Finish.

5. Distribute the password to the other people who will be joining the homegroup.

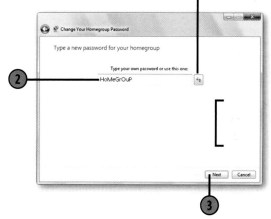

**Caution**

If other people have already joined the homegroup, make sure their computers are turned on and awake so that their computers will be aware that the password has been changed. Then go to each computer and manually change the home-group password to the new one.

**Tip**

If you just want to see the password instead of changing it, choose View Or Print The Homegroup Password in the Home-Group window.

# Setting Up Dial-Up Internet Access

Many ISPs (Internet service providers) supply installation CDs or other setup discs for setting up Internet access, and all you have to do is insert the CD or the discs into the appropriate drive and follow the instructions on the screen. However, if you don't have any installation materials, you can easily set up your connection manually.

## Set Up a Connection

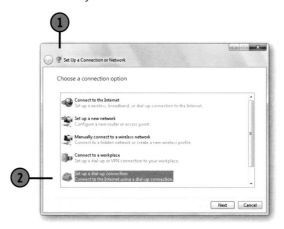

1. Click the Network icon in the notification area of the taskbar, and click Open Network And Sharing Center. In the Network And Sharing Center window, click Set Up A Connection Or Network to start the Set Up A Connection Or Network wizard.

2. Choose Set Up A Dial-Up Connection, and click Next.

3. Enter the connection information you received from your ISP.

4. Click Dialing Rules, and select the location for this connection. Click OK when you've finished.

5. Select this check box if you want your password to be entered automatically whenever you use this connection.

6. Name the connection.

7. Select this check box if you're willing to share the connection with anyone who has a user account on this computer.

8. Click Connect to try out the connection.

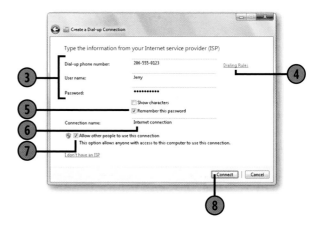

**See Also**

"Setting Up a Modem" on page 282 for information about creating or modifying the dialing rules for different locations.

## Control the Connection

(1) Click the Start button, and choose Control Panel from the Start menu. In the Control Panel, click Network And Internet, and then click Internet Options to display the Internet Properties dialog box.

(2) On the Connections tab, if you have more than one connection, select the one you want to use.

(3) Click Set Default.

(4) Specify when you want the connection to be used.

(5) Click Settings, and, in the Dial-Up Settings section of the Settings dialog box that appears, click Properties to display the Properties dialog box.

(6) On the General tab, add an alternative number in case the main number can't connect.

(7) On the Options tab, specify how many times you want the number to be redialed if the connection can't be made, how long to wait between redialings, how long the line can be idle before it's automatically disconnected, and whether you want the number to be redialed if the connection is lost.

(8) Click OK in the Properties dialog box, and click OK in the Settings dialog box.

(9) Click OK in the Internet Properties dialog box.

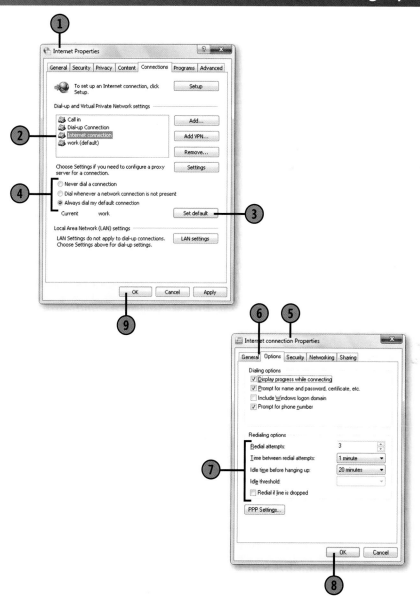

# Setting Up a Modem

When you use a phone line with your computer, whether it's for placing a voice call, sending a fax, creating an Internet connection, or connecting to a network, you can set up dialing rules that are specific to the location you're calling from.

That way, you can simplify the calling, and possibly even save yourself a little money on your phone bill by calling at times when the rates are reduced and by using a calling card.

## Set the Dialing Rules

**1** Click the Start button, type **phone** in the Search box of the Start menu, and choose Phone And Modem from the Start menu. If this is the first time you've set rules, complete the information in the Location Information dialog box that appears, and click OK.

**2** In the Phone And Modem dialog box, click New to create dialing rules for a new location, or select a location and then click Edit to modify the existing dialing rules.

**3** On the General tab, in either the New Location or the Edit Location dialog box, type a name for the location.

**4** Select the country and region, and enter the area code for this location.

**5** Enter whatever information you need to make the call.

**6** On the Area Code Rules tab, create any rules to handle specific situations for calling within a designated area code.

**7** On the Calling Card tab, select a calling card, and enter any required information if you want to use a calling card to make the calls.

**8** Click OK.

**9** Select the location you want to use, and click OK.

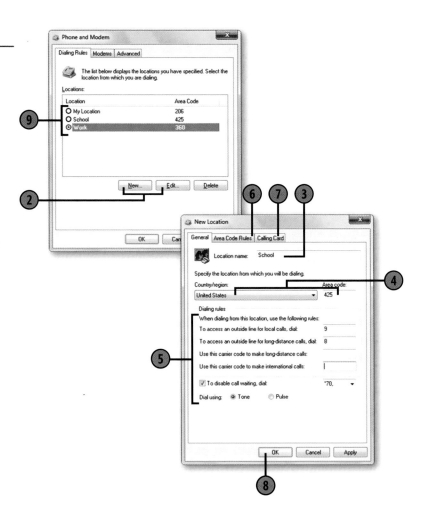

# Setting Up Internet Connection Sharing

Although most networks use a router for sharing an Internet connection, there are some circumstances—such as using a dial-up connection or in some ad hoc network connections— in which you might need to share a single connection between computers. To do this, one computer hosts the connection and the other computer or computers connect through the host.

## Share the Connection

① Click the Network icon in the notification area of the taskbar, right-click the network connection you want to share, and choose Properties from the shortcut menu to display the Internet Connection Properties dialog box.

② On the Sharing tab, select this check box to share your connection.

③ If there's more than one way the other computers can connect to your computer, select the connection you want them to use.

④ Select this check box if you want a dial-up connection to be created, if one doesn't already exist, whenever someone accesses the Internet.

⑤ Select this check box to allow other people to control or to modify this connection.

⑥ Click OK.

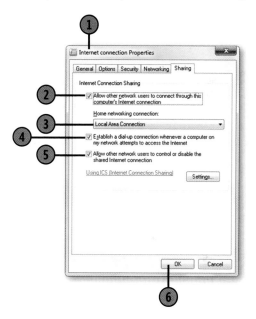

**Tip**

If the connection you want to share isn't listed in the Available Network Connections window, open the Control Panel, type Network Connections in the Search box, and click View Network Connections. In the Network Connections window that appears, right-click the connection you want, and choose Properties from the shortcut menu. Note, however, that not all network connections can be shared.

# Setting Up Windows Backup

Backing up your files is one of the most important things you can do to protect yourself and your computer in the event of a hardware failure or an accidental mishap in file management.

Fortunately, Windows Backup provides an easy and automated way to back up your files. All you need to do is set it up, and it will do the rest.

## Set Up Backup

① Click the Start button, type **back** in the Search box of the Start menu, and choose Backup And Restore from the menu. In the Backup And Restore window that appears, click Set Up Backup to start the Set Up Backup wizard.

② Select the storage device you want to use, and click Next.

③ Specify whether you want Windows to use the default libraries and folders and a system image, or whether you want to select what is to be backed up; then click Next. If you chose to select what is backed up, select the items, and then click Next.

④ Review the items to be backed up. If you want to change any of these items, click the Back button, and repeat step 3.

⑤ Click Change Schedule if you want to change whether the backup is run automatically, how frequently you want it to run, and at what time you want it to run.

⑥ Click Save Settings And Run Backup to run the backup for the first time.

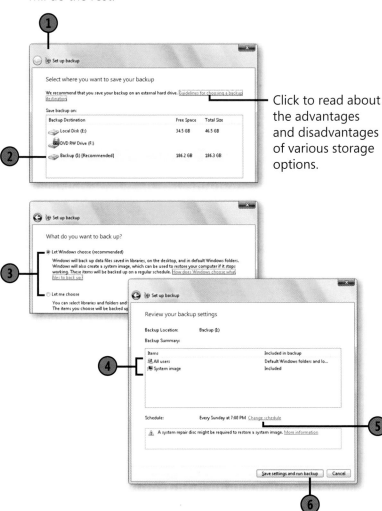

Click to read about the advantages and disadvantages of various storage options.

> **See Also**
>
> "Saving Everything" on page 354 for information about creating a system image.

# Setting Up Windows Live Essentials Programs

Windows Live Essentials is a suite of programs that don't come with Windows 7 but were designed to work seamlessly with it. And, best of all, they're free. All you need to do is download the ones you want, and you're all set. Some of these programs provide additional features if you're logged on with a Windows Live ID, but most of them will work just fine even if you aren't.

## Set Up Windows Live

1. Use your Web browser to go to *http://download.live.com*. On the Web page, read about the products, and then click Download. Follow the instructions to start the download.

2. In the Windows Live window that appears, click a program, and read the description of what it can be used for.

3. Select the check boxes for the programs you want to install, and clear them for the programs you don't want to install at this time.

4. Click Install, and wait for the programs to be downloaded and installed.

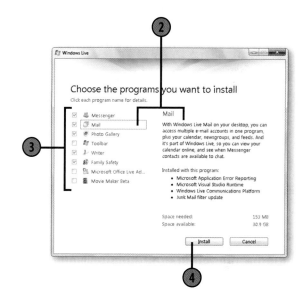

**Tip**

Downloading and installing the Windows Live Essentials programs can take substantial time, so you might want to download only the programs you want now. You can always download additional programs later.

**Tip**

A Live ID is a logon name and password for Hotmail, MSN, Xbox Live, or Live. If you don't have a Live ID and you want one, you can get a free Live ID by clicking the Sign In button on the Windows Live Web page.

# Setting Up Windows Live Mail

Windows Live Mail, one of the free Windows Live Essentials programs you can download, is a convenient mail client program that allows you to receive mail from one or multiple e-mail accounts. All you need to do is give Live Mail enough information so that you'll be able to connect to your e-mail server.

## Set Up Your E-Mail Account

① Click the Start button, type **mail** in the Search box of the Start menu, and choose Windows Live Mail from the menu. The first time you run Windows Live Mail, the Add An E-Mail Account wizard is displayed.

② Enter your e-mail address and password, and the name you want to be displayed for the account.

③ Click Next, and, if Live Mail is able to complete the connection, click Finish.

④ If Live Mail was unable to complete the connection information, provide the protocol and server information for the account.

⑤ Click Next, and then click Finish.

**Tip**

In case you're wondering, POP3 is Post Office Protocol 3, IMAP is Internet Message Access Protocol, HTTP is Hypertext Transfer Protocol, and NNTP is Network News Transfer Protocol. Now you know!

**Tip**

Gather up all your account information from your ISP before you start setting up your e-mail account. Mail protocols and server names can be complex and confusing.

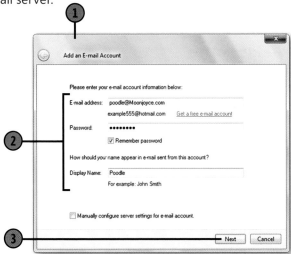

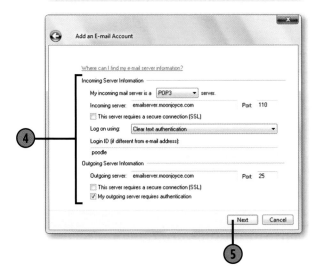

## Add an Account

1. Click Mail if it isn't already selected.

2. Click Add E-Mail Account.

3. Complete the information in the Add An E-Mail Account wizard.

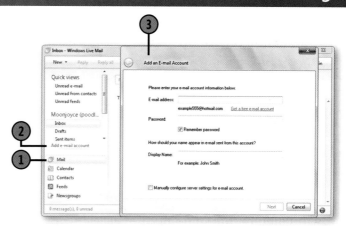

## Modify Account Settings

1. Choose Accounts from the Tools menu. In the Accounts dialog box, select the account to be modified, and click Properties to display the Properties dialog box.

2. On the General and the Servers tabs, make any changes to the account name and the logon information.

3. If the Advanced tab is present, make any configuration changes you want.

4. Click OK.

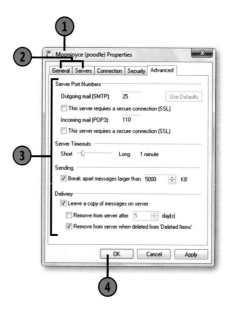

**Tip**

If the menus aren't visible, click the Menus button on the Windows Live Mail toolbar (or press the Alt key), and choose Show Menu bar from the drop-down menu.

# Setting Up for Faxing

If you're going to use the Windows Fax And Scan program to send and/or receive faxes using a fax modem on your computer, you'll need to provide the program with some basic information. You need to enter your contact information only once so that it can then be automatically inserted into all your faxes. You can also create your own fax cover pages to personalize your faxes.

## Set Up the Fax

① Click the Start button, type **fax** in the Search box of the Start menu, and choose Windows Fax And Scan to display the Windows Fax And Scan program. Click Fax to switch to Fax view if Fax view isn't already displayed.

② Choose Fax Settings from the Tools menu to display the Fax Settings dialog box.

③ On the General tab, select this check box, if it isn't already selected, to be able to send faxes.

④ Specify whether you want to receive a fax, and, if so, how you want to answer the call.

⑤ Click to modify the TSID and CSID fax identification names if necessary, to have the fax printed automatically, or to save a copy of the fax to a different location.

⑥ On the Tracking tab, specify which notifications you want to have displayed, whether you want the Fax Monitor to be displayed, and whether you want sound notifications.

⑦ On the Advanced tab, specify the location where you want your sent faxes to be archived, whether you want to include a banner containing transmitting information, and how you want to redial if the connection isn't made.

⑧ Click OK.

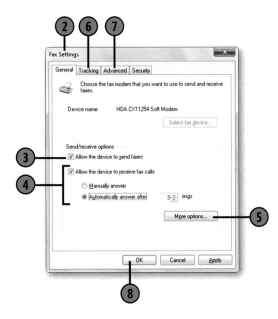

**Tip**

The TSID is the Transmitting Station Identifier and is usually sent with the fax so that the recipient can identify the source of the fax. The CSID is the Called Subscriber Identifier and is sent back to the sending fax device to confirm the recipient's identity.

## Personalize the Fax

**1** Choose Sender Information from the Tools menu to display the Sender Information dialog box.

**2** Complete the information you want to be included automatically in your fax.

**3** Click OK.

**4** Choose Cover Pages from the Tools menu, and, in the Fax Cover Pages dialog box, click New to start the Fax Cover Page Editor.

**5** Use the Insert menu to insert fields that will be filled in automatically based on your sender information. Use the other tools to format the content and to add text and other elements such as shapes.

**6** Click Save, and name and save your cover page. Close the Fax Cover Page Editor and the Fax Cover Pages dialog box when you've finished.

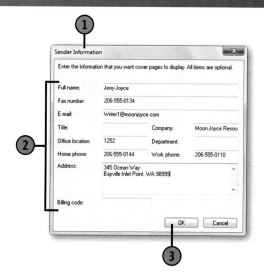

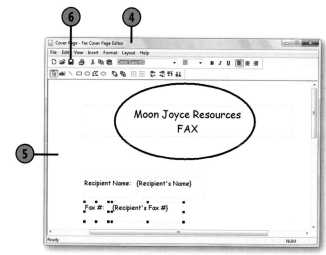

**Tip**

A *field* is a tool used by many programs to insert information automatically. On a cover page, when you insert an item from the Insert menu, you insert a *field label* and a *field*. For example, when you insert Sender's Name, you insert the field label *From:* and the field *{Sender's Name}*. When you use the cover page, the Sender's Name field is automatically replaced by the name you entered in the Sender Information dialog box.

# Setting Up a Printer

Windows 7 might or might not detect your printer, depending on how and to what the printer is attached. Windows should detect and install any printer that's attached to your computer's USB (Universal Serial Bus) or infrared port, provided the printer is turned on. If the printer is attached to a parallel or to a serial port, however, Windows might not have detected the printer when it was installed, so you'll need tell Windows about it yourself. If the printer is a wireless or a network printer, it's often detected automatically, but if it isn't, you can manually add it to your printers list.

## Set Up a Local Printer

1. If the printer came with an installation disc that's designed to work with Windows 7, follow the directions that came with the printer to run the installation program. The printer should then be installed correctly.

2. If you don't have an installation disc, with the printer connected and turned on, click the Start button, and choose Devices And Printers to display the Devices And Printers window.

3. Click Add A Printer to start the Add Printer wizard.

4. Click Add A Local Printer.

5. Step through the wizard, specifying

   - The port the printer is attached to.

   - The manufacturer and model of the printer.

   - A display name for the printer—that is, the name by which you'll identify it.

   - Whether you want to share the printer on your network.

   - Whether the printer will be your default printer.

   - Whether you want to print a test page.

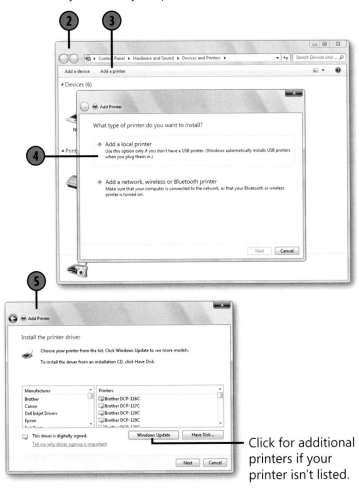

Click for additional printers if your printer isn't listed.

## Connect to a Network Printer

**①** Open the Devices And Printers window, and click Add A Printer to start the Add Printer wizard. Click Add A Network, Wireless Or Bluetooth Printer.

**②** When the search for printers on the network is complete, click the printer you want to use, click Next, and skip to step 5.

**③** If the printer you want isn't found, click here to connect manually.

**④** Choose to browse your network to locate the printer; enter its location and name; or connect using the TCP/IP address. Click Next.

**⑤** Complete the wizard by assigning a name to the printer and then printing a test page.

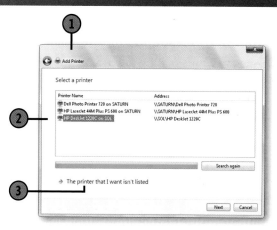

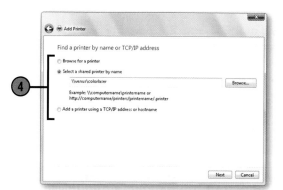

**Tip**

If a new printer is installed and is shared on a computer that's a member of your homegroup, each member of the homegroup will be notified that a new homegroup printer is available. Click the message to install the necessary drivers on your computer so that you can use the printer.

**See Also**

"Sharing a Printer over the Network" on page 292 for information about sharing your printer over a network.

**Tip**

Make sure the computer that hosts the shared printer is turned on, or you won't see the shared printer in the list of available printers.

# Sharing a Printer over the Network

If you chose not to share a printer over your network when you set up the network, and if you have computers on your network that aren't part of your homegroup (or if you decided not to share your printer with the homegroup), you can modify the printer setting if you want to so that it can be shared.

## Share the Printer

(1) Click the Start button, and choose Devices And Printers from the Start menu. In the Devices And Printers window, double-click the printer, and then double-click Customize Your Printer to display the Properties dialog box.

(2) Select this check box to share the printer.

(3) Enter a descriptive name for the printer so that other people on the network will be able to identify it.

(4) Select this check box if you want the time-consuming print processing (rendering) to be conducted on the network computer that's using this printer, or clear the check box to have all the print processing done on your computer.

(5) Click Additional Drivers if any computer on your network uses a different type of operating system from yours and needs a different print driver.

(6) Change any settings you want on the General, Security, and Advanced tabs to add identifying information, to limit the time the printer is available, and/or to include a separator page between print jobs.

(7) Click OK.

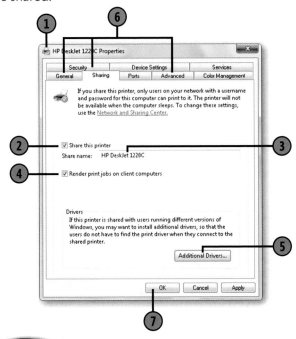

**See Also**

"Allowing Your Files to Be Shared" on page 254 for information about configuring your system to share printers, and setting the security required to access shared printers.

"Joining a Homegroup" on page 248 and "Setting Up a Homegroup" on page 278 for information about sharing your printer with others in your homegroup.

"Setting Up a Printer" on page 290 for information about sharing a printer when you set it up.

# 15 Maintaining Security

In days of old, only the Administrators of large corporate networks dealt with computer security. These days, with the proliferation of computer viruses, constant connections to the Internet, home networks, and sophisticated hacking techniques used by an ever-growing cadre of snoops and pranksters, everyone must be vigilant. In this section you'll find valuable information about the ways you can protect your files, your privacy on the Internet, and so on. If other people use your computer, you can protect your files from prying eyes by restricting user rights, by creating a password that protects the computer from unauthorized access, or by locking your computer.

Windows 7 provides many powerful built-in security features, but you have to do your part too. In this section, you'll find a useful list of actions you can take to improve your own security, including checking in periodically with the Action Center to verify that your firewall, virus protection, and software updates are working hard to protect your computer. If several people use your computer (and especially if any of them are children), you can use parental controls to restrict access to games, TV, movies, and Internet sites that contain material you consider inappropriate, and you can apply similar restrictions to movies and DVDs in Windows Media Center.

# Setting Your Password

Unless you create a password that allows you to gain entry to your user account, anyone can log on to your computer and access your files. If you want to protect the computer from unauthorized access, create a password that's easy for you to remember and difficult for others to guess.

## Create a Password

**1** Click the Start button, and click your account picture to display the User Accounts window for your account.

**2** In the User Accounts window, click Create A Password For Your Account.

**3** In the Create Your Password window that appears, type your password, and then type it again to confirm that you didn't make a typing error.

**4** Type a hint that will remind you, but no one else, of your password.

**5** Click Create Password.

> **Caution**
>
> Passwords are *case sensitive*—that is, *MyPASSWORD* and *mypassword* are two different passwords.

> **See Also**
>
> "Changing Your Password" on page 295 and "Resetting Your Password" on page 296 for information about changing and resetting your password.
>
> "Adding or Deleting User Accounts " on pages 324–325 for information about creating a new user account.

# Changing Your Password

One of the best ways to prevent others from using your account is to change your password occasionally—especially if you've given it to someone or you suspect that someone might have guessed it or watched you type it. When you change your password, create one that can't be easily guessed (don't use "password" or your well-known nickname, for example), and try to incorporate both uppercase and lowercase letters as well as one or two numerals. Of course, don't make the password so complicated that you can't remember it!

## Change Your Password

①  Click the Start button, and click your account picture to display the User Accounts window for your account.

②  Click Change Your Password.

③  In the Change Your Password window that appears, type your current password.

④  Type your new password.

⑤  Type the new password again to confirm that you didn't make a typing error.

⑥  Type a hint that will remind you, but no one else, of this password.

⑦  Click Change Password.

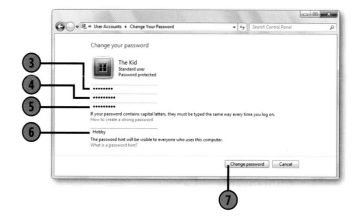

> **Tip** ✓
>
> For maximum security, use a password that's at least eight characters long and contains upper- and lowercase letters, with at least one number and one symbol, and no real words. This is known as a "strong" password.

# Resetting Your Password

Few things are more maddening than trying repeatedly to log on, only to realize that you've forgotten your password! If this happens, you have two choices: You can reset the password (or, if you're a member of the Standard group, you can ask an Administrator to reset it for you), which means that you'll lose all your settings and any security credentials and certificates; or you can use your Password Reset disk or USB storage device to log on and reset your password and save all your settings and credentials. The latter is obviously the better choice, so you should create a Password Reset disk while you still remember your password.

## Create and Use a Password Reset Disk

1. Insert a floppy disk or a USB storage device into your computer, click the Start button, and then click your account picture to display the User Accounts window for your account. Click Create A Password Reset Disk to start the Forgotten Password wizard.

2. Go through the first two steps of the wizard, and then enter your current password when prompted. Click Next.

3. Wait for the necessary information to be copied to your disk or storage device, click Next, and then click Finish to complete the wizard. Remove the disk or storage device, and label it as your Password Reset disk.

4. If you can't log on and you know that you've really forgotten your password, insert the disk or storage device, and click Reset Password to start the Reset Password wizard. Step through the wizard, typing a new password and a new (and better!) password hint. After you've completed the wizard, type your new password, and press Enter to log on with your new password.

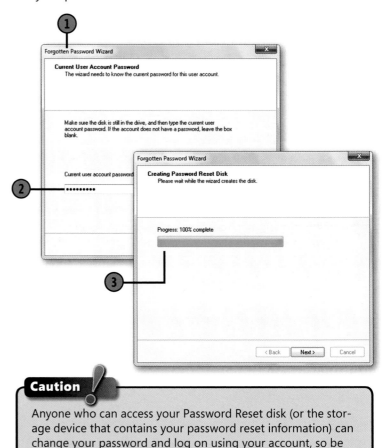

**Tip**

To create a Password Reset disk, you can use only a floppy disk (provided your computer has a drive for it) or a USB memory device. You can't use a CD, a DVD, or a removable hard drive.

**Caution**

Anyone who can access your Password Reset disk (or the storage device that contains your password reset information) can change your password and log on using your account, so be sure to keep the disk or the storage device in a secure pace.

## Force a New Password

**1** If you don't have a Password Reset disk and you've forgotten your password, have someone with Administrator credentials log on and execute steps 2 through 6.

**2** Click the Start button, type **user** in the Search box of the Start menu, and choose User Accounts from the menu to display the User Accounts window.

**3** Click Manage Another Account.

**4** In the Manage Accounts window, click the user account to be changed. In the Change An Account window, click Change The Password to display the Change Password window.

**5** Type a new password, retype it, and then add a password hint.

**6** Click Change Password.

**7** Have the Administrator log off. Click your account, and type your new password to log on. Immediately create a Password Reset disk, and then store it in a safe place. You don't want to go through this again!

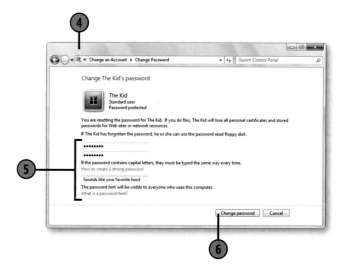

**Tip** ✓

If you're the sole Administrator on the computer and you're unlucky enough to have forgotten your own password, and if there's no Password Reset disk available, you can't reset your password. Instead, sad to say, you'll have to reinstall Windows to gain full access.

# Restricting User Rights

One of the surest ways to protect your computer from either malicious or accidental damage is to assign everyone who uses the computer to the Standard group, and to allow only one Administrator account for use in executing system changes. Often however, several people have Administrator accounts. If you're the one true Administrator of the computer, use the single Administrator account you want to keep to switch everyone else to the Standard group. Make sure that you also have a Standard User account for yourself for your normal log in, and use the Administrator account only when you need to. If you want to further restrict access to specific people, don't assign them user accounts at all; instead, ask them to sign in to the Guest account. Of course, you'll need to activate the Guest account before anyone can use it.

## Change the Type of Access

**①** Click the Start button, and click your account picture to display the User Accounts window for your account. Click Manage Another Account to display the Manage Accounts window. If the User Account Control appears, enter the Administrator credentials, and then click Yes.

**②** Click the account you want to manage.

**③** In the Change An Account window, click Change The Account Type to display the Change Account Type window.

**④** Select the Standard User option if it isn't already selected.

**⑤** Click the Change Account Type button.

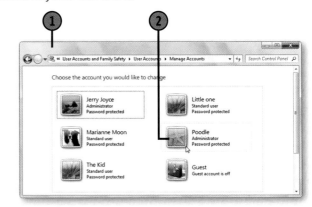

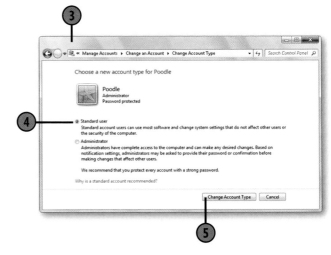

> ### See Also
>
> "Controlling the User Account Control" on page 95 for information about setting the level of security requiring Administrator authorization.
>
> "Adding or Deleting User Accounts" on pages 324–325 for information about creating a new Standard User account for yourself and deleting existing user accounts.

## Use the Guest Account

**1** In the Change An Account window, click Manage Another Account to display the Manage Accounts window.

**2** Click the Guest account.

**3** In the Turn On Guest Account window, click the Turn On button.

**4** Close the Manage Accounts window when you've finished.

**5** If necessary, inform those who want to use the computer that they don't have Standard access, and advise them to log on using the Guest account.

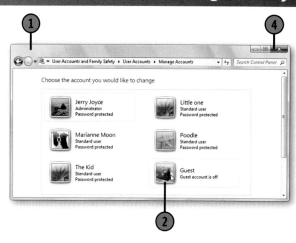

### Tip

Provided you're an Administrator, if you'd prefer someone who has an account on the computer to log on as a Guest, you can easily delete his or her account. To do so, click the account in the Manage Accounts window, and click Delete The Account. Windows 7 will give you the option of saving any of this user's files (but not his or her e-mails) to a folder on the Desktop that's accessible only by the person who deleted the account, or will give you the alternative option of deleting the files.

### See Also

"Know Your Rights" on page 300 for information about the different types of user accounts.

# Know Your Rights

Windows 7 provides several tools to help you effectively maintain security on your computer system. One of the principal ways to maintain security is to assign specific rights to each user of the computer. Those rights can range from simply being allowed to use the computer all the way up to having permission to make changes to the entire system. You specify user rights by assigning individual users to an appropriate group.

## User Groups

What you're allowed to do on your computer depends on the user group—Administrator, Standard, or Guest—of which you're a member. You can see which group you've been assigned to by choosing Control Panel from the Start menu and clicking the User Accounts category.

**Administrator Group:** Users have full control of the computer and can make whatever changes they want to the system, including adding or removing software, changing user accounts, and even modifying the Windows 7 configuration. You should log on as an Administrator only when you're certain you know what you're doing, only when you're making extensive changes to your computer, or when you're using certain administrative tools that will run only when you're logged on as an Administrator. As an Administrator, depending on your security settings, when you choose a command that executes something that Windows 7 considers a security-sensitive action, you'll be asked to confirm that you want to continue with that action. Your confirmation prevents viruses, hackers, and other malicious entities from doing something bad to your computer. The security level at which the confirmation process—called the User Account Control (UAC)—occurs depends on your UAC settings. Although the UAC is set at

a moderate level of security by default, it's possible to set it to never ask for confirmation, which is *not* a good idea! For information about the UAC, see "Controlling the User Account Control" on page 95.

**Standard Group:** Users can do most things on the computer without ever running into the need for Administrator permission, including running programs, using and creating files, and installing some programs. When a security-related task, such as making changes to the system configuration, needs to be executed, and if the User Account Control is set to notify you of this event, Windows 7 asks the user to confirm administrative approval by providing the Administrator credentials. If the user doesn't have the credentials, he or she will need to contact the person who has the Administrator account. This protects the system from being modified and possibly damaged by someone who might not have the skill or knowledge to make these changes safely. Therefore, with the User Account Control set to notify you when a security-related event occurs, there's no reason for anyone always to be logged on as an Administrator.

**Guest Group:** Users are people who don't have user accounts on the computer. By logging on as a member of the Guest group, a user can work on the computer without being able to modify the computer or any of its files. If you're a Guest user, you're quite limited in what you can do. You can run existing programs but can't install new programs or make any changes to Windows 7. You can open files that are shared on the computer and possibly shared over the network, depending on the sharing settings, but you can't save any changes to those files. You can save or delete only the files that you've created yourself. By default, the Guest account is inactive and must be activated before it can be used. There's only one Guest account on the computer, and there's no password for this account.

# Monitoring Your Security Settings

Although there are many different high-security settings in Windows 7, there are six big ones: Network Firewall, Windows Update, Virus Protection, Spyware And Unwanted Software Protection, Internet Security Settings, and the User Account Control. In the Windows Action Center, you can easily monitor your settings and can adjust them as necessary. All the items shown in the Action Center are part of Windows 7 except for Virus Protection, which you have to obtain separately.

## Check Your Settings

1. Click the Action Center icon in the notification area of the taskbar, and click Open Action Center to display the Action Center window.

2. Click the down arrow if the Security section isn't fully displayed. (The down arrow becomes an up arrow after the area has been expanded.)

3. Check the status of the security features and settings.

4. If a feature isn't turned on or isn't installed, click the appropriate button or link.

5. Close the Action Center when you've finished. If you need to make any changes, such as installing an anti-virus program or changing some of your settings, make them, and then return to the Action Center to confirm that your system is properly configured.

Click to go to a Microsoft Web site that features information and links to virus-protection software providers.

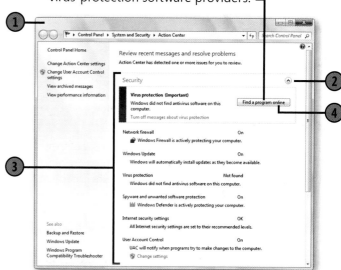

**Try This!**

Point to the Action Center icon, and note the status of your system in the window that appears. Click the icon, and read more details in the window that appears. Click Open Action Center, and click the down arrow next to Maintenance. Note whether there are any maintenance issues. If you had previously turned off messages about a feature, click the link to turn the messages back on. Close the Action Center when you've finished.

**Tip**

Another security item in the Action Center is Network Access Protection. You use this when a computer is remotely connected to a corporate network to make sure that the computer has all the proper software and settings so that it won't harm the corporate network. However, Network Access Protection doesn't function when you're connected to a home or public network.

# Configuring the Windows Firewall

A *firewall* is a program that's designed not only to prevent unauthorized and malicious access to your computer over the Internet, but also to prevent unauthorized communications *from* your computer to the Internet—for example, the communications that can be made by a spyware program.

In other words, a firewall is your defense against hackers, viruses, Trojan horses, worms, and all the other horrors that exist out there in cyberspace. You can configure the firewall for different network locations and can decide which programs will and will not be blocked.

## Configure the Firewall

(1) Click the Start button, type **firewall** in the Search box of the Start menu, and choose Windows Firewall from the menu. In the Windows Firewall window, click Turn Windows Firewall On Or Off to display the Customize Settings window.

(2) For your home or work network, specify whether you want the firewall turned on or off.

(3) If the firewall is turned on, select this check box to block everything, or clear the check box to block only connections that aren't in the list of allowed programs.

(4) Select this check box to receive a notification whenever a connection is blocked, or clear the check box to block programs without receiving any notification. If you choose to receive a notification, you can then choose to block, allow once, or always allow the connection.

(5) Make your firewall settings for the Public network location.

(6) Click OK.

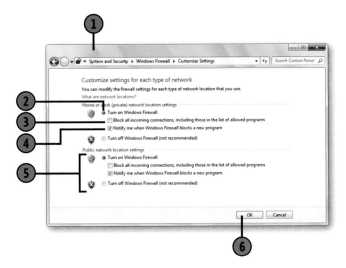

**Tip**

Many security suites come with their own firewall as well as with anti-virus tools. If you're using one of those firewalls, use the control panel that came with the security suite to adjust the firewall settings.

## Allow or Block Specific Programs

**(1)** In the Windows Firewall window, click Allow A Program Or Feature Through Windows Firewall to display the Allowed Programs window.

**(2)** If necessary, click Change Settings, and enter Administrator credentials.

**(3)** Click a program or a feature to which you might want to allow or deny access.

**(4)** Click Details for information about that program or feature. Click OK when you've finished.

**(5)** Select a check box to allow program access, or clear the check box to deny access on a private (home or work network) and/or a Public network location.

**(6)** If you want to allow access to a program that isn't listed, click Allow Another Program. In the Add A Program dialog box that appears, select the program. If the program isn't listed, click the Browse button to locate it, and then click Open. Click Add to add it to the list, and then choose to allow it on a private and/or a Public network location.

**(7)** Repeat for any other programs, and then click OK.

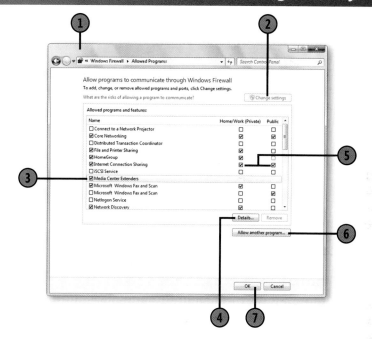

# Protecting Yourself from Spyware

Windows Defender is a Windows program that runs in the background, searching your computer for harmful and unwanted software that you might have inadvertently down-loaded or installed or that might have been downloaded and installed without your permission or knowledge. You can monitor what Defender has detected on your computer and, if you want, can modify when the program scans your computer and what it scans. If you have concerns that something evil might have found its way onto your computer, you can run a full scan immediately.

## Set Your Options

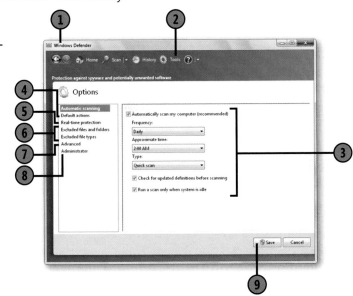

1. Click the Start button, type **defend** in the Search box of the Start menu, and choose Windows Defender from the menu to display the Windows Defender window.

2. Click Tools, and, in the Tools And Settings section, click Options.

3. Select Automatic Scanning, and then select the Automatically Scan My Computer check box, if it isn't already selected, to turn on automatic scanning. Also select the frequency, the time, and the scan type for the automatic scan.

4. Select Default Actions, and, if necessary, change any of the actions that take place when an item has been detected.

5. Select Real-Time Protection to specify whether files are to be scanned when they're downloaded and whether programs are to be scanned when you run them.

6. Select Excluded Files And Folders and Excluded File Types to specify items that you don't want to be scanned.

7. Click Advanced to specify what is to be scanned, how the scan works, and whether a restore point is to be created before Defender acts on any items that were detected.

8. Click Administrator to turn Windows Defender on or off and to show or hide scan results for other users of this computer.

9. Click Save.

**Tip**

Many security suites come with their own anti-spyware programs. Be aware that if you run two or more anti-spyware programs, the performance of your computer could be substantially slowed down.

## Take Action

(1) Click Tools in the Windows Defender window to display the Tools And Settings section.

(2) Click the feature that you want to use to take an action:

- Quarantined Items to see items that have been quarantined as suspected spyware or unwanted software, and either to remove the software if it's harmful or to restore it if you're sure it's safe

- Allowed Items to view the items you've marked as safe and to start monitoring any items whose safety you're not sure of

- Microsoft SpyNet to modify your participation in reporting spyware

(3) To conduct a scan, click the Scan Options down arrow at the right of the Scan button, and select the type of scan you want:

- Quick Scan to scan the locations on your computer that are most likely to contain spyware

- Full Scan to scan all locations on your computer

- Custom Scan to specify the locations to be scanned

(4) Click History to see items that were previously detected by Defender and to view the actions that were taken.

(5) Click Home to see the current status of your protection.

(6) Close Defender when you've finished.

**See Also**

"Fixing System Problems" on page 350 for information about using restore points to restore the computer to a previous state if changes have damaged the system.

# Limiting Access to the Computer

Allowing a child unlimited access to a computer isn't necessarily the best policy. Fortunately, with parental controls, you can set boundaries for the types of games a child can play, specify the programs a child can or can't access, and limit the days and hours during which a child can access the computer. You can use additional programs and features to control Internet access, and you can also monitor the child's Web activities. You'll just need to ignore the whining and use the parental controls to establish appropriate boundaries.

## Create the Rules

① Click the Start button, type **parent** in the Search box of the Start menu, and choose Parental Controls from the menu to display the Parental Controls window. If necessary, enter Administrator credentials.

② If the child doesn't have his or her own Standard account, click Create A New User Account, and create an account.

③ Click the child's account.

④ Click here to turn on the controls.

⑤ Select an item for which you want to create rules, and use the appropriate controls to create the rules you want. Repeat for the other items as desired.

⑥ If you've installed a Web-filtering program, click it, and make any appropriate settings. Only programs that have been installed will appear as part of the parental controls.

⑦ Click OK to turn on the controls.

**Caution**

The parental control settings can be changed by anyone with Administrator credentials, so make sure that anyone who's being restricted doesn't have access to those credentials.

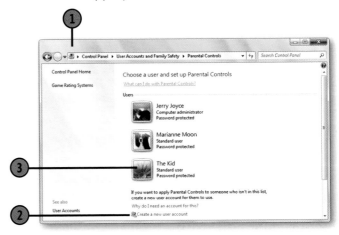

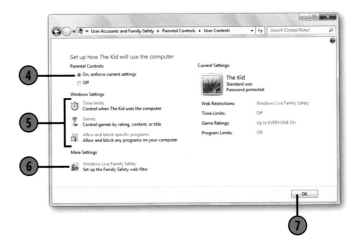

# Restricting Time on the Computer

As we've already mentioned, unlimited access to the computer isn't such a great idea, especially where a child is involved. If gaming or other computer activities interfere with more productive pursuits, such as reading, doing homework, or just having a conversation, you can limit the days and hours during which the child can access the computer.

## Restrict Access Times

**1** Click the Start button, type **parent** in the Search box of the Start menu, and choose Parental Controls from the menu to display the Parental Controls window. If necessary, enter Administrator credentials. Click the account to be managed to display the User Controls window, turn on the parental controls if necessary, and click Time Limits to display the Time Restrictions window.

**2** Use the mouse to drag over time blocks during which access is not permitted. To remove a time block, drag over it again. To change an individual square, click it.

**3** Click OK when you've finished.

Dark squares are the times when access is blocked.

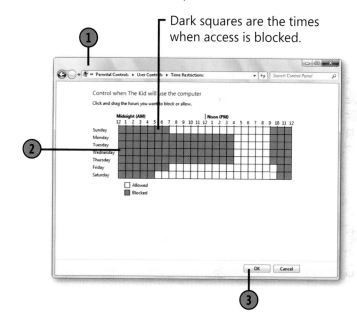

### See Also

"Setting Up Windows Live Essentials Programs" on page 285 for information about downloading Windows Live Family Safety and details about including Web filtering in the parental controls.

"Limiting Access to the Computer" on the facing page for information about turning on the parental controls and limiting access to specific types of programs and content.

### Tip

To select time blocks with the keyboard instead of with the mouse, use the arrow keys to select the time block you want, and then press the Spacebar or the Shift key to permit or deny access. To select multiple time blocks, hold down the Shift key while you use the arrow keys to select time blocks.

# Restricting Access to Games

Every parent or caregiver knows that many games are far from being child's play. With parental controls, you can prevent a child from playing all games or can allow the child to play only those games you consider to be age appropriate.

## Restrict the Games

① Click the Start button, type **parent** in the Search box of the Start menu, and choose Parental Controls from the menu to display the Parental Controls window. If necessary, enter Administrator credentials. Click the account to be managed to display the User Controls window, turn on the parental controls if necessary, and click Games to display the Game Controls window.

② Specify whether this person is allowed to play games.

③ If games are allowed, click Set Game Ratings.

④ In the Game Restrictions window, make your settings:

- Specify whether to allow or block all games with no rating.

- Specify the rating level allowed.

- Choose to block or to allow any specific descriptors of the game content.

⑤ Click OK.

⑥ Click here to block or to allow specific installed games. Select the games that you want to block or to allow, and then click OK.

⑦ Click OK to apply your settings.

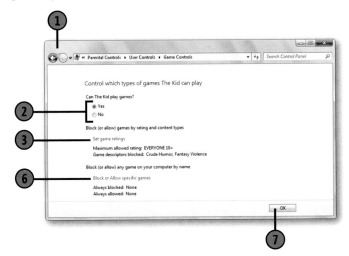

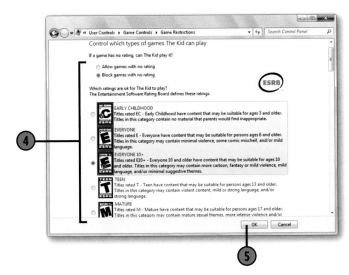

# Restricting Access to Programs

As with games, not all computer programs can be safely used by children or teenagers. If you want to restrict the programs the young people in your care are allowed to run, you can use the parental controls to limit access to the programs you consider to be inappropriate.

## Block Programs

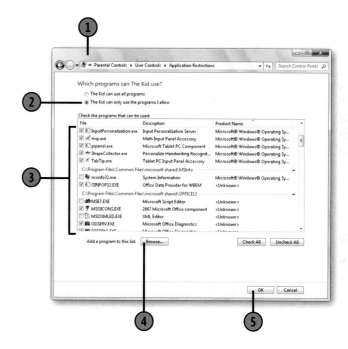

**(1)** Click the Start button, type **parent** in the Search box of the Start menu, and choose Parental Controls from the menu to display the Parental Controls window. If necessary, enter Administrator credentials. Click the account to be managed to display the User Controls window, turn on the parental controls if necessary, and click Allow And Block Specific Programs to display the Application Restrictions window.

**(2)** Select this option to specify which programs can be used.

**(3)** Select the check boxes for the programs you want to allow, and clear the check boxes for the programs you want to block.

**(4)** To add a program that isn't in the list, click Browse, locate the program, and click Open. Select the check box for the program to allow access, or clear the check box to block access.

**(5)** Click OK, and then click OK in the User Controls window.

# Restricting Internet Content

Despite its usefulness, the Internet can be a scary and dangerous place, especially when a child or a teenager has access to it. Although nothing can substitute for direct supervision, when you use Windows Internet Explorer you can set some restrictions on the type of material that a young person can access. When you set these restrictions, they apply not only to the children but to all users of the computer.

## Enable Content Advisor

1. Click the Start button, and choose Control Panel from the Start menu. In the Control Panel, click Network And Internet, and then click Internet Options to display the Internet Properties dialog box.

2. On the Content tab, click Enable and, if necessary, enter Administrator credentials.

3. On the Ratings tab of the Content Advisor dialog box that appears, select a category, and drag the slider to adjust the restrictions you want to apply to that category. Repeat for other categories.

4. On the Approved Sites tab, enter the names of the Web sites that you always want to allow or always want to block, regardless of the site's rating.

5. On the General tab, specify whether Web sites without ratings are to be allowed or blocked, and then create or change the Supervisor password so that only you will be able to change the settings.

6. Click OK, and then click OK again in the Internet Properties dialog box.

7. To modify the settings or to turn off Content Advisor, open the Internet Properties dialog box again, and, on the Content tab, click Settings to make modifications, or click Disable to turn off Content Advisor. You need Administrator credentials to do this, and you'll also need the Supervisor password.

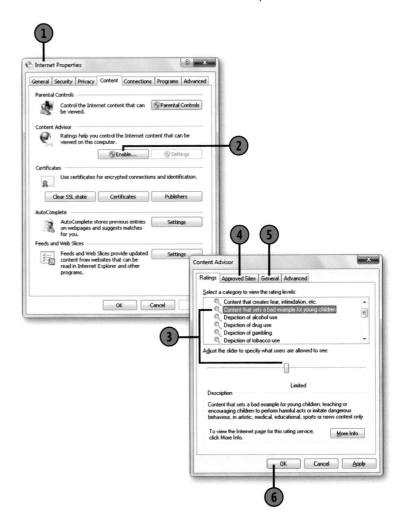

# Maintaining High Security

Windows 7 itself provides your computer with many built-in security features. However, as powerful as they are, by themselves these security features can't protect you from every type of mischief that can befall your computer. You need to be active in protecting your computer, your data, and your personal information from those who would do you harm.

## Doing Your Part

Here are some things you can do to greatly improve your security:

- Log on using a Standard account instead of an Administrator account, and use the User Account Control to authorize individual actions as an Administrator when required.

- Set the User Account Control at the default or at a higher security level so that you receive notifications when any programs attempt to modify your system.

- Use the Action Center to verify that your basic security settings are properly configured and are up to date.

- Make sure Windows Defender or a similar anti-spyware program is running, that it has up-to-date definitions, and that it scans your system frequently.

- Make sure that you have a good, up-to-date anti-virus program installed. This will add protection against viruses and worms that have figured out ways around some of the security features.

- In your e-mail program, don't download pictures and other external HTML content contained on a server unless you trust the source. Doing so can verify your e-mail address to potential authors of spam and can also introduce malicious code.

- Make sure that your Web content zones in Internet Explorer are properly set, and that you're not using custom settings that provide less protection than the recommended default levels.

- If you're using Internet Explorer, make sure you have the pop-up blocker turned on to prevent code from being loaded, to prevent a hacker from stealing information by making the pop-up look like a dialog box or other content that asks for information, and, of course, to keep those annoying pop-up ads from appearing.

- If you're using Internet Explorer, make sure that you have the SmartScreen phishing filter turned on to identify illicit Web sites that look legitimate but that are designed to steal your information.

- If you're using Internet Explorer, work in Protected mode so that Internet Explorer activities and downloads are isolated from the rest of your computer.

- Keep Windows up to date with Windows Update. Many of the important updates are fixes to outmaneuver newly detected software vulnerabilities.

- Stop and think before you do something you might regret: open an attachment, for example, or download a file, install a program, or even answer an e-mail message.

- Keep important data backed up so that if something nasty sneaks past all your security, you can recover the data.

Complicated? Absolutely! But don't be intimidated: Windows 7 is designed to be as secure as possible and will take care of most security issues. It also adjusts many of your default settings to maintain the optimum balance between security and functionality, and it monitors your security status and quickly alerts you when there's a problem.

# Setting Internet Explorer Security

Although most Web sites pose few security threats to your computer, some sites are designed with malicious intentions. In Internet Explorer, to protect your computer from these sites—and to allow access to additional features for sites you know won't cause any harm—you can set and customize your own security levels and can add sites to your list of trusted or restricted Web sites.

## Set Your Security

(1) In Internet Explorer, click Tools, choose Internet Options from the drop-down menu, and, in the Internet Options dialog box that appears, click the Security tab.

(2) Click the Trusted Sites zone, click the Sites button, and type or paste an address for a Web site you trust and to which you want full access.

(3) Click the Restricted Sites zone, click the Sites button, and type or paste an address for a Web site you believe might be dangerous and from which you want maximum protection.

(4) Click in a zone, and do either of the following:

- Use the slider to adjust the level of security. If the slider isn't visible, click the Default Level button, and then use the slider.

- Click Custom Level, and select the options you want in the Security Settings dialog box. Click OK.

(5) Select the Enable Protected Mode check box, if it isn't already selected, to use Protected mode.

(6) Repeat steps 4 and 5 for each of the zones, and click Apply.

(7) On the Privacy tab, set the privacy level you want to control the types of cookies that are stored and that contain and/or collect information about you.

(8) Click OK.

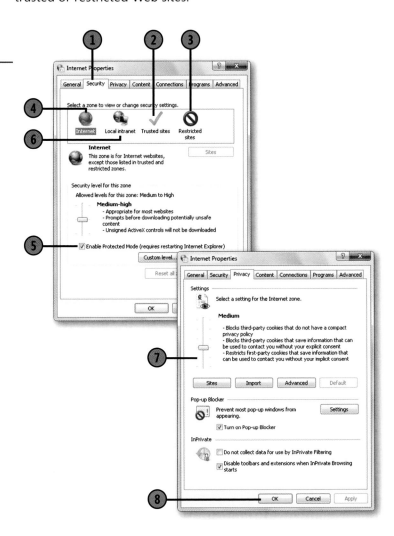

# Restricting DVD Movies in Windows Media Player

If there are DVDs that, because of their ratings, you don't want to be played on your computer using Windows Media Player, you can block them from being played based on their ratings. Note, however, that the blocking can be overridden by someone else who can provide Administrator permission from the User Account Control.

## Specify the Allowable DVD Rating

1. With parental controls set up and turned on, start Windows Media Player if it isn't already running.

2. In Library view, click Organize, and choose Options from the drop-down menu to display the Options dialog box.

3. On the DVD tab, click the Change button.

4. In the Change Rating Restriction dialog box that appears, specify the maximum rating you'll allow.

5. Click OK, and supply Administrator credentials if needed.

6. Click OK.

**See Also**

"Limiting Access to the Computer" on page 306 for information about setting up and enabling parental controls.

"Restricting Content in Windows Media Center" on pages 314–315 for information about setting access restrictions on playing DVDs and other movies in Windows Media Center.

**Tip**

To prevent access to inappropriate material, make sure that you set rating restrictions for all the programs on your computer that play DVDs.

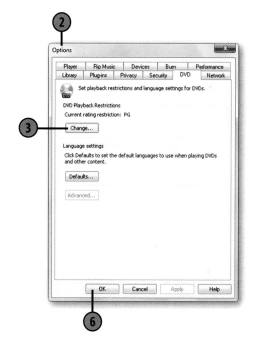

# Restricting Content in Windows Media Center

Windows Media Center has its own tools to control the type of content that can be viewed. Unlike with most of the Windows 7 controls, though, your access to the settings is controlled by the use of a *pin code* rather than reliance on Administrator access. The settings that are controlled by the pin code affect all users of the computer.

## Set the Movie and DVD Control

1. With Media Center running and the main menu displayed, choose Tasks, and then choose Settings. In the Settings window, select General, and, in the General window that appears, select Parental Controls. To control access, create and enter a four-digit PIN (Personal Identification Number) code that you'll remember.

2. In the Parental Controls window, click Movie/DVD Ratings to display the Movie/DVD Ratings window.

3. Select the Turn On Movie Blocking check box to turn on blocking.

4. Select the Block Unrated Movies check box to block any movie that doesn't have a rating.

5. Specify the maximum rating you'll allow.

6. Click Save.

**Tip**

If someone who shouldn't have access to restricted materials has managed to crack the pin code, you can easily change it. To do so, in the Parental Controls window choose Change Access Code, and enter a new pin code.

## Set the TV Control

**1** In the Parental Controls window, select TV Ratings to display the TV Ratings window.

**2** Select the Turn On TV Blocking check box to turn on TV blocking.

**3** Select the Block Unrated TV Programs check box to block any TV program that doesn't have a rating.

**4** Specify the maximum rating you'll allow.

**5** If you want to specify certain types of content, click Advanced, select your settings, and click Save.

**6** Click Save, and click the Windows Media Center button to return to the main menu.

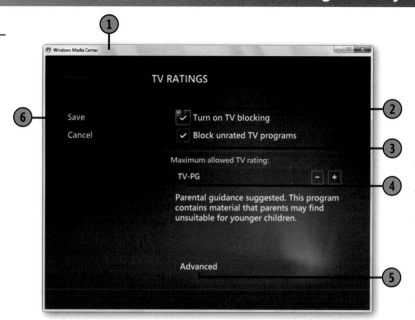

**Tip**

When a movie or a TV program is blocked, you can override the setting by entering your pin code. Therefore, you must make sure that the pin code isn't known by or available to those whose access you're trying to limit.

# Installing Critical Fixes

Microsoft continues to issue updates to Windows, fixing problems and vulnerabilities as they're discovered. To keep your computer running smoothly and to avoid new types of attacks, it's critical that you install any important updates that Microsoft issues as soon as they're available. Fortunately, the Windows Update feature does most of the work for you.

## Configure Your Downloading

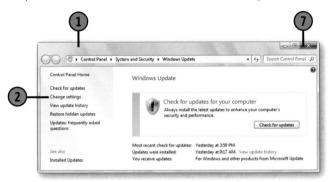

**①** Click the Start button, type **update** in the Search box of the Start menu, and choose Windows Update from the menu to display the Windows Update window in order to review the status of your updates.

**②** If the computer hasn't checked for updates recently and/or isn't set for automatic updating, click Change Settings.

**③** Specify the way you want to receive updates, if at all.

**④** If you chose to install the updates automatically, specify a frequency and a time during which you want them to be installed—preferably when the computer will be idle.

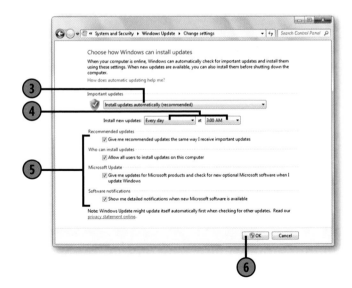

**⑤** Select these check boxes to specify whether you want to include recommended updates as well as important updates in your downloads, whether you want to receive updates for other Microsoft products, and whether you want to receive detailed information when new software becomes available.

**⑥** Click OK when you've finished.

**⑦** Wait for Windows Update to check for updates, if necessary, and then close the Windows Update window.

# 16

# Managing Windows 7

Windows 7 provides the flexibility you need to make your computer work better by making changes and fixing problems. With an Administrator account, you can create or delete user accounts. If you want to squeeze more items onto your Desktop, you can increase its virtual size by changing the screen resolution, or change its actual size by stretching it across two or more monitors. If your computer supports pen or touch input, we show you how to manage those features so that they work in the best possible way for you.

Windows 7 helps you control the power options on your portable computer and provides tools to help you use that computer at a meeting without any snafus. It also provides disk-maintenance tools to help your computer run at its best. You can schedule these tools to run periodically—they'll find and re-order bits of files that have become scattered or lost, delete unused files, and so on. If Windows won't start properly, you'll find solutions here that will either get your computer started or help you diagnose what's wrong. If you want to reverse changes you've made to your system, the System Restore tool restores your previous settings. To safeguard against the loss of files should you have any serious problems with the computer, you can back up your files and later restore them to your computer.

# Changing the Date and Time

Windows 7 and your computer keep track of the date and time, using commonly accepted formats to display them. In most cases, your computer routinely checks the date and time over the Internet. However, if the date or time on your computer is inaccurate, or if you travel with your computer into different time zones, you can quickly adjust the settings.

## Change the Date, Time, or Time Zone

1. Click the Start button, type **date** in the Search box of the Start menu, and choose Date And Time from the menu to display the Date And Time dialog box.

2. If the date or time is incorrect, click the Change Date And Time button, and, if necessary, provide Administrator credentials in the User Account Control.

3. In the Date And Time Settings dialog box, use the left or right arrow at the top of the calendar to scroll to the current month, and then click today's date.

4. To correct the time, click the hour, the minute, or the second that needs correcting, and either type a new value or use the scroll arrows to set the value.

5. Click OK.

6. In the Date And Time dialog box, click Change Time Zone if you want to change the time zone. In the Time Zone Settings dialog box, select the new time zone, specify whether you want the time to be adjusted for Daylight Saving Time, and click OK.

7. Click OK.

**See Also**

"Adding Time Zone Clocks" on page 108 for information about displaying additional clocks for different time zones.

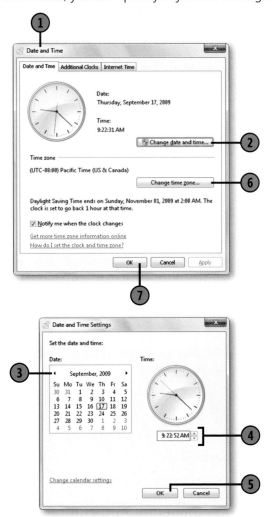

# Changing the Display

If you want to squeeze more items onto your Desktop, you can change its size...sort of. This is one of those virtual realities. You "enlarge" the available space by changing the screen resolution, and thereby the scaling, which lets you fit more items onto the Desktop even though its area on your screen doesn't get any larger. Your gain in virtual area comes at a cost,

## Increase the Computer's Screen Area

① Right-click a blank spot on the Desktop, and choose Screen Resolution from the shortcut menu to display the Screen Resolution window.

② Click the current screen resolution, and, when a slider appears, drag to select the screen-area size in pixels (the degree of screen resolution), and then click outside the slider window.

③ Select the orientation you want for the screen.

④ Click the Advanced Settings button to display the Properties dialog box for the monitor and the graphics adapter if you want to change the color depth or the color-management settings, or if you want to run a control program provided by the manufacturer of the graphics adapter (if a control program is available for your graphics adapter). Click OK when you've finished.

⑤ Click OK.

⑥ If the Display Settings dialog box appears after you've changed the Desktop's screen resolution, click Keep Changes to accept the new settings, or click Revert if you want to revert to the original settings. If you don't click Yes or No within 15 seconds, Windows 7 will restore the original settings.

though—everything will be smaller and harder to read. You can also go the other way—make the screen area smaller and make everything bigger. Another way to modify the way items fit on your screen is to change the orientation—for example, you might want to physically rotate your monitor so that it's longer than it is wide.

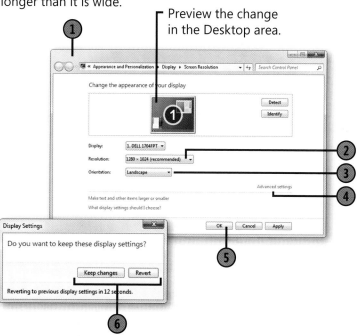

Preview the change in the Desktop area.

### See Also

"Enlarging Text" on page 87 for information about changing the size of the screen text when you change the screen resolution.

"Managing Multiple Monitors" on page 330 for information about using more than one monitor.

# Managing Windows Arrangements

Windows 7 tries to let you arrange your windows on the Desktop quickly and easily with new mouse and keyboard shortcuts. These features are called *Aero Snap* and *Aero Shake*. With Aero Snap, you can resize a window by dragging it to the left or the right edge of the screen to resize it so that it takes up half the screen, dragging it upward to maximize it, or dragging it downward to restore a maximized window. If you resize a window vertically, when it reaches the upper edge of the screen, the bottom of the window also resizes to reach the bottom of the screen. Aero Shake is a strange but useful management tool: Place the mouse pointer in the title bar and shake it—any other windows on the Desktop will be minimized. Intriguing as these features are, you might find them annoying, and they might even interfere with your use of the computer. If so, you can turn off these features.

## Turn off Automatic Window Arrangements

1. Click the Start button, type **ease** in the Search box of the Start menu, and choose Ease Of Access Center from the menu to display the Ease Of Access Center.

2. Click the Make The Mouse Easier To Use button.

3. In the Make The Mouse Easier To Use window, select this check box.

4. Click OK, and close the Ease Of Access window.

**Tip**

You can access Aero Snap features without using the mouse by pressing the Windows key+Arrow key combination.

# Changing Search Options

The Search feature in Windows is a powerful and useful tool that helps you find just what you need. You can make it even more useful to your work if you customize it for your own needs. That way, you can balance the speed of the search with the feature's ability to find the file you need.

## Set the Search Options

**1** In Windows Explorer, click Organize, and choose Folder And Search Options from the drop-down menu to display the Folder Options dialog box.

**2** On the Search tab, specify whether you want to search file names everywhere and file contents only in indexed locations, or whether you want to search file names and file contents everywhere.

**3** Select the check boxes for the options you want to use and clear the check boxes for the options you don't want.

**4** Specify whether you want to search directories that contain system files.

**5** Specify whether you want to search the contents of compressed files.

**6** Click OK.

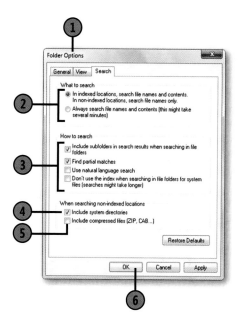

**See Also**

"Changing Indexing Options" on page 322 for information about the way files are indexed and how to change the indexing options.

**Tip**

Make sure you enable only the options you need. Searching the content of files that haven't been indexed can substantially slow down the search, and searching for partial matches can result in an extremely large number of search results. When you use Natural Language Search, your search queries can be a little less structured, and Windows will try to interpret what search parameters you're using. However, a misinterpretation of your entry might not provide the results you're looking for—or you might end up with a really long list of results.

# Changing Indexing Options

When you're not using all the resources of your computer, Windows will jump in and search your common files and folders to create an index of the folders and the file names and their contents. This index is then used to speed up your searches.

## Set Your Indexing Options

1. Click the Start button, type **index** in the Search box of the Start menu, and choose Indexing Options from the menu to display the Indexing Options dialog box.

2. Note the items that are currently indexed.

3. Click Modify.

4. In the Indexed Locations dialog box, select the check boxes for the locations you want to add and clear the check boxes for the items you don't want to include.

5. Click OK.

6. Click Advanced, and, in the Advanced Options dialog box that appears, specify whether or not to index encrypted files or files of a specific type, and how you want words with diacritical marks to be indexed. Click OK when you've finished.

7. Click Close.

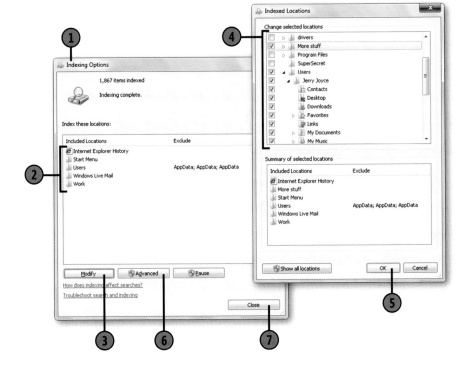

**Tip**

Sometimes an index gets corrupted and no longer functions. In that case, you can re-create the index. To do so, in the Advanced Options dialog box, click the Rebuild button.

# Managing Your Credentials

Windows 7 uses Credential Manager to store the credentials—usually your user name and password—that allow you to automatically log on to certain Web sites, services, or network computers. These aren't the same credentials that you've saved in your Web browser but are those that you explicitly asked Windows to save. For example, if you need to provide credentials each time you want to log on to a computer on the network, you can have those credentials saved. Some programs, including the Windows Live programs, can store your credentials in the *Vault*, which is a secure folder or group of folders that you manage with Credential Manager. However, many other programs and services aren't designed to access the Vault and so cannot access this information.

## Manage the Vault

1. Click the Start button, type **cred** in the Search box of the Start menu, and choose Credential Manager from the menu to display the Credential Manager window.

2. To view a credential, click the down arrow next to the credential (the down arrow changes into an up arrow after you've clicked it), and review the information.

3. Click Edit if you want to modify the credential, or click Remove From Vault to delete the credential from the Vault.

4. To add a credential, click here, and click the type of credential you want. Complete the information, and click OK.

5. To safeguard your credentials, click Back Up Vault, and step through the Stored User Names And Passwords wizard to create a secure backup of the credentials. Click Restore Vault to use your backup file if you need to recover your lost credentials.

6. Close the Credential Manager window when you've finished.

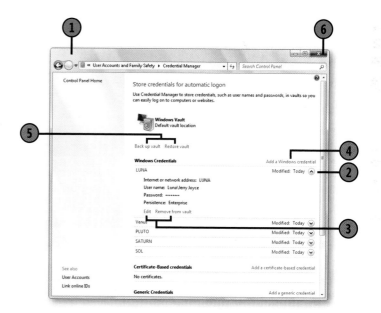

**Tip**

To add a certificate-based credential, you need to have been issued a certificate from an authorized source.

# Adding or Deleting User Accounts

If you're a member of the Administrator group or if you can authorize administrative permission, you can grant other people access to the computer by creating new user accounts and specifying what type of access the new users will be allowed. To keep things tidy, you can also delete user accounts that are no longer being used.

## Add a Standard Account

1. Click the Start button, choose Control Panel from the Start menu, and, in the User Accounts And Family Safety category, click Add Or Remove User Accounts. In the Manage Accounts window that appears, click Create A New Account to display the Create New Account window.

2. Type a name for the account.

3. With the Standard User option selected, click Create Account.

4. In the Manage Accounts window that appears, click the new account and, in the Change An Account window, change the name and the picture, add a password, or set up parental controls for the account.

5. Close the Change An Account window when you've finished.

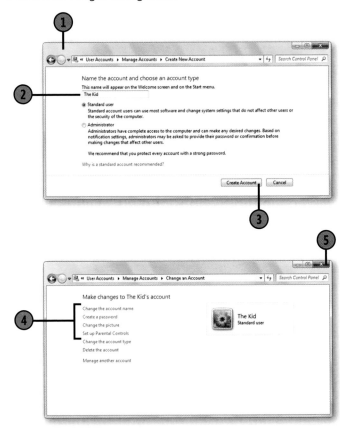

**Tip**

If you don't see the User Accounts And Family Safety category in the Control Panel, choose Category from the View By drop-down list.

## Delete an Account

**1** Click the Start button, choose Control Panel from the Start menu, and, in the User Accounts And Family Safety section, click Add Or Remove User Accounts. In the Manage Accounts window that appears, click the account you want to delete to display the Change An Account window.

**2** Click Delete The Account.

**3** In the Delete Account window that appears, click Delete Files to delete all the files, or click Keep Files if you want all the files in that account's folders saved to a Desktop folder.

**4** Click Delete Account to permanently delete the account.

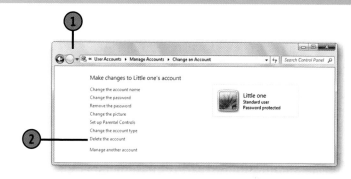

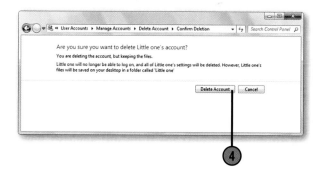

**Tip**

When you save files for an account that's being deleted, the files are saved to the Desktop of the person who's deleting the account and are accessible only when that person is logged on.

**See Also**

"Restricting User Rights" on pages 298–299 and "Know Your Rights" on page 300 for information about the reasons you should create only Standard User accounts.

# Creating a Linked Online ID

A linked online ID is a way to use your online identity credentials to authenticate access to your account on your computer. You can also link more than one online ID with your account by using different online ID providers. If you link someone else's online ID to your account, you can share files from your computer with that individual without creating a separate user account for him or her on your computer.

## Link the IDs

1. Click the Start button, and click your account picture. In the User Accounts window that appears, click Link Online IDs to display the Link Online IDs window.

2. If this in the first time you're linking to an online ID, click Add An Online ID Provider, select the Online ID provider with whom you already have an account, and follow the instructions to download and install any required software.

3. Click Link Online ID, and sign in with your user name and password when requested to do so.

4. If you've already linked an online ID to your account and you want to either use a different ID or modify an existing ID, click any of the following:

   • Update Credential to update the password so that it matches your online ID password.

   • Remove Linked ID if you want to use a different account from the same Online ID provider. Confirm that you want to delete the linked ID, and then click Link Online ID to enter the name and password for a different online ID.

   • Add An Online ID provider to use a different online ID provider. You'll need to download and install any needed software to use the online ID provider.

5. Click OK, and then close the User Accounts window.

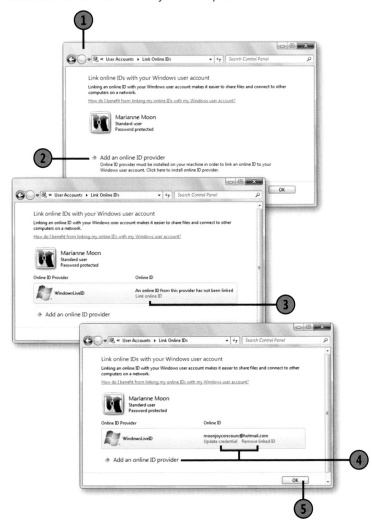

# Managing Travel Settings

Have you ever squirmed uncomfortably in a meeting when someone's computer suddenly blares out a little tune? Or when someone is about to start a presentation but can't get the computer screen to show up on an external display, and then, when the computer is finally working, the battery is exhausted and there's now a frantic search for a power cord? Windows Mobility Center brings together in one place all the necessary tools for managing your computer so that none of these nightmare scenarios will ever happen to you!

## Control the Settings

1. Click the Start button, type **mob** in the Search box of the Start menu, and choose Windows Mobility Center to display the Windows Mobility Center window.

2. Note the status of your system, and modify any of the settings if necessary.

3. If you're connecting to an external monitor or projector, with the external display connected and turned on, click Connect Display.

4. Click the way you want to use the external display.

5. To modify the way you use the external display, press the Windows key+P key combination to display the Connect To A Projector window again, and then click the display you want.

> **Tip**
>
> The Windows Mobility Center is available only on portable computers, and the items displayed will vary depending on the computer you use. The Connect To A Projector feature is available on all computers. In Windows 7 Professional and higher editions, the Mobility Center includes a Presentation Settings feature that disables system notifications, keeps the system awake, shows a custom background, and prevents the screen saver from appearing.

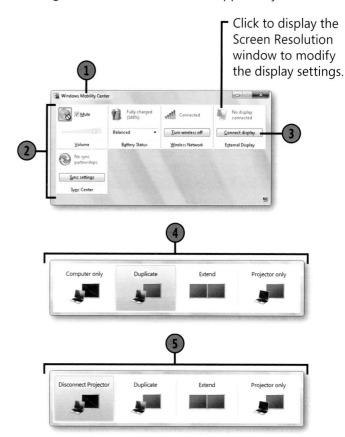

Click to display the Screen Resolution window to modify the display settings.

# Controlling the Power Options

Different computers have different power-management requirements and abilities. You might want the monitor on your main desktop computer to shut down after a few minutes of idleness, but you might also want the computer itself to "stay awake" constantly. With a portable computer, you might want everything to go to sleep after a few minutes of idleness. You can adjust the power plan so that the computer does these things automatically, or you can make the adjustments manually by specifying what you want to happen when you press a power button or close the lid of a portable computer. For your protection, you can also require that only you may unlock your account when the computer wakes up from Sleep mode.

## Use a Power Plan

**1** Click the Start button, type **power** in the Search box of the Start menu, and choose Power Options from the menu to display the Power Options window.

**2** Click Show Additional Plans if you want to see plans other than the preferred ones, including any custom plan you might have created.

**3** Select a power scheme.

**4** Click Change Plan Settings for the plan you want to use.

**5** In the Edit Plan Settings window that appears, examine the settings. If you want to modify a setting, specify a new value.

**6** If you want to make more detailed changes— for example, to specify when the hard disk is to be turned off—click Change Advanced Power Settings. In the Power Options dialog box that appears, make the changes you want, and click OK.

**7** In the Edit Plan Settings dialog box, click Save Changes.

Click if you want to create and name your own custom plan.

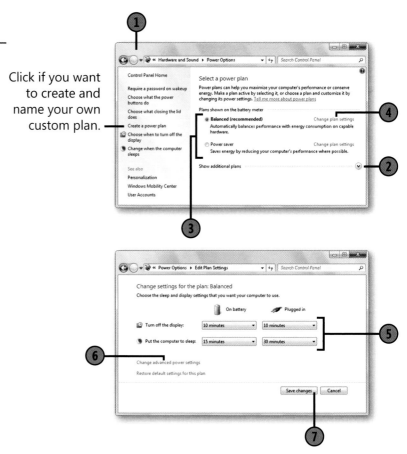

## Set the Power Buttons and the Password Requirement

**①** In the Power Options window, click Choose What The Power Buttons Do (or click Choose What The Power Button Does, if you're using a desktop computer) to display the System Settings window.

**②** Specify what you want to happen to the items available on your computer when you press a button or close the computer's lid.

**③** Click here to authorize changes to the password requirements.

**④** Click an option to specify whether you want to require a password when the computer wakes up from Sleep mode.

**⑤** Click Save Changes.

**⑥** Close the Power Options window.

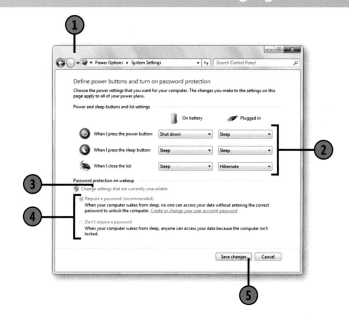

**Tip**

For obvious reasons, only a portable computer with a battery will display the On Battery settings.

**Tip**

You can quickly switch power plans or can access the Power Options window by clicking the Power icon on the taskbar, if it's displayed.

**See Also**

"Customizing the Start Menu" on page 99 for information about setting the default action for the power button on the Start menu.

**Tip**

If you require a password when the computer wakes up, you'll see the standard logon screen, from which you can log on to your currently locked account.

# Managing Multiple Monitors

Sometimes a single video monitor just isn't enough. If you need a larger-than-usual working area, or if you want to view your Desktop on one screen while other people can see it on a different screen, you can set up multiple monitors to display your Desktop. To use multi-monitors, you need the proper equipment. Many laptop computers support two monitors—the built-in display and an external display. For other computers, you need to have either a display adapter that supports more than one display, or one display adapter for each monitor you want to use.

## Configure the Displays

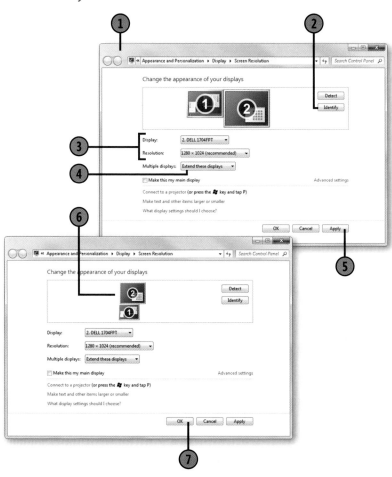

**①** With your monitors connected, right-click a blank spot on the Desktop, and choose Screen Resolution to display the Screen Resolution window.

**②** Click Identify to see which monitor is which.

**③** Select a display, and set the screen resolution for the monitor. Repeat the process for your additional display or displays.

**④** Specify the way you want to use the multiple monitors:

- Duplicate These Displays to have the whole Desktop shown on all monitors. This is available only on some displays.

- Extend These Displays to spread the Desktop across all the displays.

- Show Desktop Only On *display number*, where *display number* is the monitor number you identified in step 2 to show the Desktop on only one monitor.

**⑤** Click Apply.

**⑥** If you want to change the arrangement of the monitors, drag them into the position you want.

**⑦** Click OK, and, if the Display Settings dialog box appears, click Keep Changes.

## Manage the Extended Desktop

**1** With your multiple displays configured to have your Desktop extended across the displays, open a window or start a program on your primary monitor (monitor 1 is your primary monitor and contains the taskbar).

**2** Drag an open window or program to whichever edge of the primary monitor is adjacent to the other monitor, as shown in the Screen Resolution window. Continue dragging the window or program until it appears on the other monitor. Move it and/or resize it so that it looks the way you want.

**3** Use standard techniques to switch among your windows and programs—pressing the Alt+Tab keys or clicking items on the taskbar—regardless of which monitor the windows or programs are located on.

**Tip**

If you want a window to fully extend across two or more displays, drag a border to resize it. If you maximize a window, it will be maximized but will appear on only one monitor.

**Tip**

Use the Windows key+the arrow direction keys to move the active window quickly between monitors.

With the monitors arranged one above the other, you see this on your secondary monitor...

...and this on your primary monitor.

# Configuring a Pen or Touch Computer

If you have a Tablet PC or another system that uses pen or touch input, you can configure the computer so that it works best for you and the way you use it. Unless you want to change the way things are working, you'll need to configure most of these settings only once.

## Change the Settings

**①** Tap or click the Start button, type **tablet** in the Search box of the Start menu, and choose Tablet PC Settings from the menu to display the Tablet PC Settings dialog box.

**②** On the Display tab, tap or click the Setup button if the display isn't properly set up yet. Click or tap the Calibrate button to align your touch locations with the positions interpreted by the display.

**③** On the Other tab, specify which hand you use to enter most of your input.

**④** Tap here to open the Pen And Touch dialog box to adjust your pen, your *flicks* (navigational and editing gestures), and your handwriting, touch, and *panning* (touch scrolling) options.

**⑤** Tap here to open the Options dialog box for the Input Panel, and adjust the way you want the Input Panel to work.

**⑥** Tap OK.

**Tip**

The Tablet PC Settings dialog box is available only if Windows recognizes your computer as having pen or touch input.

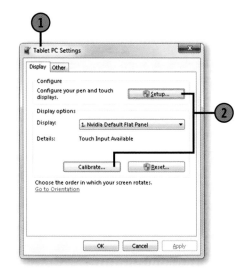

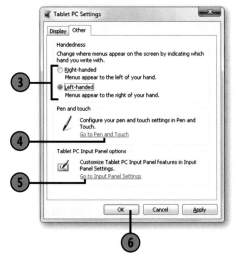

# Managing Pen Settings

If you have a computer that has the capability of using pen input—a Tablet PC or a computer with a digitizer pad, for example—you can adjust the way it responds to the pen.

## Set the Pen Options

① Tap the Start button, type **pen** in the Search box of the Start menu, and choose Pen And Touch from the menu to display the Pen And Touch dialog box.

② On the Pen Options tab, select a pen action.

③ Click Settings.

④ In the Settings dialog box, adjust the settings you want. Each of the pen actions has different settings.

⑤ Use the pen action on the test graphic to test your settings. Adjust the settings if necessary.

⑥ Click OK.

⑦ Repeat steps 2 through 6 for other pen actions.

⑧ Select or clear the check boxes for other pen options.

⑨ Click OK.

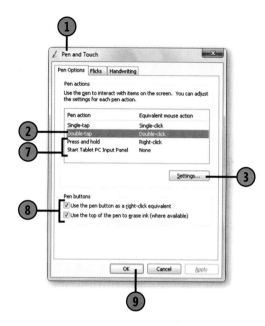

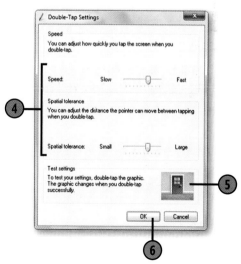

# Managing Navigational and Editing Flicks

On a computer that has pen or touch input, you can use *flicks* to accomplish specific actions. A flick is a short gesture that you make with a pen or a finger, in a specific direction, to accomplish a certain action. You can also customize flicks to perform many different actions.

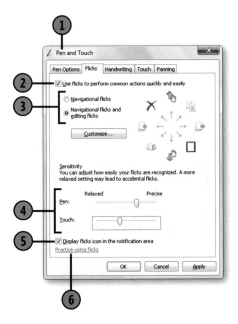

## Control Your Flicks

**①** Tap the Start button, type **flick** in the Search box of the Start menu, and choose Turn Flicks On Or Off from the menu to display the Pen And Touch dialog box.

**②** On the Flicks tab, select this check box, if it isn't already selected, to enable flicks.

**③** Specify whether you want to use flicks for navigation only, or whether you want to use them for editing and various other actions.

**④** Use the slider or sliders to adjust exactly how precise your flicks must be in order to be recognized.

**⑤** Select this check box if you want to be able to tap or click the Flicks icon in the notification area of the taskbar to see your current flicks settings.

**⑥** Click here to start the Flicks Training wizard. Step through the wizard to fine-tune your flicking ability.

 **Tip**

Not all pen-computer configurations support flicks, so use the Flicks Training wizard to see whether flicks work on your computer.

**Tip**

Flicks are cool shortcuts for accomplishing tasks on a pen or touch computer. However, flicks can be quite frustrating until you've mastered the motion, duration, and direction of the flick. Because of this, it's important to step through the Flicks Training wizard to hone your skills so that you can get the most from your pen or touch computer.

## Customize the Flicks

**1** On the Flicks tab, with the Navigational Flicks And Editing Flicks option selected, click Customize to display the Customize Flicks dialog box.

**2** Click the flick action that you want to change, and select the new flick action you want from the drop-down menu that appears. Repeat for other flick actions.

**3** Click a flick action. If you don't see the action you want listed, select Add from the list.

**4** Enter a name for the action.

**5** Click in the Keys box, and then press the key or key combination for the action you want to assign to the flick.

**6** Click Save.

**7** Customize any of the other flicks, and then click OK when you've finished.

**8** Click OK again in the Pen And Touch dialog box to close it.

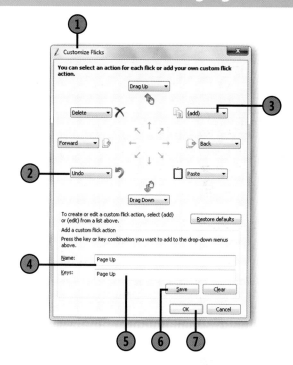

**Tip**

To disable a single flick while still being able to use the other flicks, click the flick action, and choose None from the list.

# Managing Touch Settings

If your computer has touch capabilities, you can customize the way the computer responds to your touch, and the way windows and programs respond when you pan to scroll the window with your finger.

## Customize Your Touch

(1) Touch the Start button, type **touch** in the Search box of the Start menu, and choose Change Touch Input Settings from the menu to display the Pen And Touch dialog box with the Touch tab selected.

(2) Select these check boxes, if they aren't already selected, to enable the touch and multi-touch features.

(3) Select the Double-Tap touch action, and then tap the Settings button. In the Double-Tap Settings dialog box that appears, use the sliders to adjust how fast you need to tap twice for your taps to be recognized as a double-tap; if necessary, adjust how close the two taps need to be. Use the graphic to test your settings, and then tap OK to close the dialog box.

(4) Select Press And Hold, and then tap the Settings button. In the Press And Hold Settings dialog box, select the check box to enable Press And Hold if it isn't already selected. Use the sliders to adjust the speed and duration of the press and hold. Use the graphic to test your settings, and then tap OK.

(5) Select this check box if you want to show the touch pointer on your screen, or clear the check box if you don't want to see the touch pointer.

(6) If you chose to display the touch pointer, tap Advanced Options, and, in the Advanced Options dialog box, specify where you want the pointer to appear. Use the sliders to adjust the transparency, size, and speed of the touch pointer. Tap OK to close the Advanced Options dialog box.

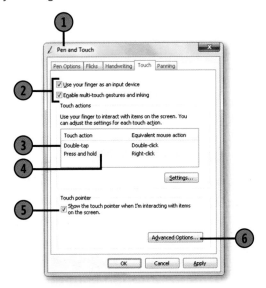

**See Also**

"Playing Microsoft Touch Pack Games" on page 154 for information about using touch to play special games that are part of the Microsoft Touch Pack add-on.

**Tip**

The touch pointer is an arrow (selection) pointer with an image of a mouse. You can drag the mouse image to move the pointer, and you can tap its left or right mouse button to execute an actual mouse-click.

## Customize Panning

1. Click the Panning tab of the Pen and Touch dialog box.

2. Select this check box to enable panning by dragging a single finger on the screen.

3. Select this check box to allow panning rates to be affected by the speed of your panning gestures.

4. Select this check box to have your window move a bit when you've reached the end of the area in which you can pan.

5. Use the slider to adjust how much the window pans when you use a panning gesture. With less resistance, you'll have more area panned than you would if the slider were set for higher resistance.

6. Click OK.

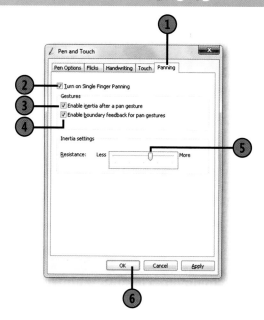

**Tip**

Touch capabilities on a computer change some of the ways Windows 7 works. It's a good idea to read the background information that came with your computer so that you'll understand the way the touch features work with the special programs that came with the computer.

**Tip**

Panning is similar to using the scroll bars in a window, but panning recognizes the speed and duration (the inertia) of your panning gesture, so you can scroll just a little bit or a long way with a single gesture.

**Try This!**

With the Enable Multi-Touch Gestures And Inking check box selected on the Touch tab, click OK. Open Paint. Click Brushes, and then draw a line with your finger. Now use two fingers to draw two lines simultaneously. Try more fingers and see how many touch points your system supports. In your Pictures Library, open a photo in Photo Viewer. Use two-finger gestures to zoom in and out and to rotate the photo. Use flicks to display other photos. Open WordPad, and either open or create a long document. Try different panning gestures to scroll through the document. Continue having fun with your touch features!

# Checking the Performance Status of Windows

In order for Windows 7 to be able to use all its features, it demands a lot from your computer. If your computer just isn't performing the way you want it to, try checking to see how the different parts of your computer perform with Windows 7.

## Check the Performance Status

1. Click the Start button, type **perform** in the Search box of the Start menu, and choose Performance Information And Tools from the menu to display the Performance Information And Tools window.

2. Note your system's score. You need a score of at least 3 to obtain full functioning of the Aero Glass effect, and you need a score of at least 4 to support all the Windows 7 features and programs that demand high graphics performance. A score of 6 or higher is needed for high-end multimedia and games.

3. Click here to see and print the details about your system.

4. Click a link to find out more about scores and how you can improve your computer's performance.

5. Close the window when you've finished.

6. Click the Start button, type **system** in the Search box of the Start menu, and choose System from the menu to display the System window.

7. Review the information about which edition of Windows is on your computer, the type and speed of the processor, the availability of any pen or touch input, and the network information.

8. Click here to learn about using Windows Anytime Upgrade to upgrade your edition of Windows.

9. Close the window when you've finished.

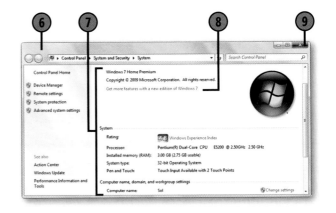

# Maintaining Your Hard Disk

With time and use, your computer's contents can become a bit disorganized. As the information stored in the computer gets used, moved, copied, added to, or deleted, the computer's hard disk, or drive, can become cluttered with useless or inefficiently organized files. Windows 7 provides a group of maintenance tools whose occasional use can make your computer run more smoothly, more efficiently, and (usually) faster. The table below describes what each of these tools does.

## Maintain a Drive

①  Click the Start button, choose Computer from the Start menu, click the drive that needs attention, and click Properties on the toolbar to display the drive's Properties dialog box.

②  Click the appropriate button to use the tool you need, and follow the instructions provided by the program:

* On the General tab, click Disk Cleanup.

* On the Tools tab, under Error-Checking, click Check Now.

* On the Tools tab, under Defragmentation, click Defragment Now.

## Disk-Maintenance Tools

| Tool | What it does |
|------|-------------|
| Disk Cleanup | Checks the disk for unused files that can be deleted. |
| Error-Checking | Scans the disk to see whether there are disk errors in any files or folders. Optionally, fixes file-system errors and attempts to recover bad sectors on the hard disk. If the disk is in use, error-checking will be scheduled for the next time you log on. |
| Defragmentation | Analyzes the disk to see whether defragmentation is necessary. Re-orders the items on your disk so that files aren't separated into several noncontiguous parts. Can take a long time to run but speeds up disk performance. |

**Tip** ✓

By default, the Defragmentation program is set to run automatically every week. If it doesn't run, or if you want to change the schedule, click Modify Schedule in the Disk Defragmenter dialog box.

# Troubleshooting Problems

Windows 7 is filled with troubleshooters—little wizards that analyze a situation and try to provide guidance to help solve problems. Although troubleshooters aren't a substitute for this book, or even for a knowledgeable friend, they can really help when things are just not going right. If you run into a problem, Windows will often suggest a particular troubleshooter. However, you can choose a troubleshooter and can run it whenever you want.

## Find a Troubleshooter

1. Click the Action Center icon in the notification area of the taskbar, and choose Open Action Center to display the Action Center window. In the Action Center window, click Troubleshooting near the bottom of the window to display the Troubleshooting window.

2. Select a category to view the troubleshooters for that topic.

3. Click a troubleshooting topic to start the Troubleshooting wizard.

4. If you can't find the troubleshooter you want, click the Back arrow to return to the Troubleshooting window.

5. Click View All to see a complete list of troubleshooters, and then click the troubleshooter you want.

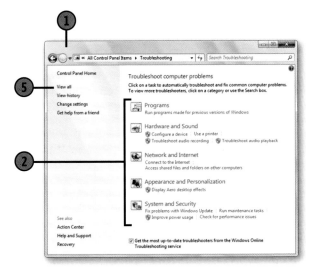

> **Tip**
>
> When you select a category, Windows checks on line (provided you're connected to the Internet) for new troubleshooting packs. With new troubleshooters being written to address recently discovered problems, what you see here is likely to be different from what you see on your computer.

## Run a Troubleshooter

**1** Click the troubleshooter you want to use to start the Troubleshooting wizard.

**2** If you want to run the troubleshooter as an Administrator, or if you want to disable automatically applying fixes, click Advanced.

**3** Click Next, and wait for the Troubleshooter wizard to gather information and run any diagnostics.

**4** Continue to step through the wizard.

- If additional information is required, supply it, and click Next.

- If you're given the option to take an action, click the action to apply a fix.

**5** If a fix or fixes were applied, click here to see a report on the troubleshooting and what fixes were applied.

**6** If the troubleshooter didn't fix the problem, click here to see what else you can do.

**7** Click Close if you've solved the problem, or if you want to use a different troubleshooter to investigate other problems.

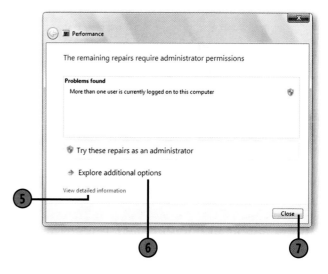

# Helping Each Other

How many times have you screamed "Help!" (or worse) when your computer was being an uncooperative brat, only to be met by silence? Now your pleas for help won't disappear into the void. Using the Remote Assistance feature, you can contact someone on your network or over the Internet for help. Your friend or coworker can view your computer Desktop, review your system information, and even chat with you to help you figure out what's wrong. Likewise, if a friend or colleague has a problem that you know how to solve, you can be the expert who provides the oh-so-welcome assistance.

## Start the Session

1. To ask for help, click the Start button, type **remote** in the Search box of the Start menu, and choose Windows Remote Assistance from the menu to display the Windows Remote Assistance window. Click Invite Someone You Trust To Help You.

2. Choose the way you're to going to invite your helper:

   - If you're using Webmail or if you'll deliver the invitation on a flash drive, click to create a file.

   - If you have an e-mail client on your computer, click to e-mail the invitation as an invitation.

   - If your helper is on your network, click Easy Connect.

3. Provide your helper with the password Remote Assistance creates, and, unless you're using Easy Connect, provide your helper with the invitation.

4. To give help, open Windows Remote Assistance from the Start menu, choose to help someone, and specify whether you'll connect by issuing an invitation or by using Easy Connect. If you're using an invitation, open the file. When prompted by Remote Assistance, enter the password that was provided to you.

5. On the computer that's asking for help, click Yes when you're asked to allow your helper to connect.

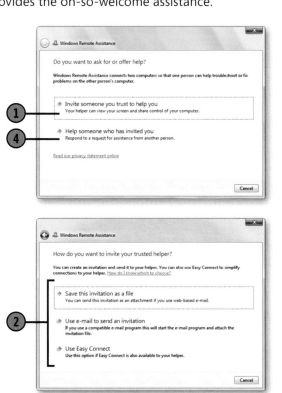

## Solve The Problem

**①** When you're connected, click Chat on each computer, and use the chat area to discuss the problem and the expected action.

**②** To give help, click Request Control (the Request Control button changes into the Stop Sharing button after you've clicked it). Wait for the person you're trying to help to confirm that you can take control. Click OK to confirm that you have control, and use your mouse to explore the other computer, to open menus and programs, and to do whatever trouble-shooting and problem-solving is necessary. When you no longer need control, click the Stop Sharing button.

**③** To receive help, when the helper asks to take control of your computer, click Yes to allow him or her full access to the computer and permission to make changes to the system. Click No if you want to retain control and make the changes yourself. If you've allowed the other person to take control of the computer, click Stop Sharing or press the Esc key when you want to terminate that control.

**④** When you've finished (and solved the problem, we hope!), click Close to end the remote assistance.

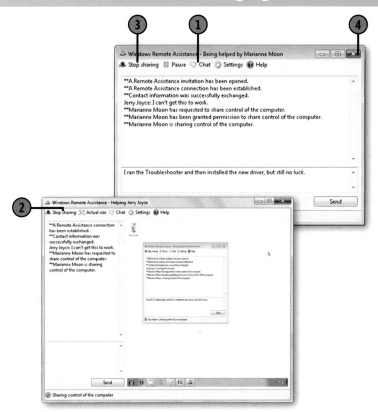

### Tip

Windows 7 also provides the Remote Desktop Connection tool that makes it possible for someone to control your computer from another computer. However, a computer running Windows 7 Home Premium edition can allow only an incoming Remote Desktop Connection and is unable take control of another computer.

### Tip

Your system must have Remote Assistance enabled to establish a connection. If Remote Assistance isn't already enabled, click the Start button, type **remote** in the Search box of the Start menu, and choose Allow Remote Assistance Invitations To Be Sent From This Computer. On the Remote tab of the System Properties dialog box that appears, select the check box for allowing Remote Assistance connections. Click OK.

# All Those Tools and Settings!

Windows 7 is loaded with tools and performance settings, some of which you can use productively and others that require major translation from techspeak into plain English. In most cases, the settings have already been optimized to achieve the correct balance between power and performance, but they might need some changes based on your computer equipment and your needs.

Although the tools are accessible in several locations, you'll find that you can access many of them in a single location by opening the Action Center and clicking View Performance Information. In the Performance Information And Tools window, click an option at the left side of the window to adjust settings and run diagnostic tools. For most diagnostic tools, click the Advanced Tools link to display the Advanced Tools window and a list of information-gathering tools. You can also start many of the tools by typing each one's name in the Search box of the Start menu. We'll discuss some of these tools below, but you might want to spend a little time exploring all of them. Note that in many cases you'll need to be signed in as an Administrator in order to use the tools.

## Information-Gathering Tools

**Event Viewer** shows by category the different events that have been recorded in Windows logs. Information displayed is usually highly technical and isn't intended for casual use. However, if your system is having problems, you might be able to find out what's happening. If you choose View Performance Details In Event Log in the Advanced Tools window, the Event Viewer will open, displaying a performance diagnostics log.

**Performance Monitor** shows, in its basic form, the current activity of the system processor. You can monitor additional parts of the system by adding them to the graph. You can also view past logs of previous tests. Although it's interesting to see the current performance of elements, you'll find the System Health Report much more comprehensive and usable—and even a bit more readable. You start Performance Monitor by choosing Open Performance Monitor from the Advanced Tools window.

**Reliability Monitor** graphs a stability index for your computer over time. The index is based on hardware and software problems. Also shown are the times when problems have occurred. If you click one of the problem markers, you'll see details about the event. You start Reliability Monitor by choosing View Reliability History in the Maintenance section of the Action Center.

**Resource Monitor** shows the activity of different pieces of hardware and the sources of that activity. It's a useful tool for finding a misbehaving program that's hogging the resources of your computer. Although you can stop a misbehaving running program by using Resource Monitor, doing so can be quite dangerous and could make your system unstable, so avoid taking this action unless you're certain there's no other way to end the program. You start Resource Monitor by choosing Open Resource Monitor from the Advanced Tools window.

**System Health Report** is a comprehensive report generated by running a 60-second test, using both Performance Monitor and Resource Monitor. The test includes a basic pass/fail result for the different parts of the system, which can really help in figuring out problems. Although most of the information is quite technical, you can print the information, save it as a file, or e-mail the information to someone who can make sense of the details. You create the report in the combined Resource And Performance Monitor by choosing Generate A System Health Report from the Advanced Tools window.

**System Information** provides full details of all the hardware and software on your computer. It's a really good idea to use this tool to print or export to a file all the information about your system, and to save this information for future reference and repair. You open the System Information window by choosing View Advanced System Details In System Information from the Advanced Tools window.

**Task Manager** is a venerable tool that's lived through many generations of Windows. It shows the status of the computer, including the running programs, computer processes, Windows services, CPU and Memory usage, network traffic, and logged-on users. Previously, Task Manager was used extensively to terminate misbehaving programs and processes, but Windows 7 has taken over most of those tasks. Stopping a program with Task Manager can be quite dangerous and could make your system unstable, so you should avoid doing this unless you're certain there's no other way to end the program. You can start Task Manager in several ways, including right-clicking the taskbar and choosing Start Task Manager; choosing Open Task Manager in the Advanced Tools window; or, if the computer isn't responding, pressing the Ctrl+Alt+Delete key combination and then choosing Start Task Manager from the menu on the Security screen that appears.

**Windows Memory Diagnostic** examines the physical memory of your computer. You'd normally run this tool if you believe that there's some malfunction in the memory modules that's causing serious problems. It runs after the computer has been restarted, and it generates a report. If you want to find out how much memory is installed on your computer, you don't use this tool. Instead, in the Control Panel, click System And Security, and, in the System And Security window, click System. To start Windows Memory Diagnostic, click the Start menu, type **mem** in the Search box of the Start menu, and choose Windows Memory Diagnostic. If Windows detects a problem possibly associated with memory, you'll also be prompted to run Windows Memory Diagnostic.

## System Settings Tools

**Device Manager** provides access to all the hardware devices on your system. You can use it to identify the devices installed on your computer; to disable, enable, or uninstall a device; to install a new driver or return to a previously installed driver; and to find and fix resource conflicts between devices. You can start Device Manager by choosing Hardware And Sound in the Control Panel and then clicking Device Manager.

**Performance Options** adjusts settings for the best visual effects, for the best performance, or for a combination of settings. If you make custom settings, you can turn on or off such features as animation of windows when they're minimized, using Aero Peek to preview the Desktop, and so on. Therefore, this tool not only lets you maximize performance for your system but also gives you customization options for features that you might not like. This tool also adjusts the system to get the best performance for running programs or background services and for using virtual memory. It also sets whether Data Execution Prevention is used only for essential Windows 7 programs and services or is used for all programs and services except the ones you exclude. You open the Performance Options dialog box by choosing Adjust Visual Effects from the Performance Information And Tools window.

**System Configuration** is a powerful tool that modifies the way Windows starts up, which services are enabled, and which system programs start at startup. It also provides tools to modify the system, including an editor to change the system Registry. System Configuration is a valuable tool that you can use to prevent a program that isn't listed in the Startup folder of the Start menu from starting when Windows starts. To start System Configuration, click the Start button, type **sys** in the Search box of the Start menu, and choose System Configuration from the menu.

# Speeding Up Your System

Windows can use a fast USB flash-memory drive or flash-memory cards to increase the speed of using virtual memory. Virtual memory is a method whereby Windows temporarily writes down information that's stored in the computer's memory when programs ask for more memory than is available. By writing to a flash-memory device instead of to a relatively slow hard drive, Windows speeds up the swapping of information between the computer's memory and the virtual memory, thus making the computer work faster. This feature is called *ReadyBoost*. Because computers that use solid-state drives, such as some Netbooks, have storage speeds similar to those of flash-memory drives or cards, ReadyBoost might not be available on those systems.

## Use ReadyBoost

1. Plug in your USB drive or the memory card. In the AutoPlay dialog box that appears, click Speed Up My System to display the Properties dialog box. If the AutoPlay dialog box doesn't appear, click the Start button, and choose Computer from the Start menu. In the Computer window, right-click the drive or the card, and, in the shortcut menu that appears, choose Properties to display the Properties dialog box.

2. On the ReadyBoost tab, specify the way you want to use the memory:

   - Dedicate This Device To ReadyBoost to use the device exclusively for ReadyBoost

   - Use This Device to use a portion of the device for ReadyBoost and the remaining storage area for other types of files

3. If you choose to use only a portion of the device for storage, use the slider to specify how large a portion you want to be reserved for ReadyBoost.

4. Click OK.

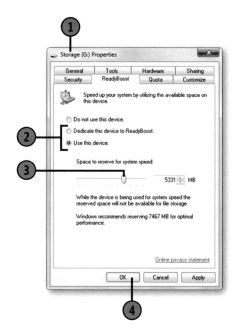

**Tip**

To stop using the device for ReadyBoost, choose Computer from the Start menu, click the drive, and click Properties. On the ReadyBoost tab, choose Do Not Use This Device, and click OK to free up the space reserved for ReadyBoost.

# Removing a Software Program

Most programs are *registered* with Windows 7 when you install them. You can—and should—use Windows tools when you want to remove a program. If you simply delete the files, you might leave accessory files you don't need or even delete files you need for other programs. When you uninstall a program using Windows tools, Windows 7 keeps track of the files, and only when a file is no longer needed by any of your programs does Windows 7 delete the file.

## Uninstall a Program

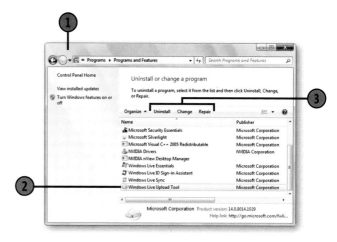

1. Close all your running programs, and make sure that no one else is logged on to the computer. Click the Start button, choose Control Panel from the Start menu, and, in the Programs section, click Uninstall A Program to display the Programs And Features window.

2. Select the program you want to uninstall.

3. Click the appropriate button:

   • Uninstall to remove the program

   • Change (if available) to modify the installed elements of the program or to repair the current installation

   • Repair (if available) to reinstall all or part of the program or to correct errors in the current copy of the program

4. If you're asked to, confirm the action you took. If another program starts and offers you a choice of actions, use this program to remove the selected program, to change the installed elements, or to repair the program.

5. Wait for the program to be removed or modified, and then close the Programs And Features window when you've finished.

> **Tip**
>
> Various programs provide different ways to remove or modify an installed program. Some programs display only the Uninstall button; others include the Change button, the Repair button, and even an Uninstall/Change button.

# Starting Up When There's a Problem

If you have any problems starting up Windows 7 correctly, you can use one of several startup procedures, either to determine what's wrong or to start Windows with minimal features so that you can adjust or restore settings. Then, after you've been able to start Windows, you can use a variety of techniques to fix whatever's wrong with the system.

## Control the Startup

1. Restart your computer. When the Windows Error Recovery screen appears, press Enter to start up in Normal Mode. If the computer doesn't start correctly, shut it down and then restart it, and wait for the Windows Error Recovery screen to appear again.

2. Use the Up arrow key to select Safe Mode, press Enter, and make changes to correct the problem.

3. Restart your computer, and see whether it starts correctly now.

4. If it doesn't, restart it again, and, just as Windows starts loading, hold down the F8 key. The Windows Advanced Boot Options menu appears. Experiment with different settings until you get the system working.

## Windows Error-Recovery Startup Options

| Option | What it does |
| --- | --- |
| Safe Mode | Starts with no network connections and without most of its drivers. |
| Safe Mode With Networking | Starts with network connections but without most of its drivers. |
| Safe Mode With Command Prompt | Starts without network connections, without most of its drivers, and with the command prompt only. |
| Start Windows Normally | Starts Windows, assuming that nothing is wrong. |

## Additional Options Using the Windows Advanced Boot Options Menu

| Option | What it does |
| --- | --- |
| Enable Boot Logging | Starts normally; records startup information to the *ntbtlog.txt* file (in the Windows folder). |
| Enable Low-Resolution Video Mode | Starts normally, using only the basic VGA video driver. |
| Last Known Good Configuration | Starts normally, using the settings stored in the Registry when the computer was last shut down properly. |
| Debugging Mode | Starts normally but sends the debugging information to another computer over a serial cable. |
| Disable Automatic Restart On System Failure | Prevents the computer from restarting repeatedly if a system failure occurs each time the computer restarts. |
| Disable Driver Signature Enforcement | Allows all drivers to be loaded even if they don't have the proper driver signatures. |

# Repairing the System

If your computer is having really serious problems starting up and you can't find the offending driver, setting, or any other issue by booting into Safe Mode, then you might need to ask Windows to help you figure out and repair your problems. Repairing covers a wide range of actions, from asking Windows to run diagnostics and apply fixes to your startup settings, to restoring your computer to previous settings, to replacing the entire contents with a copy you created earlier, to running a diagnostic on your memory chips.

## Repair the System

1. Start your computer, holding down the F8 key as Windows starts loading to display the Windows Advanced Boot Options window. If your computer manufacturer installed the repair program on your computer, select Repair Your Computer, and press Enter. Select your keyboard layout, and enter your user name and password.

2. If the Repair Your Computer option isn't available, insert your System Repair Disc or your Windows 7 DVD into your DVD drive, press the Esc key until your computer restarts, and, when prompted, press a key to boot from the DVD. In the Install Windows window that appears, click Next, and then click Repair Your Computer. In the System Recovery Options wizard that appears, make sure your Windows 7 operating system is selected, and, with the option to use the recovery tools selected, click Next. If your computer isn't set to boot from a DVD, consult your documentation for information about modifying the computer's BIOS settings.

3. In the System Recovery Options window, select the recovery tool you want to use.

4. After using a tool, if the System Recovery Options wizard is still visible, either choose another tool or remove the DVD if you used it, and choose Shut Down or Restart.

## Repair Tools Available from the Repair Your Computer Wizard

| Tool | What it does |
| --- | --- |
| Startup Repair | Runs diagnostics and applies fixes if available. After running, click View Diagnostic And Repair Details to see which tests were run, to view the results of those tests, and to see what, if any, fixes were applied. |
| System Restore | Restores the system files and settings to their status at an earlier time, when they were saved as a restore point. |
| System Image Recovery | Replaces everything on the hard disk with a copy of the hard disk, including the operating system and all the files that you created at an earlier time. |
| Windows Memory Diagnostic | Runs diagnostics on the memory hardware on your computer, and, if it finds a fault, identifies the issue. Requires that the computer be restarted. |
| Command Prompt | Displays the command prompt so that you can enter DOS commands. This is a very powerful and dangerous technique by which substantial damage can be done. It should be used only by a knowledgeable Administrator. |

# Fixing System Problems

An invaluable feature of Windows 7 is the System Restore tool, which makes it possible for you to undo whatever changes you and/or various programs have made to your computer system. Periodically, and also whenever you make changes to the system, Windows 7 records all the system information. If you've made changes to the system but the effect isn't what you wanted, you can tell Windows to revert to the previous settings.

## Restore the System

**1** Close all your running programs, and verify that no one else is logged on to the computer.

**2** Click the Start button, type **restore** in the Search box of the Start menu, and choose System Restore from the menu to display the System Restore wizard. If requested, provide Administrator credentials. Click Next to start the wizard.

**3** Review the dates and times, the descriptions, and the types of restore points available.

**4** Select a restore point that occurred just prior to when you experienced problems, or a restore point that was made just prior to an action that might have caused the problem.

**5** Click Next.

**6** Review the information about the restore point, and make sure this is the one you want to use.

**7** Click Finish to use the restore point, or click Back to select another restore point.

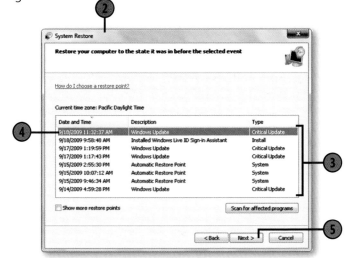

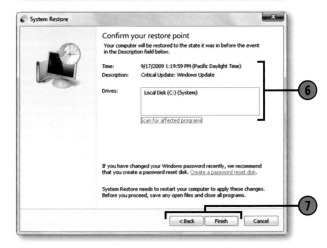

**Tip**

A restore point contains a record of the system settings that were in effect when the restore point was created, and you can use the restore point to restore the system settings to the way they were then. Most restore points are created automatically, but you can create your own restore points. To do so, click Recovery in the Action Center.

# Managing Everything

Windows 7 provides you with a powerful administrative tool called the Computer Management Console, which gives you access to almost everything on your computer system. You can use this tool to explore your computer and to learn about the various adjustments you can make, and—armed with a little knowledge—you can then use the tool to maintain and improve your system.

## Use the Console

**1** Log on as an Administrator, click the Start button, type **man** in the Search box of the Start menu, and choose Computer Management from the menu to display the Computer Management Console.

**2** Click an item to see a subtopic or category, and then click an item to see the details.

**3** Use the items in the main pane to gather information or to adjust settings. Close the console when you've finished.

## Computer Management Console Items

| Item | What it does |
|------|--------------|
| Task Scheduler | Manages computer tasks that are run automatically. |
| Event Viewer | Displays the system log and other event logs. |
| Shared Folders | Monitors which items are shared on the network and by whom. |
| Performance | Provides technical data about the running of the computer. |
| Device Manager | Provides the ability to manage all hardware devices on the system. |
| Storage | Provides information about and management of all storage devices. |
| Services And Applications | Provides management of all services available on the computer. |

**Tip**

To access many of the tools mentioned here without using the Computer Management Console, and to access some additional tools, click the Start button, type **admin** in the Search box of the Start menu, and choose Administrative Tools from the menu to display the Administrative Tools window.

**Tip**

Another powerful management tool available in Windows is PowerShell. This is a technical tool for creating and using scripts that automate administrative tasks. Therefore, this tool should be used only by those who are expert in such matters.

# Backing Up Your Files

If losing important files every now and then is simply not an option, backing up your files is critical. After you have Windows Backup set up, you can control what's backed up and when, as well as being able to run a backup whenever you want. You might also want to back up to a different device—a USB memory drive, for example—to create an additional backup that you can store in a safe location.

## Back Up Now

① Click the Start button, type **back** in the Search box of the Start menu, and choose Backup And Restore from the menu to open the Backup And Restore window.

② With the device you're going to use to store your backup attached to your computer, verify that there's adequate room on it for another backup. If there isn't enough room, click Manage Space, either to manually delete non-backed-up files on the device or to delete selected backed-up files. Click Close when you've finished.

③ If you want to change which device you use, change what's backed up, or modify the schedule for automatic backups, click Change Settings, and step through the Set Up Backup wizard.

④ Click Back Up Now to run the backup.

Click if you want to suspend automatic backups.

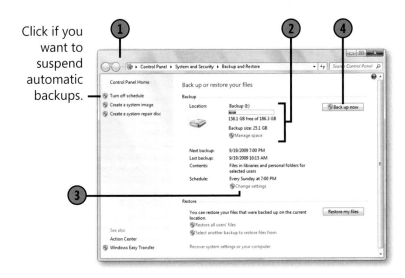

**Tip**

Just about everything you do in Backup normally requires Administrator permission, so this is one instance where you might want to log on as an Administrator, modify and run the backup, and then log off as an Administrator.

**See Also**

"Setting Up Windows Backup" on page 284 for information about setting up Backup.

# Restoring Backed-Up Files

Have you deleted or otherwise lost files that you now realize you need? If those files were backed up from your computer, you can restore them from the backup onto your computer.

## Restore the Files

**①** With the storage device you used for your backup attached to your computer, click the Start button, type **back** in the Search box of the Start menu, and choose Backup And Restore from the menu to open the Backup And Restore window. Click Restore My Files to start the Restore Files wizard.

**②** Specify whether you want to search for specific files, browse for files, or browse for folders.

**③** In the window that appears, search for or otherwise locate the files or folders you want, and then select the ones you want. Click OK if you clicked Search, click Add Files if you clicked Browse For Files, or click Add Folder if you clicked Browse For Folders, to add the selected item or items to your list of items to be restored. Use the Search button or the Browse buttons to locate any other files or folders you want to restore until the list of items to be restored is complete.

**④** Click Next, and specify whether you want the items to be restored to their original location or to another location you specify. Click Restore to restore the items to your computer.

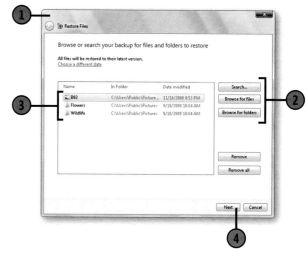

**Tip** ✓

If the backup that you want to use isn't stored on your default backup device, attach the device, and then, in the Backup And Restore window, click Select Another Backup To Restore Files From. Use the Restore Files (Advanced) dialog box to select the backup you want to use.

**Tip** ✓

To restore a backed up version of a file that you still have on your computer, right-click the file in Windows Explorer, and click Restore Previous Versions. On the Previous Versions tab of the file's Properties dialog box, click the version of the file you want, and then click Restore.

# Saving Everything

Sometimes your whole system can go down and you won't be able to piece it back together using Windows 7 repair tools. This disaster can happen when your hard disk fails; when a particularly nasty virus attacks your system; or when someone, somehow, makes enough changes to really mess the system up. As a last resort, provided you have a system image of your hard drive, you can return the system to exactly the way it was when you created the system image. However, anything that you added after you created the system image, including any files that you saved or copied, will be lost.

## Create a System Image

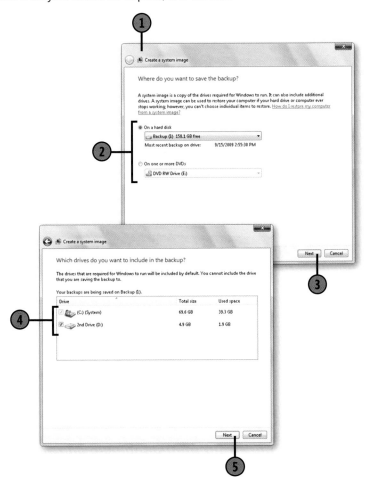

**①** Click the Start button, type **back** in the Search box of the Start menu, and choose Backup And Restore from the menu to open the Backup And Restore window. Click Create A System Image to start the Create A System Image wizard.

**②** Specify where you want to store the system image.

**③** Click Next.

**④** Specify which drives, in addition to the drive or drives required to run Windows, you want to include in the image.

**⑤** Click Next, review the settings, and click Start Backup to create the system image.

> **Tip** ✓
>
> If you haven't yet created a System Repair Disc or you don't have one provided by your computer manufacturer, create one when prompted to do so after you've created the system image.

> **See Also**
>
> "Repairing the System" on page 349 for information about using the Repair Your Computer wizard to use the system image to restore your previous configuration and files.

# Downloading Free Software

Microsoft and its partners are continually developing tools, utilities, and other items that make it possible for your computer to work better, run more effectively, and just do more things. Many such items are available as free downloads from the Microsoft Web site. True, you'll need to wade through listings of many technical downloads, but it's worth it—your search can yield some pretty interesting items related to just about any Microsoft product, including trial versions of many of Microsoft's games.

## Download the Software

(1) Use your Web browser to go the main Microsoft Web page *(microsoft.com),* point to Downloads And Trials, and choose Download Center from the drop-down menu to display the Microsoft Download Center Web page.

(2) Click one of the menus to find the category for the item you want, and then click the category. On the Web page that appears, click the download you want.

(3) On the Download page, review the information about the download and the instructions for downloading and installing the item.

(4) Click Download, and follow the directions on the screen.

**Tip**

Web pages change frequently, so what you see on the Microsoft Web page might be a bit different from what's pictured here. If you can't find the downloads, use an Internet search for "Microsoft downloads."

**See Also**

"Setting Up Windows Live Essentials Programs" on page 285 for information about downloading the Windows Live programs.

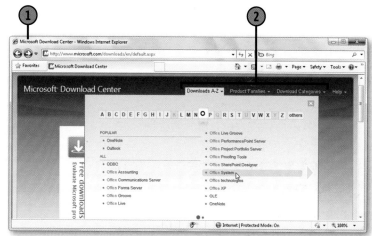

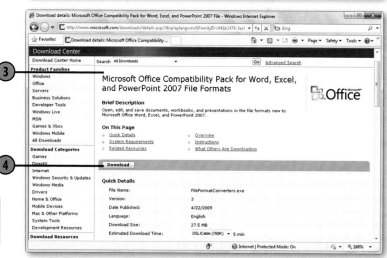

# Index

**D**

# U

# X

# Z

# About the Authors

**Jerry Joyce** is a marine biologist who has conducted research from the Arctic to the Antarctic and has published extensively on marine-mammal and fisheries issues. He developed computer programs in association with these studies to simplify real-time data entry, validation, and analysis that substantially enhanced the quality of the research. He has also had a long-standing relationship with Microsoft: Prior to co-authoring 16 books about Microsoft Windows, Word, and Office, he was the technical editor for numerous books published by Microsoft Press, and he wrote manuals, help files, and specifications for various Microsoft products. Jerry is a Seattle Audubon volunteer and is involved in citizen-science programs, as well as consulting on oil-spill prevention and response.

**Marianne Moon** has worked in the publishing world for many years as proofreader, editor, and writer—sometimes all three simultaneously. She has been proofreading and editing Microsoft Press books since 1984 and has written and edited documentation for Microsoft products such as Microsoft Works, Flight Simulator, Space Simulator, Golf, Publisher, the Microsoft Mouse, and Greetings Workshop. In another life, she was chief cook and bottlewasher for her own catering service and wrote weekly food and cooking articles for several East Coast newspapers. When she's not chained to her computer, she likes gardening, cooking, traveling, writing, and knitting sweaters for tiny dogs. She volunteers for Seattle Audubon's History Committee, and there's a children's book in her head that she hopes will find its way out one of these days.

Marianne and Jerry own and operate **Moon Joyce Resources,** a small consulting company. They've been friends for 28 years, have worked together for 24 years, and have been married for 18 years. They are co-authors of the following books:

*Microsoft Word 97 At a Glance*

*Microsoft Windows 95 At a Glance*

*Microsoft Windows NT Workstation 4.0 At a Glance*

*Microsoft Windows 98 At a Glance*

*Microsoft Word 2000 At a Glance*

*Microsoft Windows 2000 Professional At a Glance*

*Microsoft Windows Millennium Edition At a Glance*

*Troubleshooting Microsoft Windows 2000 Professional*

*Microsoft Word Version 2002 Plain & Simple*

*Microsoft Office System Plain & Simple—2003 Edition*

*Microsoft Windows XP Plain & Simple*

*Microsoft Windows XP Plain & Simple—2nd Edition*

*Microsoft Office Word 2007 Plain & Simple*

*The 2007 Microsoft Office System Plain & Simple*

*Windows Vista Plain & Simple*

If you have questions or comments about any of their books, please visit *www.moonjoyce.com.*

# What do you think of this book?

We want to hear from you!

To participate in a brief online survey, please visit:

**microsoft.com/learning/booksurvey**

...and enter this book's ISBN number (appears above barcode on back cover).

Tell us how well this book meets your needs—what works effectively, and what we can do better. Your feedback will help us continually improve our books and learning resources for you.

Thank you in advance for your input!

**Where to find the ISBN on back cover**

ISBN: 000-0-0000-0000-0

90000

0  000000  000000

Example only. Each book has unique ISBN.

**Microsoft®**
*Press*

# Stay in touch!

To subscribe to the *Microsoft Press® Book Connection Newsletter*—for news on upcoming books, events, and special offers—please visit:

**microsoft.com/learning/books/newsletter**